Music Rituals
in
the Temples of South India

Music Rituals
in
the Temples of South India

Vol. 1

Geetha Rajagopal

D.K. Printworld (P) Ltd.
New Delhi

Cataloging in Publication Data — DK
[Courtesy: D.K. Agencies (P) Ltd. <docinfo@dkagencies.com>]

Rajagopal, Geetha, 1948-
Music rituals in the temples of south India /
Geetha Rajagopal.
v. 1 cm.
Includes bibliographical references (p.)
Includes index.
ISBN 13: 9788124605370 (set)
ISBN 10: 8124605378 (set)
ISBN 13: 9788124605387 (vol. 1)
ISBN 10: 8124605386 (vol. 1)

1. Temples, Hindu — India, South — Dedication.
2. Hindu music — India, South — History and criticism.
3. Hinduism — India, South — Rituals. I. Title.

DDC 294.535 095 48 22

ISBN 13: 978-81-246-0537-0 **set** **ISBN 10: 81-246-0537-8**
ISBN 13: 978-81-246-0538-7 **vol. 1** **ISBN 10: 81-246-0538-6**
First published in India in 2009

Published and printed by:
D.K. Printworld (P) Ltd.
Regd. Office: 'Sri Kunj', F-52, Bali Nagar
Ramesh Nagar Metro Station
New Delhi-110 015
Phones: (011) 2545 3975; 2546 6019; *Fax*: (011) 2546 5926
E-mail: dkprintworld@vsnl.net
Website: www.dkprintworld.com

I dedicate this book to

my late mother-in-law Smt. Vedam
who had supported me in each and every endeavour of mine,

my late father Sri S.R. Srinivasan
a voracious reader, and writer — one who encouraged me
from my childhood to write and appreciate art,

my mother and guru Smt. Shakunthala Srinivasan
who has been instrumental in my attempt to take
my music to the research level;

and last but not least

to my husband Sri K.S. Rajagopalan and **my family**
without whose support this book
would not have been possible.

Preface

A TRIP to a number of temples in Tamil Nadu while doing a documentary film — "A Tryst with Trinity" — was what inspired me to take up this project. Born into a Vaiṣṇavite family I had the opportunity of learning a number of *Pāsurams* and the *Tiruppāvai* at a very young age. I was also fortunate to learn the *Tevārams* and a number of *Tirupugazh* hymns. I sang them wherever and whenever I was asked to sing. Sadly I did not know the background of their divinity.

The documentary film on the Trinity again was an eye-opener. Before I ventured into this project I had no idea about the biographical details of the holy composers, even though I had learnt the songs of the Trinity from my seventh year. While doing the documentary, visiting a number of temples was a very divine experience. It happened to be unique as it was a musical journey (down memory lane) done by the Trinity. During the documentation I interviewed temple artistes like the *pañcamukha vādyam* player, the *nādasvaram* artistes, etc. and an interesting factor I hit upon was that the musical traditions of temples distinctly differed from temple to temple, particularly from Vaiṣṇavite to Śaivite temples. That is when I decided to explore further to get more facts about these rituals. Sanjay Subramanian, a leading Carnatic vocalist and also Treasurer of "Sampradāya" at that time, suggested I apply for the Senior Fellowship to Sangeet Natak Akademi. I was pleasantly surprised when I got my fellowship and then for two years it was travelling all over south India visiting one temple after another, collecting information on the music rituals.

Seeing temples in a different light and learning about the mythological background of each and every temple (the *Sthala Purāṇam*), getting to know the art forms practised in the temple along with the regular religious rituals was an exhilarating experience and cannot be explained in a few words. It was nothing but the Divine Grace of Almighty that took me on this most wonderful journey.

Through volume one, I hope to familiarize the reader with the worship patterns of the temples in four south Indian states — Tamil Nadu, Karnataka, Kerala and Andhra Pradesh — and how music has brought humanity and God together. Volume two will be a combination of spirituality, divinity, beauty and art — worship of the Almighty and Nature and appreciation of Art. In the second volume I hope to focus on the two beautiful states — Karnataka and Kerala — in detail.

Though Andhra Pradesh has contributed immensely to Carnatic music through its composers and their songs, very little temple music rituals survive today, when compared to the other south Indian states. The nine famous Narasiṁha Swamy temples — the Ahobila Temple, the Maṅgalagiri Narasiṁha, Siṁhacalam, etc. — the famous Bhadracalam Rāma temple, and the Śiva temple of Śrīśailam will be covered with their rituals.

God's own land Kerala with its breathtaking landscape, the beautiful sea and lofty mountains, the simple yet majestic temples — where traditions play a very significant and dominant role with a variety of art forms — classical and folk — will feature in volume two. The soul stirring music known as "Sopānam" (Aṣṭapadī singing) is a part of music ritual in a number of temples in Kerala. It has also a rich tradition of art forms like Theyyam and Thullal that continue to be part of the worship pattern in temples. Another aspect of Kerala music tradition is their instrumental music — the drum-beats — the *pañcavādyam* and *tāyambaka* that continue to be an integral part of the temple festivals. The world famous "Trissur Pooram" festival where the entire city vibrates with these drum-beats finds a special place in volume two.

Besides these, other art forms like Kathakali, Chākyar Koothu, Nangiyar Koothu, Thōlpāvai Koothu, etc. are a part of rituals practised in temples. A special auditorium known as "Koothu-Ambalam" (performing-temple) is found in many temples where these art forms are performed on special occasions. These auditoriums mostly as old as the temples themselves help in promoting these art forms in a big way.

Coastal Karnataka where one sees nature at her best — the lofty mountains on one side, the breathtaking valleys on the other side, a gushing water fall here and there, is a feast to the pilgrim as well as the tourist. A number of temples are situated among these mountains, like Śṛṅgeri, Uḍupi, Mookambika, Subramaṇya, Kattil, etc. as we travel through the Kudremukh National Park, a long stretch of nearly 250 km.

Apart from vocal music (singing of Purandara Dasa's songs) instrumental music like the *mukha vīṇā,* the art forms like *yakṣagāna* and puppetry give the temple traditions here a unique flavour. The "Malai-Madeśwar" temple situated in the mountainous region of Kollegal district near Mysore where the "Khamsale" folk songs are dedicated to the presiding deity as a ritual, the "Araiyar Sevai" at the Melkottai temple near Māṇḍya and some of the temples around Mysore where *nādasvara* traditions are followed will also feature in volume two.

It is also to be noted that in spite of the common thread of Classical music that runs through them, the local flavours of the four different states make them unique in their own way. It would give me great pleasure if the book is of use not just to a researcher or pilgrim but also to a traveller interested in our celebrated temple history.

I feel grateful to the omnipresent to be born in India. That I belong to a country with such a rich, ancient, glorious culture makes me proud but also a little sad because I was not aware of so many traditions related not only to religion but also to art.

Working in an Archive for the past few years where we are trying our best to preserve music for posterity it is saddening to know that there is a lot of information on several art forms that are lost for lack of facilities in archiving and also the cultural changes that are forcing their way in. I felt I should present in this book some of the information I have gathered with a hope that it will inspire or at least interest a few people to visit the places I have been very fortunate to visit and see them as not only places of worship but also as places of art and culture, in short in a different light and feel proud that we belong to this country of rich cultural heritage. With a sincere and fervent hope let us try to revive or at least relive a little of this our past — a glorious one at that.

I thank the Sangeet Natak Akademi for giving me this wonderful opportunity; all the artistes of the temples; the temple priests, who with a lot of zeal and enthusiasm gave me a lot of information related to their temples; the Sampradāya Library; my colleagues Padma Viswanathan, Bharath and Govindan who gave me a lot of support, and my daughter-in-law Jyothi who travelled with me to a number of places and helped me in a big way to compile.

Finally one word to all the readers — there is a popular saying in Tamil — *yaan peṭra inbam peruka ivvaiyagam* (Let this world experience the moments of happiness I enjoyed). A visit to a temple just does not end with the entry and exit from the *sanctum sanctorum*. I am sure if one looks beyond the *gopuram* of a temple one will agree with me, because there are mightier and more magnificent matters contained within other than the impressive edifice.

Contents

	Preface	vii
	Acknowledgement	xiii
	Key to Transliteration	xiv
	Introduction	1
1.	Role of Music in the Vedas	5
2.	Music as a Form of Worship	11
3.	The Bhakti Movement	14
4.	The Role of Temples in Promoting Music	18
5.	The Nāyaṉmārs	24
6.	The Āḻvārs	51
7.	Temple of Lord Veṅkaṭeśvara-Tirumala (Music Rituals in detail with Photographs)	74
8.	Comparisons between the Works of Āḻvārs and Nāyaṉmārs	111
9.	Contribution of the Devadāsīs to the Temple Music Tradition	114
10.	Music Traditions in the Temples of Tamil Nadu	119
11.	Vocal Music	124
12.	Instrumental Music	136
13.	Dance Forms as Rituals in Temples	152
14.	Festivals in Temples	160
15.	Inscriptions of Information on Music in the Temples	170
16.	Sculptures of Dance and Music in Temples	173

17. Unique Music traditions in Some Temples 175
18. Centres that Promoted Temple Art Forms 184
19. A few Important Centres to Visit 204
Conclusion 209

Plates 211
Bibliography 251
Index 253

Acknowledgement

I thank the following who have helped me in my research and to understand the innumerable aspects of the music traditions discussed in the book. This book would have been impossible without them.

- Sri Chinna Thambi, Nādasvaram Artiste, Āchalupuram.
- Dr John A. Loud, Retd. Prof. Music Deptt., Harvard University.
- Smt. Padma Vishwanathan, "Sampradaya," Chennai.
- Sri P.D. Govindan, Librarian, "Sampradaya," Chennai.
- Sri Muthu Kumaraswamy, Nādasvaram Artiste, Semponnār Koil.
- Sri Selvaganapathy, Pāri Nāyanam artiste, Thiruvārūr.
- Sri Selvaraj, Pañcamukha Vādyam artiste, Thiruvārūr.
- Sri Muthuswamy, Cheyyūr Temple.
- Sri Azhagiri Swamy, Thavil Artiste, Kāñcīpuram.
- Dr N. Ramanathan, Madras University, Music Deptt.
- Dr Medasani Mohan, Director, Annamācārya Project (TTD, Tirupati).
- Dr Dwaram Lakshmi, HOD, Music Deptt, Music College, Tirupati.
- Sri Dasarathy, Mattapalli Temple, AP.
- Sri Thiruvengadu Jayaraman, Vocalist, Thiruvengādu.
- Sri Subramaniam, Ghoṭṭu vādyam artiste, Āvadiyar Temple, TN.
- Sri Sivacarya, *Oduvār*, Thiruvalangāḍu Temple, TN.
- Sri Lalgudi Swaminathan, *Oduvar*, Kapālīśvārar Temple, TN.
- Arayar Sri Śrīnivāsa Iyengar, Arayar, Melkoṭe Temple, Karnataka.
- Arayar Sri Siṁha, Arayar, Melkoṭe Temple, Karnataka.
- Arayar Śrīnivāsa, Arayar, Srivilliputtur Vatapatrasāyī Temple, TN.
- Sri Rajarathnam, *Oduvar*, Thiruvānmiyur Temple, Chennai, TN.
- "Sampradaya" Library, Chennai.
- Madras University Library, Chennai.
- Madras Archives, Chennai.
- Artistes and priests from various temples who gave us, interviews that were recorded.

Key to Transliteration

VOWELS

अ *a*	आ *ā*	इ *i*	ई *ī*	उ *u*	ऊ *ū*	ऋ *ṛ*	ॠ *ṝ*[1]
(Roman)	(palm)	(it)	(police)	(put)	(rule)	(rig)	
ऌ *ḷ*	ॡ *ḹ*[1]	ए *e*	ऐ *ai*	ओ *o*	औ *au*		
(able)		(there)	(aisle)	(no)	(loud)		

CONSONANTS

Guttural	क *ka*	ख *kha*[2]	ग *ga*	घ *gha*[2]	ङ *ṅa*
	(skate)	(blockhead)	(gate)	(ghost)	(sing)
Palatal	च *ca*	छ *cha*[2]	ज *ja*	झ *jha*[2]	ञ *ña*
	(chunk)	(catch him)	(john)	(hedgehog)	(bunch)
Cerebral	ट *ṭa*	ठ *ṭha*[2]	ड *ḍa*	ढ *ḍha*[2]	ण *ṇa*
	(start)	(anthill)	(dart)	(godhead)	(under)
Dental	त *ta*	थ *tha*[2]	द *da*	ध *dha*[2]	न *na*
	(path)	(thunder)	(that)	(this)	(numb)
Labial	प *pa*	फ *pha*[2]	ब *ba*	भ *bha*[2]	म *ma*
	(spin)	(philosophy)	(bin)	(abhor)	(much)
Semi-vowels	य *ya*	र *ra*	ल *la*[3]	व *va*[4]	
	(young)	(drama)	(luck)	(vile)	
Sibilants	श *śa*[5]	ष *ṣa*[5]	स *sa*	ह *ha*	
	(shove)	(bushel)	(so)	(hum)	
Others	क्ष *kṣa*	त्र *tra*	ज्ञ *jña*		
	(*kṣatriya*)	(*triśūla*)	(*jñānī*)		

अं (ं) *ṁ anusvāra* is a nasal off-glide that immediately follows the pronunciation of a vowel as in *saṁskṛti.*

अः *visarga* = *ḥ* consists in abrupt release of breath after a vowel as in *prātaḥ.*

ऽ *Avagraha* shows non-pronunciation, that is, deletion of "a" after "e" or "o" as in *ime 'vasthitāḥ*. In Vedic ṣanskrit, it can also show word division.

HINDI LETTERS (extras)

ँ = *m̐*	ं = ṅ	ड़ = *ṛa*	ढ़ = *ṛha*
(*candrabindu*)	(*anusvāra*)		

---

1 Longer form of the preceding vowel.

2 Aspirated forms of the preceding consonants. The compound words given as examples should be pronounced without a syllabic break at the underlined places. "tha" and "pha" should not be pronounced as fricatives.

3 retroflexed and written as "L *ḷa*" in certain phonetic contexts.

4 Pronounced like "w," without aspiration.

5 "śa" is palatal; "ṣa" cerebral or retroflex.

Introduction

We the people of India are heirs to a hoary heritage enriched and handed down to us, from generation to generation, from the dawn of civilization. Indians are welded together by strong bonds of culture, common ideals and traditions. Our history runs back to remote antiquity. Devoid of this, India is like a body without life. The backbone of Indian life is religion. Spirituality is the life-blood of this sacred land, sanctified by the footprints of great sages. This is our precious inheritance. We should strengthen these ethical and spiritual values.

The eternal fountain of our religion, philosophy, Vedas, Upaniṣads, Purāṇas and the sacred *kṣetra*s and temples have withstood the shocks and ravages of several foreign invasions and upheavals of the past. They have preserved our culture and unity. They have led to the rejuvenation of our faith. Temples express an unseen power and the presence of it. God's manifestation in the idol is the basis of our religious worship. Many are the names of God and infinite are the forms that lead us to know Him. You will see Him in the very name and form. According to the Hindu philosophy God is *sarvavyāpī* — omnipresent and pervades the entire Universe and can be realized in any place through prayers, *anuṣṭhāna*s (rituals), meditation and spiritual *sādhanā*s (practices). His presence is always more explicitly felt and realized in a temple. Therefore visits to such holy and sacred places has been our tradition that is being followed to this day. The holy pilgrimage is conducted with utmost humility, purity in thought, word and deed. Keeping this in mind our forefathers had set up time- honoured traditions, customs and tenets in the form of meditation, *nāmasaṅkīrtana*, *bhajana*s, reading of sacred books, *satsaṅga*, etc. These rituals were prescribed to us thousands of years ago, with the sole idea that an ardent devotee and an earnest seeker can feel the presence of God and derive much spiritual benefit.

According to Hindu mythology, music and gods have always been identified with each other. We cannot imagine any god without a particular instrument. Many of the important deities have their own instruments and are worshipped as embodiments of music or art. Lord Śiva is the embodiment of *nāda* playing the *ḍamuru* and also the performer of the *tāṇḍava* (the cosmic dance). Lord Brahmā is the origin of music inspired by *Sāmaveda*. From the word *OṀ* (the *praṇava mantra*) the following concepts were emanated.

Sadyojātam

Vāmadevam

Tatpuruṣam

Īśānam

Aghoram

These five factors are identified as the five faces of Lord Śiva and it is believed that the musical notes emanated from them and were passed on to posterity. Lord Śiva was supposed to have taught these to his prime disciple and consort Pārvatī and from there on it was passed on to his other disciples Sage Nārada, Tumburu, Nandikeśvara (the *mṛdaṅgam* exponent) and Goddess Sarasvatī, the eternal Vaiṇika.

Goddess Sarasvatī, the goddess of knowledge, is always associated with the *vīṇā*. Lord Kṛṣṇa, the flutist, also claims that he is the *Sāmaveda* among the Vedas. Goddess Pārvatī is the embodiment of *lāsya*. Lord Viṣṇu plays on the percussion while his consort Goddess Lakṣmī, the goddess of wealth is a connoisseur of music. Sage Nārada can never be imagined without his *thampura* and he is also known as the *vaiṇika-gāyaka* (an expert in vocal music and *vīṇā*). Nandī, the bull, is the master of *laya*. Almost all the demi-gods like the *gandharva*s, the *yakṣa*s and the *kinnara*s are believed to be proficient in music and musical instruments. Music is also known as *Āndhra Vidya*. Hanumān was supposed to be proficient in the instrument called *hanumad vīṇā* and this is the predecessor of the present-day *vicitra vīṇā*.

There has always been a perfect unison of *nāda* with *Paramātmā* (supreme power) and in this unison one can find the "Transcendental Power" — *nādopāsanā*. The one who created us is the Almighty. He can only be seen from within. This is the philosophy of our life, and a man who acts according to this philosophy is believed to see this Power within himself and shun suffering for himself as well as others.

Classical music and dance had a natural affinity with the temple and religion. Not only are the themes almost always religious, the performances of dance and music were carried on in temples where it was free for the public. The implication is that those who came to the temple, at least while they were within the temple, are in an elevated form of mind and do not look for cheap entertainment. Almost all the rulers (kings) in south India gave importance to the fine arts. They built many fine temples in those days (we must remember that in those days temples served the same purpose as the modern auditoriums), and patronized artistes. Traditionally a balance was struck between the king, who ruled like a feudal lord and patron, and the power of religion. All arts and sciences prospered under the wings of the temple generously supported by the king. On the other hand, the king's holy goals, i.e. to be victorious, maintain peace within his own territory, enhance rain and rich crops, etc. were sustained by the temple priests who served in both the temples and the court.

The *utsava*s (festivals) are considered highly pleasing to the Lord. Various arts and crafts depend on temples and festivals. The insistence on the recitation of the sacred texts, as part of the festivals (rituals), apart from propagating them, help in preserving their form. The rituals instil in the devotee a sense of spiritual involvement either directly or indirectly. Great ritual care is taken to keep all the divine forces embedded in the temple area peaceful and content. Like a royal lord, the Divine Lord holds a court, receives visitors, listens to their requests, is awoken with the auspicious sounds of music, is bathed, dressed and amused, and, what is more important, He is emotionally involved with His devotees. One of the reasons for the many Hindu temple rituals may be the fact that this cultural religious syncretism has absorbed traditions of very divergent nature, divergent in all respects, time and social stratum.

Temples in south India particularly have played an important part in the preservation and development of music. In India, music and dance were never conceived of as mere items of entertainment. Even the greatest men and women of the land treated music and dance as subjects worthy of serious study and practice. These two arts were elevated to the status of *vidya*. They helped the thinking men and women to understand something of the Infinite.

At a time when the habit of recording songs in notation was not cultivated, the only method by which the music compositions were handed on to posterity was through oral tradition. Hymn singers among the Śaiva and Vaiṣṇava saints like Seramān Perumāḷ (*circa* CE 700) in Śaivism and Kulaśekara Āḻvār (*circa* CE 800) in Vaiṣṇavism had sung wonderful compositions in their respective canons which are held sacred even in the present day. Temple festivals have given rise to a large number of new poetic patterns and motifs.

1

Role of Music in Vedas

The Hindus owe allegiance to the Vedas, which are their holy scriptures. The Vedas present a complete and panoramic view of life in all its facets. They contain within themselves the philosophical conclusions of the life of great saints and *ṛṣis* and also serve as a guide for the art of living with a detailed record of conduct for the ordinary man.

The Vedas are divided into four parts — the Saṁhitās, the Brāhmaṇas, the Āraṇyakas and the Upaniṣads. The Saṁhitās are hymns sung in exquisite poetry, in praise of the Vedic gods like Indra (rain), Agni (fire), Varuṇa (water), Vāyu (air), Pṛthvī (earth), etc. The Brāhmaṇas are the liturgical portion of the Vedas and contain details about the *yāga*s (rituals) and sacrifices to be performed by everyone. Āraṇyakas are the mature thoughts of persons, who having experienced richly all its aspects, and not being satisfied with the earthly pleasures of the senses, seek the salvation of the spirit through renouncement from the worldly pleasures in the quietude of the forests (*āraṇya*s).

The Upaniṣads, also called as the Vedānta, represent the quintessence and the acme of the philosophic thinking, and the mystic realization of the ancient seers. All these four forms, put together, present a pattern or a way of life, to which the Hindus, right up to the present day, owe their rituals and traditions and their allegiance broadly.

According to the Vedas and their ideals, a man's life is a sum total of the result of all his actions or *karma* in his previous births. For the Hindus, life and religion are so entirely mixed up that it is difficult to separate them.

The Vedas, particularly the *Ṛgveda,* represent the earliest and the most important phase of the sacred language and literature of India. The *Ṛgveda* is undoubtedly the oldest literary monument of the Indo-European languages. The exact period when the hymns were composed is a matter of conjecture. We can say that any approach to certainty is that the oldest of the hymns cannot date from later than the thirteenth century BCE. This assertion is based upon the following grounds — Buddhism that began to spread in India about 500 BCE presupposes the existence of not only the Vedas, but also the intervening literature of the Brāhmaṇas and Upaniṣads. The development of language and religious thought apparent in the extensive literature of the successive phases of the two Vedic periods renders it necessary to postulate the lapse of seven or eight centuries to account for the gradual changes, linguistic, religious, social and political, that this literature displays. On astronomical calculations, one Sanskrit scholar concluded that the oldest Vedic hymns dated from 3000 BCE, while another dated them as far as 6000 BCE. These calculations are based on the assumption that the early Indians possessed an exact astronomical knowledge of the sun's course such as there is no evidence, or even probability, that they actually possessed. On the other hand, the possibility of such extreme antiquity seems to be disproved by the relationship of the hymns in the *Ṛgveda* to the oldest part of *Avesta,* if it were known at a stage some five centuries later. We must thus rest content with the moderate estimate of the thirteenth century BCE as the approximate date for the beginning of the Ṛgvedic period. This estimate has not been invalidated by the discovery in 1907 of the names of Indian deities Mitra, Varuṇa, Indra and Nāsatya, in the inscription of about 1400 BCE found in Asia Minor. For the phonetic form in which these names appear may belong to the Indo-Iranian period when the Indians and Persians were still one people. The date of the inscription leaves two centuries for the separation of the Indians, their migration to India, and the commencement of the Vedic hymn literature in the north-west of Hindustan. When the Indo-Āryans entered India, they brought with them a religion in which the gods were chiefly personified powers of Nature, a few of them, such as Dyaus, going back to the Indo-

European, and others such as Mitra, Varuṇa and Indra, to the Indo Iranian period. They also brought with them the cult of fire and *soma*, besides the knowledge of the art of composing religious poems in several metres, as a comparison of the *Ṛgveda* and the *Avesta.* The purpose of these ancient hymns was to propitiate the gods by praises accompanying the offering of melted butter poured in the fire and the juice of *soma* plant placed on the sacrificial grass.

Hereditary priesthood exclusively composed the hymns, which survived in the *Ṛgveda* from the early period of the Indo-Āryan invasion. They were handed down in different families by memory, not by writing, which could have hardly been introduced into India before about 700 BCE. These family groups of hymns were gradually brought together till, with successive additions, they assumed the earliest collected form of the *Ṛgveda*. Then followed the constitution of the Saṁhitā text, which appears to have taken place about 600 BCE, at the end of the period of the Brāhmaṇas, but before the Upaniṣads, which form appendages to those works, came into existence. The creators of the Saṁhitā did not in any way alter the diction of the hymns that were collected together. They only applied to the text certain rules of *saṁdhi* that prevailed in their time, and by which, in particular, vowels are either contracted, or changed into semi-vowels, and *a* is often dropped after *e*, and *o*, in such a way, as constantly to obscure the metre. Soon after this work was concluded, extraordinary precautions were taken to preserve from loss or corruption the sacred text thus fixed. The earliest expedient of this kind was the formulation of the *pada* or "word" text in which all the words of the Saṁhitā text are separated. They were then given in their original form as unaffected by the rules of the *saṁdhi* (combination) and in which most compounds and some derivatives and inflected forms are analysed. This text, which is virtually the earliest commentary of the *Ṛgveda,* was followed by other and more complicated methods of reciting the text, and by various works called *anukramanta*s or indexes. These enumerate from the beginning to the end of the *Ṛgveda* the number of stanzas contained in each hymn, the deities, and the metres of all the stanzas of the *Ṛgveda*. Thanks to these various precautions the text of the *Ṛgveda* has been handed down for 2500 years with a fidelity that finds no parallel in any other literature.

Sāmavedic Music

Sāma refers to the *tejas* aspect of *Brahman.* Lord Kṛṣṇa in *Bhagavad-Gītā* says, *vedānām sāmavedosmi* (of the Vedas "I am the *Sāmaveda*"). In the Upaniṣads we find the mystic meaning for *sāma.* It means a song. The *Chāndogya Upaniṣad* explains *Sāma* as follows: *Sāma* is composed of *Sa+ama.* The *sa* signifies *vāk* or form and *ama* signifies *prāṇa* (life-force).

> *yad etad sa ca amasca sāmavedatam tat sāma abhavat* ।
> *tat samnah sāmatvam* ॥

When there is *Sama* or harmony between *sa* and *ama* then we have *sāma. Sāma* is thus the cosmic music of *Brahman.* We have *Sāma* whenever there is harmony between form and life, word and metre, note and rhythm and centre and circumference. *Sāma* is the musical rendering of the hymns occurring in the *Ṛgveda.* In the technical language of music literature we can say that *Sāmaveda* has borrowed the *mhatu* (text) of the song from the *Ṛgveda* and given the *dhātu* or musical rendering itself. The characteristic feature of *Sāma* is not the words but the musical rendering. The hymns of the *Ṛgveda* were set to music in *Sāmaveda* but certain structural changes were made in the text of the hymns when they were given musical setting in *Sāma.* There are five components of a Sāmavedic song, i.e. *Huṅkāra* or *Hiṅkāra, Prastava, Udgītha, Pratihāra* and *Nidhāna.* A Sāmavedic song is sung by a group of three singers — the *prastotā, udgata* and *pratihārata.* All the three first utter *huṁ* in the key-note. Then the *prastotā* sings the introductory portion of the song together with *auṁ.* Next the *udgata* sings the *udgaitha* portion of the *Sāma.* This is the main portion of the song. *Udgaitha* means songs in higher notes. The *pratihāra* catches up the last syllable of *udgaitha* and starts singing the *pratihāra* portion. The concluding portion of the song is then sung by all the three together. After this, i.e. the concluding part of the song (*nidhāna*) all the three singers together jointly get together to chant *auṁ. Tālam* was not used in *Sāma* but this concept was developed later. Though there was no *tālam* in *Sāma* there was definitely the rhythm, which was expressed by the metre (*chanda*) of the particular hymn, and in the actual singing of the hymn the rhythm was determined by the *mantras*.

From the time of the Vedas and during the period of the Itihāsas, Purāṇas and Āgamas (ancient texts and literature) the *bhakti* movement spread all over India. It became very powerful during the medieval times. In the south, particularly in Tamil Nadu the "Vaiṣṇavite" and the "Śaivite" mystics (the 12 Āḻvārs and the 63 Nāyaṉmārs, Śaṅkarācārya, Rāmānujācārya, Madhvācārya, etc.) took the new manifestation of spiritual force to dizzying heights through their spiritual hymns. The tremendous tidal waves rocked the other parts of the country, in the form of a number of saints like Caitanya, Tukārāma, Tulasīdāsa, Mīrābhāī and hundreds of others. They created the pathway to the Almighty through music and lifted the devotees to sweet and sublime spiritual heights. It should be remembered that Indian music and dance influenced South-East Asia, particularly the island of Bali and also the other Western countries. While some of them recognized the curative and therapeutic power of music the Indians realized the spiritual value of music.

A popular Sanskrit verse says *śruti-mātā-pīṭhā-laya* — *śruti* (pitch) is the mother and rhythm (*laya*) is the father. Music has never been looked upon as a form of entertainment but as a means of *mokṣa* (eternal salvation). Music for the Indians has always been the resource, from which they always seek comfort or solace in joy or grief, for prayer or praise. We can now understand the importance Indians have given to music, and why they have this religious passion for the fine arts, and why the fine arts have religion as their very centre of heart and life. We can also understand how and why temples have played an important role in promoting all the fine arts.

Music is holy art in India. The spiritual side of music has taken deep roots in our land as the people have all along been more prone to spirituality. It is primarily because of the spiritual influence of the temples. South India is a land of temples and every village invariably has a temple. In fact, the temple is the centre around which a village developed. These temples have not only been functioning as places of worship but also as centres of all fine arts. These art forms grew adjuncts to religion and the temples with their vast endowments had a regular establishment with artistes like singers, composers (musicians, dancers, instrumentalists, etc.) for offering musical service in its sacred precincts. The abundant epigraphical and inscriptional evidence bear testimony to all these fine arts and the hymns that have been preserved over the years. Thus all forms of music and dance became indispensable items of worship (rituals) in the temples of south India.

2

Music as a Form of Worship

Music is equated with worship and *sādhanā* (spiritual practice). Music is the finest of the fine arts. It is also *vidyā* (knowledge). This is why in the earlier days it was called Upaveda that helps to realize the Supreme Being. Music is claimed to possess the power to "purify him that chants and him that listens." Congregational musical recital of God's name helps even the inanimate, immovable and inert objects of God's creation to get imprints of the name of God by ethereal vibrations, that in due time will bring liberation to them also. Self-recital elevates the individual soul, whereas the congregational singing of mystic names of God elevates the Universe, the sacred creation of God Divine. Singing the name of God is the most effective remedy for all ailments of the human body and soul. Music is the best therapy for any ailment — physical or mental. Temples are like beacon lights and they lure people to come and taste the nectar of divine bliss. There is a saying "that a place without a temple is unsuitable for human habitation." The famous poetess Auvvayār has quoted:

> *kovil illādha ūril kuḍi irukka venḍām* ॥
> *ālayam thoḻuvadu sālavum nanru* ॥

> Do not reside at a place where there is no temple.
> Worshipping in a temple is extremely virtuous.

Temples were designed to create environments congenial to the expansion of one's mind and soul and above and beyond the drab realities of life, into a region where the temporal pre-occupations of man dropped off and he stood in nakedness before God, as God made him. They are constructed and equipped with the best treasures of all fine arts.

Classical music and dance had a natural affinity with the temple and religion. Not only were the themes almost always religious, the performances of dance and music were carried on in temples where they were free for the public. The implication is that those who came to the temple, at least while they were within the temple were in an elevated form of mind and did not look for cheap entertainment. Almost all the rulers of south India gave a very great impetus to the fine arts. They built temples with the sole idea of promoting *bhakti* and the fine arts and also patronized artistes. One should bear in mind that in those days, temples served the same purpose as the modern auditoriums and *sabhās*. All arts and sciences, astronomy, etc. prospered under the wings of the temples generously supported by the kings. Traditionally, an equal balance was struck between the kings who ruled like feudal lords and patrons with the power of religion. Temples in south India particularly have played an important part in the preservation for posterity the traditions of dance, drama and music. In India music and dance were never conceived of as mere items of entertainment. Music in its triple aspect of *gīta* (vocal), *vādya* (instrumental music), and *nṛtya* (dance) were given a prominent place in temple traditions (rituals). From the *Kāmikāgamam* one can see that the performance of music and dance was not something optional but an integral and compulsory part of rituals in worship. Temples have thus been the home of static dance and dynamic dance and music. The insistence on the recitation of hymns from sacred texts as part of rituals, apart from propagating it, instils in the devotee a sense of spiritual involvement either directly or indirectly. Great ritual care is taken to keep all the divine forces embedded in the temple area peaceful and content. Like a royal lord, the Divine Lord holds a court, receives visitors, listens to their requests, is awoken to the auspicious sounds of music, is bathed, dressed, and amused (all through with music as the medium). What is more important is that He is emotionally involved with His devotees right through the music rituals. It is also very significant that the "divinities" and "celestials" have been associated with music, musical instruments and dancing. The concept of God as *Nāda Brahma* (embodiment of musical sound) is highly significant. This concept implies that one can reach Him through the path of "Absolute Music." The significance of the *Holy Trinity* being associated with musical instruments deserves special attention. Śiva is associated with the *ḍamaru* (percussion), Kṛṣṇa an *avatāra* of Viṣṇu with the flute, and Sarasvatī the consort of Brahmā with the *vīṇā* and Nārada with the *tānapūrā*.

3

The Bhakti Movement

THE *bhakti* movement that rose in the ancient Tamil land more than 1500 years ago opened with the hymns of Poygai Āḻvār, Bhūtath Āḻvār and Pey Āḻvār. By the time we came to the seventh century, Periāḻvār had electrified our approach to the Divine by positioning the Supreme as the baby Kṛṣṇa. Kṛṣṇa's childhood and boyhood as seen in Periāḻvār verses inspired a new genre in Tamil literature, called *Piḷḷai Tamiḻ*. The picture of the flute-player of Bṛndāvan has continued to haunt us with all its loveliness even today.

From the second half of the first millennium CE till today Hinduism has been dominated by the monotheistic religion of *bhakti* — devotion. The devotee (*bhakta*) surrenders himself to God's grace. This self-surrender is called *prapatti*. It is made with faith in God's boundless love and sympathy for all His creatures and in particular for His dedicated, self-effacing devotee. This form of *prapatti-bhakti* began in south India. From the beginning of Tamil religious literature, in the early centuries CE, poets mention God as present in temples and shrines in His full glory, even while at the same time they believe in His transcendence. This divine presence is localized in images. The *bhakti* religion discouraged complicated rituals in favour of simple services to God and the spontaneous display of pious emotion. Overwhelmed by his love for God, the devotee craved for His nearness and felt it to be available in the temples, where God had taken up residence to favour His devotees and enjoy their love. Tamil poet-saints, both Śaiva and Vaiṣṇava, moved from one holy place to another to pour out their religious feelings in beautiful hymns to the forms of God manifest in the temples. Often, such a saint remained associated with a particular temple. The songs or hymns composed by these poets, invariably addressed to a deity belonging to a particular temple, were fine examples of a classical heritage. Sanskrit and Tamil were the most suitable medium to convey the complex religious ideas borne by these hymns. The complex synthesis resulting from this exchange was more than a thousand years old. During that long period many sects and cults were created and these further developed and changed their original forms, and the Hindu religion went through much metamorphoses. A traditional art like Indian music can only be studied in its own cultural context, that is to say, on the basis of its own philosophical and religious concepts. In Indian devotional hymns, the musical development runs parallel to that of the historical development of the Indian religious rituals.

Whatever the form of the particular temple deity (image), to the ecstatic devotee it was his own chosen deity who appeared in it. In all theistic religions the worshipper communicates to his God or Gods through some form of prayer. The most compact form of Hindu prayer is *mantra*. For a believer will often repeat his *mantra* not only in the course of ritual devotions but also when he is emotionally disturbed. However a *mantra* is only a formula, and allows very little scope for expressing emotion. It was hymns of praise — *stuti, stava,* and *stotra* — (the terms are synonymous) through which devotees came to express their understanding of God and their feelings for Him. South Indian devotion produced the vernacular hymns of the Tamil saints, the Āḻvārs and the Nāyaṉmārs. As this *prapatti-bhakti* spread through India, it gave rise to new forms of prayer hymns variously known as *kīrtana, bhajana* and *dohā*. The characteristic feature of these lyrical hymns is a declaration of total surrender to one's chosen deity, who is envisaged as both infinitely loving and exquisitely beautiful. In these lyrics, the poet's religious experience has become identical with aesthetical experience as defined by the classical Indian literary tradition. This type of lyrical hymn developed most among the Vaiṣṇavites, whose religion valued and encouraged ecstatic experience. The two most important north Indian Vaiṣṇava sects, founded by Vallabha and by Caitanya, have produced marvellous poets in this genre. But the earliest example of such lyrical poetry in Sanskrit is the *Gītagovindam*, which can be said to have been the main single source of inspiration for all later religious poet-singers, irrespective of cult or sect. *Kīrtana* like *stava* or *stotra*, literally means "laudatory hymns." *Kīrtana*s are of two types. In the *nāma-kīrtana* the deity is extolled by singing His or Her names. The *līlā-kīrtana* recalls the deity's exploits described in the mythological texts (Purāṇa). The *kīrtana* evokes the aesthetic experience of love for the divine (*bhakti rasa*). Among the various moods which may be experienced by the devotees, the Smārta and the Tāntric mainly accept three, namely the moods of repose — (*śānta rasa*), of total surrender like a bonded slave — (*dāsya rasa*), and the tender love like that of a mother to a child or vice versa — (*vātsalya rasa*). (These moods are found in the hymns of the Āḻvārs and the Nāyaṉmārs). The *bhakti rasa* of the devotee derives from his realization that his deity is of perfect beauty, transcending worldly experience. In Indian aesthetic theory, the perfection of a beautiful object evokes in the beholder emotions so acute that they transport him from his mundane existence to the transcendent state of pure bliss. The exquisite beauty and charm of the deity evokes in the devotee feelings of wonderment and love, that transport him to the realm of transcendent bliss. To the devotee his adored deity is beautiful and to love a marvellously beautiful God is no more than natural. That is why in later Vaiṣṇavism so much emphasis is laid down on the beauty of Kṛṣṇa and his favourite companion Rādhā. Tantrism is a form of Indian religion in which ritual (known as external worship) and meditative practice (also known as internal practice) are indissolubly linked. Salvation consists in the realization that ultimately one is identical with the Supreme Godhead, the object of one's adoration. To each of these stages of mental progress, corresponding ritual actions are carried out as one meditates. These ritual actions conspicuously involve stereotype gestures (*mudrā*), formulaic utterances (*mantra*) and music in different forms. All these are rituals that are observed in temple worship. In order to understand the position of *mantra* in Hindu religion, we must return for a moment to the earliest Indian religious speculations. These aimed to explain not only the efficacy of a sacrifice but also why the words accompanying a sacrifice were necessary. As early as the *Ṛgveda*, the *mantra* is praised as the form of Agni (the fire-God) hidden in the sacrificer's heart; it is also said to guard important deities like Agni. In the hymn of Speech (Vāc), Speech is said to be all-pervasive; it supports such exalted deities as Mitra, Varuṇa, Indra, and Agni. In the Upaniṣad, a close link is established between consciousness, which on the empirical level is homogeneous with the life-breath (*prāṇa*), the mind which is the faculty for discursive thought and speech.

The grammarians of Sanskrit and the Mīmāṁsakas, the theorists of the Vedic ritualism, developed closely related theories of the nature of speech and language. Patañjali, the ancient Indian grammarian, in the introduction to his great commentary on *Pāṇini*, of the fifth century BCE, developed the theory that there exists an external sound, which is the basis of any mental assessment of the meaning of significant sound. This essence of significant sound is called *śabda-sphoṭa*, the bursting/illuminating sound, which contains the meaning of all meaningful sounds of human language.

The Development of the Hymn as a Musical Form

Before the *kīrtana* became a specific type of musical composition with a characteristic form, the word *kīrtana* was used in its general sense of praising to denote all kinds of religious hymns in praise of a favourite God (*iṣṭa-devatā*). This type of *kīrtana* singing, which was specially cultivated by the Indian Vaiṣṇava devotees of the middle-age, has been mentioned in the *Bhāgavata Purāṇa* as one of the eight obligations of a true devotee *(bhakta)*. By this time the *bhakti* cult had already spread in various forms all over India. The large collections of devotional hymns composed from the eighth century CE onwards are the outcome of a religious revival that was favoured by the stable political situation of the Indian Empire during the Gupta dynasties (third to sixth century CE). Generally scholars distinguish two main types of eulogies, the descriptive-speculative type and the lyrical-devotional type. There is no doubt that the second type of hymns were sung and sometimes accompanied with dance as well. But even with regard to the first type we cannot exclude musical performance. It is very unlikely that these descriptive, speculative (sometimes didactic, sometimes philosophical) hymns were purely literary products for reading only. In the period of the eighth to the tenth century CE *bhakti* was very productive in south India.

4

The Role of Temples in Promoting Music

TRADITIONS are often regarded as sacrosanct and monolithic. The making of India's religious tradition has been one of the most complex processes in the development of its culture and civilization. The traditions in performing devotional music in the temples could be traced back to the earliest composers of *bhakti* or devotional music, the Tevāram trinity and the Āḻvārs.

It is said that the soul of a nation is enshrined in its religious places, literature and all its fine arts. All these are thus represented as having been born from the Almighty and are highly venerated in our land. Fine arts in India have always been looked upon as a part and parcel of the religious and devotional mindset prevalent in the past.

When one traces the evolution of devotional music one must necessarily take a peep into the past. Temples would be the most obvious choice as the starting point, since they have been the important centres which promoted music. The Hindu temple is a religious institution enshrining various objects of worship. The human tendency to venerate objects that are endowed with superhuman traits gradually led to the evolution of a place to enshrine them. This paved the way for the birth of temples.

The temples that initially served as places of solace, blossomed into full-fledged social institutions embracing many aspects of human life. As seats of learning, the temple gave an impetus to the study of Vedas, Purāṇas and many aspects of human life. A galaxy of scholars assembled in the *maṇḍapam* (temple halls) to indulge in literary and philosophical discourses. The temples gave a fillip to the development of fine arts and also served as repositories of architecture, sculpture and painting. They preserved the royal and the official orders in the form of stone inscriptions and copper plates. Parts of the temples served as granaries and distributed grains in times of distress. The *maṇḍapams* also served as venues for the meetings of the village assemblies and of the officials of the court. The temples sometimes maintained dispensaries also. Thus, temples acted as benevolent social institutions. In short, as a nucleus that gathered around itself all that was best in the art of civilized existence and regulated them with humaneness born in the spirit of *dharma*, the Indian temple has few parallels in the annals of mankind. Besides being an abode of the Divine, these temples also served as the true symbol of the cultural unity of the country, comprehending within them all classes of society.

About 3000 years back, that is, even earlier than the Saṅgam Age, Jainism and Buddhism were predominant religions. In the south especially these religions were spreading slowly and steadily and there were many kings who were (both Śaivites and Vaiṣṇavites) encouraging and patronizing Jainism and Buddhism. Even though Hinduism was older to Jainism and Buddhism, these religions were slowly spreading because of the disciplined lives and the intellectual knowledge of the heads of these religions. Their sermons on self-control, disciplined way of living and *ahiṁsā*, made people respect them and also slowly change from their own religions and religious convictions. This period (the black period of Hinduism) lasted for a very long time.

Revival of Hinduism

Even though Buddhism and Jainism were able to impress tremendously upon the people on the disciplined way of life and debating on means to achieve happiness, these religions were not able to reach out to the hearts (soul) of the common man. These religions were only able to pave a path for righteousness but not the path for the Ultimate Salvation (bliss) that is yearned and pined for by every human being. Also the rigidity in these religions and some of the strict conditions to attain salvation made the people feel that there was no religious depth in them.

The advent of Ādi Śaṅkara (Śaṇ-matha) and Rāmānuja (Vaiṣṇavism) introduced the *bhakti mārga* that came along with them in the form of the Nāyaṉmārs and the Āḻvārs. These saints impressed on the people the importance of communicating to God directly through prayers and songs and also chanting. They impressed upon people that not only could they pour out their happiness to God but also their grievances and even anger and thus seek comfort and solace.

During the Renaissance period of Hinduism the Trinity — Sambandar, Appar and Sundarar — wanted to show to the world the greatness of Hinduism (particularly Śaivism). They felt that the easiest way to commune with God could be only through music in a very simple but comprehensive way. For the devotees to understand the concept of God they set to tune hymns with simple words and sweet tunes with a lot of emotion in them. This movement of communicating with God through music was not only a comeback to Hinduism but also the beginning of all fine arts in south India in a very big and positive way.

With a perfect understanding of the unique psychology of each human being, Hinduism provides unfettered freedom for each individual to adopt religious worship according to his own light, so that each soul could chalk out his own path to salvation. Innumerable paths — the *jñāna yoga, karma yoga, dhyāna,* etc. — exist. The individual can choose his own *mārga* (path). Śaivism, one of the classifications of Hinduism has striven to resist the corrupting influences of material forces. The essence of Hinduism as a religion consists in describing the ultimate base of the Universe, not in any anthropomorphic terms, but as a pure ultimate power, the source of all power and life. The rising tide against the growing influence of Jainism and Buddhism found expression in the widespread *bhakti* movement. The outpourings of the Āḻvārs and Nāyaṉmārs in the course of their propagandist peregrinations constitute the most priceless treasure in Tamil literature. This great volume of popular devotional literature couched in simple diction and catchy tunes when set to music, ravished the hearts of the commoner also.

Simply by venting out one's feelings to God one can easily communicate with Him, and this path is the easiest and simplest way of reaching Him. This is what these saintly poets proved to the people and thus brought about a new revival in Hinduism. They also revived the art and culture through their poems that had both spiritual value and literary value. Chanting of God's names with deep emotion and soulful music brought about a great feeling of confidence and faith in man, and also the feeling that he is able to commune with Him, that He is there always for him to protect him.

This feeling of emotion (*bhakti*) and the faith and solace that it gave the devotees was something that Buddhism and Jainism could not give. This then was the main cause for the revival of Hinduism in a big way. It should also be noted that the essence of the Buddhist and Jaina philosophy however was not neglected. Instead it was respected and absorbed by these great saints into their works and merged with it.

Thus Ādi Śaṅkara's philosophy and the hymns of the Āḻvārs and the Nāyaṉmārs won over all the new religions and revived Hinduism. If Śaṅkara's philosophy can be compared to the intellect of Hinduism, the hymns of these saint-poets can be compared to the soul of Hinduism.

The Tevāram-trinity (Śaivism) and the Āḻvārs (Vaiṣṇavism) have composed beautiful hymns that have melodic beauty, emotional depth and literary techniques. Their total surrender has come in the form of Tevārams and Pāsurams, which are performed or offered to the deities as a part of rituals in almost all the temples of the south. The 274 Śaivite shrines lauded in the hymns of the three savants (Nāyaṉmārs) Tirujñāna Sambandar, Tirunāvukarasar and Sundarar are held in high esteem. Known as *Pāḍal Petra Sthalaṅgal* (temples eulogized by the Trinity in their hymns) they embrace the whole of India although a majority of them are located in the south. In addition to these temples, a number of Śaivite shrines sanctified in the later *Tirumuṟai* hymns and glorified by the savants of later ages also exist.

Similarly the Āḻvārs have lauded 108 Vaiṣṇava shrines in their hymns. Known as *maṅgalaśāsanam* these temples are eulogized in the

Āḻvār Pāsurams (hymns) and were held in esteem by the 12 Āḻvārs. These temples are also called the *108 Tirupatis* and embrace the whole of India and Nepal.

In the north also one sees the emergence of devotional outpourings from Gorakhnātha, Mīrābāī, Sūrdās and Kabīr. In the east Jayadeva of Orissa (twelfth century CE) and Annamācārya of present Andhra Pradesh (1408–1503 CE) have made outstanding contributions.

Spiritualism has been the key content of Indian music. The beautiful interweaving of the devotional element and aesthetics has always made it ethereal and eternal. The basic idea behind compositions has been to visualize and seek God. In fact, it has been said that the easiest way to attain salvation is to sing the greatness of the Almighty.

The saints, seers and composers of classical music have basically composed songs only as a means of expressing their devout feelings and also to communicate with the "self" and "soul." Music, when presented to God as an offering, inspires the person and the devotional feelings therein, giving rise to torrential and tuneful outpourings. Singing and chanting in praise of God awakens the singer's consciousness of the Divine and makes one sensitive to the Divine message. Music therefore, establishes a direct contact between the spiritual and the phenomenal realms. Music is the element of motion that brings forth the desired union. This vital element and the glorification of God through religion in the tradition of devotional music indicate that the Hindu *bhakti* movement must have been initiated and advanced by poet singers.

Music, whether vocal or instrumental, is the most spontaneous form of human expression. The words of a song represent its rational basis, while the melody brings forth the emotion concealed in poetry. The saintly poets never composed their devotional verses as merely literary pieces but weaved them into intricate melody yarns and sang them before their chosen and personified deities. The fundamental corollary to elucidate, present and advance this spiritual exercise and the sure attainment of the goal rested not only on the selection of that specific instrument that would produce the expected results and could also be handled with ease and certainty by the initiated, well-versed artiste but also on the layman. Easy accessibility, ready availability and the communicative potential of this means were the primary criteria for selection. And music has been tested and found the most satisfactory medium as it attracts, enchants, enthralls, enriches and easily appeals to all segments of the society.

5

The Nāyaṉmārs

THE Nāyaṉmārs are the sixty-three saints who expounded the Śaivite philosophy all over south India. They are regarded with utmost respect in the Śaivite temples and homes until today. The hymns of the Nāyaṉmārs were popularized by Nambiāṇḍār Nambi, a staunch Śaivite. These saints belonged to different communities (castes) and economic backgrounds. But they were all ardent devotees of Lord Śiva and paved the way for righteousness through their soulful hymns and became one with Him. Special festivals are conducted in the temples all over south to celebrate their birthdays and it is observed with offering of their hymns as an important ritual.

The *Aruvathīmūvar Utsavam,* the festival of the 63 Nāyaṉmārs is observed in all the Śiva temples in south India during (March–April) the *Panguni* month on the star of *Utharam.* On this day the images of the 63 Nāyaṉmārs are taken out in procession by the devotees and paid tributes with due reverence.

"Nāyaṉmār" means the head or a leader — A "Leader who became one with God." The Nāyaṉmārs were also known as Śivan Aḍiyārs — the devotees of Lord Śiva and the Āḻvārs as Tirumāl Aḍiyārs — the devotees of Tirumāl or Viṣṇu. Given below are the names of the 63 Nāyaṉmārs and some details about them.

The 63 Nāyaṉmārs

S. no	Names	Birthplace
1.	**Adi-patta Nāyaṉmār**	Nuḷaipāḍi near Nāgapaṭṭinam
2.	**Appūdiyaḍigaḷ** He took Appar as his *guru* when he met him in his hometown at Tirumunaipāḍi	Tiṅgaḷūr (near Kumbakoṇam)

3.	**Amarnīdiyār**	Paḻayāṟaī
4.	**Arivāḷ Tāya Nāyaṉār** He tried to kill himself with his sickle (*arivāḷ*) as an offering to God.	Gaṇamaṅgalam (between Tiruthuraipūṇḍi and Tiruvārūr)
5.	**Āṉāya Nāyaṉār** Was also an accomplished flautist.	Tirumaṅgalam (Trichy)
6.	**Isai Jñāniyār** Wife of Saḍaiyanār and mother of Sundaramurti Nāyaṉār. Sundaramūrti Nāyaṉār has sung in praise of his parents in his hymns	
7.	**Idaṅ Kaḻhiyār** King of a small state in Coḻanāḍu	Koḍuṁbāḷūr
8.	**Iyaṟ Pagaiyār**	Poompuhar in Coḷanadu
9.	**Iḷaiyāṉ kuḍimāṟar**	Iḷyaiyāṅkuḍi near Tirunaḷḷāṟu but some say near Paramakuḍi near Ramanathapuram as his name sounds like a traditional Pāṇḍyanāḍu name.
10.	**Rudrapasupatiyār** Was very proficient in the Rudra Veda and hence was known as Rudrāpati.	Tiruthalaiyūr between Mayilāḍuthurai and Pēralam
11.	**Yeṟipattar**	Karūr near Erode
12.	**Eyarkon Kalikāmar Nāyaṉār**	Tiruperumaṅgalam, 1 km north of Tirupunkūru
13.	**Enādi Nādhar**	Eyinannūr (Coḷanāḍu)
14.	**Aiyaḍigaḷ Kādavarkon** Was a Pallava king. He patronized fine arts, Sanskrit, and Iyal, Isai, and Nāṭakam. Renounced his kingdom at an early age and went on long pilgrimage.	Kāñcīpuram
15.	**Gaṇanāda Nāyaṉār**	Sīrkāḻi
16.	**Gaṇam Pullar** Chieftain of his community	Irukku Vellur-now known as Bellūr
17.	**Kaṇṇappa Nāyaṉār** Was highly respected and revered by Appar, Sundarar, Paṭṭinnathār and others	Uduppur (now known as Udukur) near Rasampeṭṭai on Arakoṇam–Gunṭakkal railway route

18. **Kalikkambar**	Tirupennagaḍam, famous for its Śiva Temple
19. **Kaliyār**	Tiruvoṟṟiyūr
20. **Kaḻaṟiṟṟaṟivār** Also known as Seramān Perumāḷ Nāyaṉār. A close friend of Sundaramūrti Nāyaṉār. He has composed *Ponvannathu Andhādhi, Tiruvārūr Mummaṇi Kovai* and *Tirukayilai Gñāna Ulā*. All these are included in the eleventh *Tirumurai.*	Koḍungallūr near Trichūr
21. **Kaḻaṟsiṅga** Was a Pallava king dated CE 825-50. Kazharsingar was the name given to him by his devotees since he offered his queen's arm (cut) to the Tiruvārūr God.	Kāñcīpuram
22. **Kāriyar**	Tirukaḍavūr
23. **Kāraikāl Ammaiyār**	Kāraikkāl
24. **Kuṅguliyakkalya Nāyaṉār** Worked in the temple as the torch-bearer while the deity was taken out. He would keep filling the torch with kunguliyam (incense).	Tirukadavūr
25. **Kulaccirai Nāyaṉār** Chieftain of a small state in Pāṇḍiyanāḍu. He invited Tirugnāna Sambandar to propagate Śaivism in Madurai and revived Śaivism in Pāṇḍiyanāḍu in a big way.	Manamerkuḍi between Aranthāngi and Āvuḍaiyār Kovil
26. **Kūṟṟuva Nāyaṉār** Was a Kurunila Mannan (king) and was a staunch devotee of Lord Naṭarāja.	Tirukalandhai near Cidambaram
27. **Koccenġaṭcoḷa Nāyaṉār** This king was the son of Coḷa king Subhadevar and queen Kamalavathi. Built the famous temple at Tiruvānaikkāval.	Tiruvānaikkāval

He also built seventy Śiva temples and three Vaiṣṇava temples in Coḷanāḍu. He died at Tillai.	
28. **Koṭpuliyār** Minister in the court of Coḷa king	Nātyathankuḍi in Coḷanāḍu
29. **Saḍaiyanār** He was the father of Sundaramūrti Nāyaṉār	Tirunāvalūr
30. **Caṇdeśvarar** He taught people the importance religious of worshipping Śiva. All the rituals performed in the Śiva temples were performed in his name as can be seen in a lot of inscriptions in temples.	Tiruchenjanallūr near Tirupanaithāl on Kumbakoṇam–Chennai highway.
31. **Śaktiyār Nāyaṉār**	Kāñcīpuram
32. **Sākkiyār Nāyaṉār**	Tiruchaṅgamaṅgai
33. **Siṟappuli Nāyaṉār**	Tiruvakkūr
34. **Siṟuttoṇḍa Nāyaṉār** His name was Paranjothiyār and was the general in the court of Narasiṁhavarma Pallava CE 630-68. He defeated Pulikesi II — the Cāḷukya king	Tirucheng-kattangudi
35. **Sundaramūrti Nāyaṉār** He was born to Saḍayanār and Isaignāniyar and brought up by Narsingamunai Araiyar. His famous composition *Pittā pirai sūḍi* was composed at Tiruveṇṇ-ainallūr. He composed the Tiruthoṇḍai-thogai at Tiruvārūr. There are several myths and stories about his life. According to one, he married Sangili at the Tiruvoṟṟiyūr temple near Chennai. The day is still observed as an annual festival there. He lost both his eyes against a wager. They were restored at Kāñcīpuram and Tiruvārūr. He adopted the two daughters of Koṭpuliyār. His close	Tirunavallūr

associates were the following Nāyaṉmārs — Eyarkon, Seramān Perumāḷ, Somāsi Mārar, etc. He is supposed to have attained mukthi at Tiruvañchikuḷam where he rode a white elephant to Tiru Kailai (Kailāsam).	
36. **Seruthuṇai Nāyaṉār** Was the king of a small state near Tiruvārūr and lived at Kumanakoṭṭam.	Tañjāvūr
37. **Somāsimārar** Original name was Marai Nāyaṉār. He had performed a number of *soma veḷvi*s (*yāga*s) and hence was called Somāsi Mārar.	Tiruvambār
38. **Daṇḍi Aḍigaḷ** A blind poet	Tiruvārūr
39. **Tirukkuripputoṇḍar**	Kāñcīpuram
40. **Tirugnāna Sambandar** He came to Tirukolakka and began singing at a very tender age. He visited temples in and around the village and composed a number of songs. His wife and Tirunīlakaṇṭa Yāḻpāna Nāyaṉār always accompanied him. They played the yāḻ for him. He was supposed to have been fed by Goddess Pārvatī and Lord Dhoniappan and hence came to be known as the chosen one of the Celestial couple (Āḻuḍai Piḷḷaiyār). From Tirukolakka he visited a number of Śiva shrines like Tirunanipaḷḷi (his mother's home town and there on to Tiruvalampuram, Pallavanīśvaram, Tiruchayakāḍu, Tiruveṅgāḍu, Tirumullaivāyil and came to Cidambaram. He visited a number of	Thirukaḻmalam (Sīrkāḻi). The deity is Dhoni Appār. This temple is 1 km from Sīrkaḻi and is also known as Tiruthālamuḍaiyār Kovil as God is said to have gifted him with golden tālam (plate) and he was supposed to have been fed by Goddess Pārvatī withmilk and enlightenment, when he cried out in hunger and hence he was named Tirugnāna Sambandar.

shrines in Coḷanāḍu. In between he met Appar and together they visited a lot of Śiva shrines. His marriage was fixed and the bride was the daughter of Nambi Āṇḍār. The wedding was to be held at Tirunallūrperumanam. Though Appar agreed to get married his mind was working only on renouncing all worldly pleasures and he begged to God to give him *mukti* in the song that begins *Nallūr perumanam* and he and his wife disappeared in the temple in the sanctum sanctorum of Lord Śiva. This (temple) village is very near Sīrkaḻi.

41. **Tirunāvukarasar** (Appar)
Was christened Marulnīkiyār when he was born. Was brought up by his sister Tilakavati. She was a staunch Śaivite. Marulnīkiyār went to Pāṭaliputra to study Buddhism and became a Buddhist. A serious ailment made him change his mind and he recovered only due to his sister's prayers. He became a devout Śaivite like his sister. The Lord Himself was supposed to have given him the name Tirunāvukarasu. They say that a lot of attempts were made by Buddhist monks to kill him and each time he had a miraculous escape. In one such attempt a Pallava king was approached to help them. But when this attempt too was foiled, the Pallava king realized his mistake and begged his forgiveness and became a Śaivite himself. He began visiting temples and singing hymns in praise of God. From Tirupāpuliyūr Appar took off once again and travelled for and wide up to Rāmeśvaram and other places visiting various Śiva shrines. He also met Tirugnāna Sambandar again at Tirupūnthuruthi. From Kāñcīpuram to Rāmeśvaram he had travelled singing in praise of deities in all the Śiva shrines. Among the Nāyaṉmārs he had covered the most

number of temples, like Tirumaṅgai Āḻvār who was the most widely travelled Āḻvār. He finally came to Tirupugaḻūr and breathed his last there.	Tirumunaipāḍi (Pallava State)
42. **Tirunāḷaipovār Nāyaṉār** He used to make percussion instruments like perigai (made out of skin) and chords (animal products) for instruments like *vīṇā* and *yāḻ*. He was not permitted to enter temple as he belonged to the Pulaiyar community (untouchable).	Ādanūr now known as Aadhamangalam across the Koḻḻiḍam (Colroon) River
43. **Tirunīlakaṇḍar**	Cidambaram (Tillai)
44. **Tirunīlakaṇḍa Yāḻpāna Nāyaṉār** Was an untouchable and played the *yāḻ* and accompanied by his wife, also a *yāḻ* player, he would stand outside the Śiva temples and sing. Tirugnāna Sambandar spotted him and he began to live with him. He set tunes to his hymns and accompanied him on his instrument.	Tiruerukatthaampuliyūr
45. **Tirunīlakka Nāyaṉār**	Tiruchhatha-maṅgai, 7 km from Nannilam
46. **Tirumūlar**	Tiruvāvaḍuthurai
47. **Namanandi Aḍigalar Nāyaṉār**	Ema Perūr between Tiruthuraipūṇḍi and Tiruvārūr (now known as Tiruneyaperu)
48. **Narasiṅgha Munaiyarayar Nāyaṉār** King of a small state called Tirumu naipāḍi and propagated Sundaramūrti Nāyaṉār	Tirunāvalūr
49. **Ninṟasīr Neḍumāṟa Nāyaṉār** Pāṇḍya king also known in history As Maravar Manari Kesari (CE 600-60)	Madurai
50. **Nesar**	Kāmbilli in Bellary District
51. **Pugaḻ-Kodi Nāyaṉār** Was a Coḷa king and changed his capital from Uraiyūr to Karūr. He worshipped	Uraiyūr

Paśupathīśvara at Ānilai temple. Renounced his kingdom after seeing the outcome of the war and became a *saṁnyāsī*.	
52. **Pugaḻttuṇai Nāyaṇār** Minister to a Coḷa king	Śrīvilliputhūr
53. **Pūsalār Nāyaṇār**	Tiruniṉravūr near Chennai
54. **Perumiḻalaik-kuṟumbar**	Perumiḻalai, 4 km north of Pudukkoṭṭai
55. **Maṅgaiyarkarasiyār** She was the queen of a Pāṇḍya king and daughter of a Coḷa king. She invited Tirugnāna Sambandar to the court and converted her husband to a Śaivite from a Buddhist (Samanan).	
56. **Mānakañjāra Nāyaṇār**	Kanjāru near Mayilāḍuthurai
57. **Muruga Nāyaṇār**	Tirupugaḻūr between Nannilam and Nāgapattinam
58. **Munaiaḍuvār Nāyaṇār**	Tirunidūr
59. **Mūrkka Nāyaṇār**	Tiruverkaḍu near Chennai
60. **Mūrtt Nāyaṇār**	Madurai
61. **Meypporul Nāyaṇār**	Tirukovilūr (one of the famous Virattānaṅgal eight Śiva temples)
62. **Vāyilār**	Tirumayilai (Mylapore — Chennai near Kapālīśvarar temple)
63. **Viraḷmiṇḍa**	Tiruchenkunnūr in Kerala (Ceranāḍu) near Quilon, now known as Cengannūr

Beside these 63 Nāyaṉmārs there were eight others whose works are also in the compilation of the *Tirumurai*s.

They blended religion and music with *bhakti* and *bhāva*. We find repeated reference of the word *isai* (music) throughout their works. Sambandar in a number of songs has expressed that music should be melodious and sweet (*innisai*) and we find this in eight important hymns:

> *isai pāḍal/isai pāḍu bhaktar/isai pāḍum jñanam vaḻḻār/isaiyāl urai seyvar/isai mālai/innisai pāḍal/innisaiyavar/tamiḻ innisai/*

Eḻuisai-Eḻunarambinosai — Sambandar here compares the seven strings of the *yāḻ* to the seven notes. According to Sambandar, devotees should always worship God through songs. *isai pāḍiye iraivana vaṇaṅga venḍum.*

Sundarar has also used the word — *Innisai/iyaḻisai/isai kilavi* in a number of songs.

Appar in a song says

> *salambuvoḍu dūpam marantha riyen, thamiḻodisai pāḍal marandariyen.*

> I will not forget to worship him with flowers and camphor; neither will I forget my offering of sweet songs to Him.

The holy trinity paid equal importance to music and lyrics.

Appar had composed hymns in the following formats: nerisai, viruttam, kuruntogai and thāṇḍakam.

We also find references to a number of instruments in the *Tevāram* like the *yāḻ , vīṇā, kuḻal, sangu, muḻavu, nagari, parai, kinnāram, thuḍi,* etc. Music thus became a part of religion during this time and developed as fine art in a big way.

How the Tevārams were Unearthed

Raja Abhayakula Sekaran was a Coḷa king whose capital city was Tiruvārūr. He was a very staunch devotee of the Lord Tyāgarāja, the presiding deity of the Tiruvārūr Temple. His court musicians sang songs in praise of Lord Tyāgarāja and he also learnt to sing them. He wanted to compile all these hymns and spread the message but did not get authentic information on the composers of these sacred hymns. There was a small village near Tiruvārūr called Tirunāraiyūr (also known as Nāchiar Kovil — it is one of the 108 Tirupatis — between

Kumbakoṇam and Tiruvārūr). There lived a Śaiva devotee who performed daily rituals for the local Lord Gaṇeśa (known in this temple as Pollā-Piḷḷayār) with immense faith and fevour. One day he had to leave the village on an important work and asked his little son to do the rituals. The boy offered *neivediya* (*prasāda*) that was not very pure and the God did not accept it. Repenting his mistake the boy felt he should pay for his sin and kept hitting his head on a rock nearby. God forgave him and accepted the *prasāda*. The boy at this stage stopped going to school and was supposed to have taken the God as his teacher and learnt from him. From then on he came to be known as Nambi-Āṇḍār. He also composed a sacred text called *Tiru Iraṭṭai Maṇi Mālai.* The Coḷa king heard about this miraculous story of Nambi Āṇḍār and Pollā Piḷḷayār. He also came to know that all the *Tirumurai*s written by the Nāyaṉmārs were housed in the Cidambaram Temple. He immediately came to Ponnambalam (Cidambaram) and opened the closed vaults and found that quite a few were infested by termites. He handed over the good ones (inscribed on copper plates) to Nambi Āṇḍār and asked him to compile them. Though they managed to find the hymns, they were not able to get the singing formats for the hymns and the king was very perturbed. They say that the king was informed of a lady who belonged to the lineage of Tirunīlakaṇṭa Yāḻpānar who at that time was living at Tiruarukathampuliyūr. The king immediately dispatched someone to bring her and she was the one who formatted the tunes (*paṇṇ*s for all the hymns and to her goes the credit for those timeless hymns that we hear to this day in all the temples in Tamil Nadu. Nambi Āṇḍār edited and compiled the sacred hymns into *Tirumuṟai*.

Classification of Tirumuṟai

Nambi Āṇḍār composed the first *Andāthi* and compiled the entire lot, including his own, into twelve *Tirumuṟai*s as follows:

- The first three *Tirumuṟai*s are the *Tevāram* hymns composed by Tirugñāna Sambandar.
- The fourth, fifth and sixth *Tirumuṟai*s are the *Tirupadigangal* by Tirunāvukarasar.

- The seventh *Tirumuṟai* is the *Tevāram* by Sundaramūrti Nāyaṉār.
- The eight *Tirumuṟai* is Māṇikavāsakar's *Tiruvācakam* and *Tirukovai.*
- The ninth *Tirumuṟai* comprising the *Tiruvisaipākal* and *Tiruppalāṇḍu* by the following Nāyaṉmārs:
    1. Tirumāḷigaithevar
    2. Tirchendanār
    3. Karuvūrthevar
    4. Pūnduruthi Nambikaḍa Nambi
    5. Sundarādhitar
    6. Vennath Aḍigal
    7. Tirmūla Amudhar
    8. Purudhothama Nambi
    9. Sediraiyar

Along with these nine Nāyaṉmār's hymns, Tirumūla Nāyaṉār's *Tirumandiram* also was included.

Tenth *Tirumuṟai* — *Tirumuga Pāsurams* composed by Tiruvālavāi Uḍaiyār

Eleventh *Tirumuṟai* — Nambi Āṇḍār Nambi's *Tiruvandādi*

Twelfth *Tirumuṟai* — Sekiḻār's *Periya Purāṇam*

From the eighth century these twelve *Tirumuṟai*s were edited into seven and began to be sung in all Śaiva temples by singers especially designated for this purpose known as the *Oduvār*. This tradition continues in most of the temples to this day.

The Origin of the Panniru Tirumuṟai — The sacred Hymns of the Śaivites

Tevāram (*Teva* + *Āram*) *Teva* means God and the hymns that were sung in praise of God became *Tevaram.* It also means to love and worship Him. In the eleventh and twelfth century *Tevāram* was referred to as worshipping of God in some of the temples according to stone inscriptions. Tirumūlar, Kāraikāl Ammaiyār, Sambandar, Appar,

Sundarar, Seramān Perumāḷ, Aiyaḍigaḷ, Kāḍavarkon, Māṇikkavāsagar, Tiruveṅgattu Aḍigal, Nambi Āṇḍār Nambi, Tirumaligai Tevar, and Sekiḻar, are some of the important Śaivite savants who had composed sacred hymns to be sung in temples and called *Tirumuṟai* and *Tiruneri Tamiḻ*.

The word *Tevāram* can also be split as *The* meaning *Deivam* — God and *Varam* depicting the grammar of music:

The Grammar in *Tevāram*

1. Mudal Naḍai: *Mudal naḍai* is also known as *manda naḍai* and is sung in the *vilamba kālam* (slow speed). This is a slow paced, melodic music sung in a proper technical order.
2. Varam: *Varam* lays emphasis on clarity and also clear tune.
3. Thiral: *Thiral* lays the regulation for fast beats
4. Kūdai: *Kūdai* highlights the wealth of words and wealth of music in the hymns.

The Coḷa kings enforced the singing of the *Tevāram*s as a part of daily worship. The kings had given specific names for these music rituals and singers who sang these hymns in the temples everyday. The kings treated them with utmost respect and reverence and they were compensated generously by way of money, land, paddy and honoured positions in their courts.

Classification of the Tevārams

The presentation of *Tevāram* is classified into two — the *paṇṇ-muṟai* and the *tala-muṟai*. In the *paṇṇ-muṟai* the songs have a formatted tune and *tālam*, and are sung at specific times as prescribed. Though a number of meanings have been given for the word *Tevāram*, they say the most relevant and significant is the word ā*rithal* which means singing together. Most of the *Tevarams* are formatted in such a way that they are more effective when sung in groups.

2. *Tala-muṟai*: A number of these hymns are set in three speeds *mukkālam*. Some of them are set in such a way that they begin in the first speed, then the second, and pick up more tempo, go on to the third and then again decline to second and come to first. This format

later became popular with the *bhajanai sampradāyam* and singing in the three-speed pattern became a part of the exercise in *abhyāsa ghanam* (*alaṁkāram*). There was another format in *Tevāram* singing known as the *suddhaṅgam* where importance was given only to the clarity and presentation of verses and also highlighting of the *rāgam*. This format led the way for singing the *viruttham* and is very popular in Carnatic music concerts and is normally sung towards the tail end of the concert. The *suddhaṅgam* method is sung in particular *Tevāram padhikams* like *Tiruthāṇḍagam, Tirukurunthogai* and *Tiruviruttham*. A tradition that has been followed for centuries till today is singing some of the *Tevārams* in the Harikambhodhi *rāgam* by the *Oduvār*.

There was also another method of singing in groups without *tālam*. Appar's *Tirunerisai pāḍal* was formatted in this way. This would sound more like a Vedic chanting and had a very divine feel to it.

But some of these savants composed hymns in praise of the deities they worshipped and the temples (*mūrti, sthalam,* and *tīrtham*) they were associated with.

The Cidambaram temple and Sirkāḻi temple are considered as the two important temples that follow the *thala muṟai*. Specifications also on when the *rāgams* should be sung were prescribed.

For example, *rāgams* to be sung in the morning were Bhūpāḷam, Navaroj, Bhairavi, Kambodhi, Nāṭai, etc.

Some of the *paṇṇs* are Kousikam, Thakkesi, Pañcama, Nāṭṭa Rāgam, Inthalam, etc.

Rāgams to be sung in the evenings and at nights were Śuddha Saverī, Sowrāṣṭram Sāma, Nīlāmbari, etc.

The *paṇṇs* were Sīkamaram, Kolli, Kuriñji, Kowvanam, etc.

Sambandar's first hymn *Thodudaya Seviyan* is a self-explanatory hymn and is known as *Meymai Moḻi Tirupadikam.* In this *padikam* the letter *oṁ* (the *praṇava mantra*) has been replaced by the Tamil letter *tha* and added to *o* it becomes *tho* and the entire *padikam* is set in the Nāṭṭapaḍai — the Nāttai *rāgam* and comprises 136 hymns or songs. According to musicologists the *Tevārams* were the first musical compositions in the history of Indian music and the youngest music composer ever was Tirugnāna Sambandar. They followed the hearsay method as in those times notations were unheard of. The *guru* taught his *śiṣya*s the hymns as he had learnt from his teacher before him without changing the tune. All arrangements to teach youngsters were made in those days at the temples and the *oduvār mūrti* taught them with utmost dedication and sincerity. The kings and later patrons compensated these people generously to ensure that the traditions did not change in any way. *Tevāram* concerts and *Tevāram* community singing were organized in temples all through the year to ensure that these traditions should continue. That is why we find the divinity in them even today when they are sung in temples.

There are 240 very important Śiva temples and these savants have sung in praise of these temples and the deities of the temples. We will also find some of the hymns inscribed on the walls of the temples giving in detail as to who was the Nāyaṉār who had visited that particular temple and some of the hymns composed by him.

It will be interesting to note that not all Nāyaṉmārs were brāhmaṇas or Śaivites, some belonged to the backward community, some were farmers, business people, ministers, generals, and a few were also royalty.

Tevāram from time immemorial has been referred as *Deiva Tamiḻ Isai* (divine Tamil music).

Four of the Nāyaṉmārs find a special and significant place in all the important Śaiva temples. They are Tirugnāna Sambandar, Tirunāvukarasar, Sundaramūrti Nāyaṉār, and Maṇikkavācakar. They are always referred to as *Samaya kuravargaḷ* and in most of the temples we will find their icons in a very conspicuous part of the temple.

Tirugnāna Sambandar, Tirunāvukarasar (Appar) and Sundaramūrti were called the *Tevāra Mūvar* (Trinity). Kāraikāl Ammaiyār, also one of the 63 Nāyaṉmārs, was always referred as the *Deiva Thamiḻ Isaiyin Thāi* (mother of Tamiḻ music). She has contributed a lot for Carnatic music by way of creating *rāgam*s like Nāṭṭai, Māyāmāḷavagouḷa, etc. She was older to Tirugnāna Sambandar and Tirunāvukarasar.

Tevāram is also known as the oldest form of music in Tamil Nadu, and Carnatic Music has originated from the *Tevāram*. People known as *pāṇar*s were musicians who belonged to the Saṅgam Age and the word *paṇṇ* (*rāgam*) is derived from this term. Most of the present-day *rāgam*s have originated from these *paṇṇ*s and composers like Muthu Tāṇḍavar, Tyāgārāja, etc. had composed their songs using these *paṇṇ*s. Musicologists also claim that a number of *paṇṇ*s are found in the Hindustani Music.

Yaḻmuri Paṇṇ Isai

There were twenty-three prescribed *paṇṇ*s (among the 103 prescribed *paṇṇ*s) for the *Tevāram* that are popular and common and had been handed over from generation to generation by the *Oduvār Mūrti*, which are sung in the same tune to this day. The *Yaḻmuri paṇṇ* is the only one that does not come within these prescribed 103.

Tirugnāna Sambandar's *Tevaram Madhar Madapaḍiyum* has been set in this *paṇṇ*. Strangely this *paṇṇ* is not found in any of the hymns composed by his contemporaries before him like Kāraikāl Ammaiyār and after him like Appar, Sundarar, and also in the Āḻvār *Pasuram*s. They are also not found in the *padigam* of *Tiruvisaipa* and *Tirupallāṇḍu* composed during the tenth and eleventh century. This goes to show that this *paṇṇ* must have been a creation of Sambandar.

This was like the rebirth period for Hinduism with the Āḻvārs (Vaiṣṇavite Saints) and the Nāyaṇmārs (Śaivite Saints) setting a new trend of introducing the tradition of hymn singing in temples. They provided a very simple means of communicating with God through singing and also prescribed ways on how and when these hymns should be sung. They went from temple to temple followed by their devotees singing with depth and emotion the praises of the Gods in beautifully tuned and set verses. They say among all these the earliest or the trend-setter was Sambandar who had set most of the hymns in *paṇṇ*s like Mahārāja Kuriñji, Vyāḻa Kuriñji, Sevāḻi, etc. He also had a devotee by name Tirunīlakaṇṭar Yāḻpāṇar who used to play the string instrument called the *Sakoda Yāḻ*. He belonged to the Perumpāṇar community. Sambandar's singing accompanied by Nīlakaṇṭar

Yāḻpāṇar's *Yāḻ* was so divine that people went into ecstatic raptures. Once during a visit to Tirudharmapuram Sambandar was welcomed by Nīlakaṇṭar Yāḻpāṇar's relatives. A close relative wanted to prove to the people around that Sambandar's singing was popular only because of the accompanying *Yāḻ*. He challenged Sambandar (much against the wish of Nīlakaṇṭar Yāḻpāṇar) to compose a tune which the *Yāḻ* would not be able to follow. Sambandar immediately composed a hymn, *mādhar madapidiyummada annamum annadhor-pozhil kuyil payil dahrumarampadhiye*. When Nīlakandar tried playing the tune he was unable to do so. He was about to break the instrument as he had defied Sambandar. Sambandar however stopped him and said that he would surely be able play that tune in his instrument. This is how Sambandar created the *Yāḻmuri paṇṇ*. We find reference to this incident in Sekiḻar's *Periya Purāṇam*.

Tiruvācakam

Tiruvācakam is the eighth *Tirumurai* and is compiled along with *Tirucirrambalakovai*. Mānickavāsagar composed these hymns in Tamil. *Tiruvācakam* means "the holy verses." It comprises 656 songs and they come under the following themes:

Śiva Purāṇam

Kīrti Tiruthagaval

Tiruvānda paguthi

Porri Tiru agaval

Tirusadagam

Nīthal Viṇṇappam

Tiruvembāvai

Tiru Ammānai

Tirupor kinnam

Tiru kothumbi

Tiru thell Yenam

Tirupaḷḷi Eḻuci

Koil mūtha Tirupadigam

Kanda Pathu

Sendilā Pathu

Arpuda Pathu

Kuil Pathu

Acho Padigam

When these hymns were composed they were also set to tune and musicologists have given a lot of evidences for this from the hymns themselves.

pāda venḍum nān potri ninnaiye — *Tirusadagam*

sodhiyai yām pāḍa — *Tiruvembāvai*

Though we have evidence that Mānickavāsakar sang them we do not have any prescribed tunes for them unlike the other hymns from the *Tirumuṟai*. Māṇikkavācakar was supposed to have visited a lot of temples like Tiruperunthuṟai, Tillai (Cidambaram), Madurai, Uttarakosamaṅgai, etc. singing with deep devotion and emotion in praise of those gods and goddesses. Most of those songs were set in the Mohana *rāgam* and sung in the *suddhaṅgam* method (*viruttham*) laying emphasis on the tune and clarity in a very slow tempo. Some of the hymns from the *Tiruvācakam* are also sung in the *Pannangam* method (singing with rhythmic counts in groups). Some songs (*Tiruammānai*) have more of a folk touch and can be compared to the *Kāvadi Sindu*, and the *Tiruponnūñjal* songs are in Ānanda Bhairavī and in some temples they are also sung during nights in the Nilāmbarī *rāgam*. Like Āṇḍāḷ's *Tiruppāvai* the *Tiruvempāvai* are also meant to be sung early in the morning during the *Mārgaḻi* month and there is a very ancient tradition of group singing of the *Tiruvempāvai* (*Pannangam*) in the Bhūpāḷam *rāgam*.s Both Āṇḍāḷ's *Tiruppāvai* and Mānickavāsakar's *Tiruvempāvai* end with *Empāvāi*. These songs were meant for young women to observe ceremonial fasting, wake up early in the morning during the *Mārgaḻi* month (15 December – 14 January) and join women of their own age group, bathe in a nearby river and go to the temple praying for prosperity of their land and also praying to get husbands of their choice. There are thirty songs for the thirty days. Even today the tradition of waking up very early during this cold season and singing in groups and visiting temples is followed both by Śaivites and Vaiṣṇavites.

The Singing of Tevārams in the Temples

The ritual of singing the *Tevārams* while the deity was taken around the temple was known as *Tevārathu-Cuṟṟukallūṟi* and the artiste who sang these was known as *Tevāra Nāyagam.* The singers who sang the *Tevārams* were also known as *Pidaran.*

During the reign of Rājarāja Coḷa II in the thirteenth century these singers were given huge portions of land and money. They performed the regular worship and rituals in the Tanjāvūr Bṛīhadīśvara temple and used to sing accompanied by instruments like *Uḍukai, Matthalam,* etc. The temple inscription says that there were 49 *pidarans* or *oduvars* during this time. It also talks about the accompanists for these singers. The names of all these artistes appointed by Rājarāja Coḷa are also inscribed on the walls of the Tanjāvūr temple. Another noteworthy point here is that most of these singers had prefixes of towns or villages added to their names like Ārūr, Vāimūr, Maraikāḍu, Aiyyāru, Tiruviḍaimarudūr, Ānaikā, Vengādu, Tillai, etc. These places were noted for *Tevāram* singing in those days and by adding the names of their hometowns we come to know that these artistes were honoured, recognized and brought all the way to Tanjāvūr to perform in the temple at the request of the king. Like the prefixes, suffixes are also found in the names of these *Oduvārs* in the temples. All the names had Śivan added to their names. Sadā Śivan, Pūrva Śivan, Agora Śivan, Rudra Śivan, Tatpuruṣa Śivan, Dharma Śivan, Oṁkāra Śivan, Jñāna Śivan, are some of the names we find in these inscriptions. It is also evident that such names are not available before or after the reign of Rājarāja Coḷa. Rājarāja Coḷa had appointed 400 dancers in the Tanjāvūr Periya Kovil and had added the name *Nakkan* to their names as suffixes, and honoured them and their profession. Likewise by adding the *Śivan* as suffix to the *oduvars* he put them above all the others indicating their contribution to the presiding deity of the temple. He also wanted to ensure that the tradition of the *Tevāram* should always be prevalent and the clan of these hymn singers should continue forever. An inscription to this context is also in the temple which says that even if one of them dies the next of his kin should continue and be given the same respect, reverence and remuneration. Hence they came to be known as the *Oduvar Mūrti* and also *Śivan.*

The singers also sometimes sang the hymns in groups with accompanying instruments. There were more than 10,000 such hymns and these were in palm leaf and were preserved in a special *maṇḍapam* (hall) called *tirukoṭṭu-maṇḍapam.*

The *oduvar*s (musicians) of the Śaivite temples decided the *rāgams* for the *Tevārapadikam*s from some of the *paṇṇ*s as given below:

Paṇṇ	*Rāgam*
Kolli	Navaroj
Sīkamaram	Nāganāmakriyā
Kousikam	Bhairavī
Senduruthi	Madyamāvathī
Takkesi	Kambhodi
Naṭṭapadai	Nāṭṭai
Paḻamañjaram	Śaṅkarābharaṇam
Sadhari	Panthuvarāḷi
Mega Kuriñji	Nīlāmbārī
Kuriñji	Kuriñji

Tiruvāimoḻi and Paṇṇs

Tiruvāimoḻi are the hymns composed by the twelve Āḻvārs. These differ from *rāgams* suggested for *Tevārams* as below:

Paṇṇ	*Rāgam*
Takka	Toḍī, Mukāri, Panthuvarāḷi
Pañcarram	Bilahari/Śaṅkarābharaṇam
Naṭṭapadai	Dhanyāsi/Begaḍa/Śrīrāgam
Kousikam	Chenchuriti
Viyantham	Madyamāvathi

Thirteen *paṇṇ*s are common for both *Tiruvāimoḻi* and *Tevāram.* Six *paṇṇ*s not seen in *Tevāram* are seen in *Tiruvāimoḻi,* and eight *paṇṇ*s not seen in *Tiruvāimoḻi* are seen in *Tevāram.*

Kaṭṭalai (Commandments)

The traditions of the *Tevārams* are formatted by certain principles known as *kaṭṭalai*. *Kaṭṭalai* is the compiling and formatting of lyrics, *svara* — pronunciation and clarity to get the right sound from the human body while singing the *Tevāram*. *Kaṭṭalai* is the grammar that lays emphasis, and prescribes in which *paṇṇ* it is to be sung and from which *padigam* (chapter). They say that the *Tevārams* have spiritual powers and to attain or master this one has to strictly adhere to these *kaṭṭalais*.

Muṟai means a book. *Tiru* is a prefix that is used as a mark of respect. Hence it came to be known as the *Tirumuṟai*. While our most sacred hymns, the Vedas, were not in the written format, these *Tirumuṟais* are considered to be the most precious and sacred scriptures by the Śaivites from the past to this day. Also known as the *Tiruppadhikam* these had been referred as *Padhiga Peruvaḻi* from the time of the Kulothunga Coḷa III. Later they began to be called as *padhigangal*. The term *padhigam* is supposed to have been used by Tiruvaḷḷuvar for depicting a chapter. Each *padhigam* contains ten sacred hymns. Towards the end of the *padhigams* the results of singing these *padhigams* have been explained. *Seikkiḻār Purāṇam*, the biography of the sixty-three Nāyaṉmārs, and nine devotees also known as the *Thogai Aḍiyārgal*, was written by Umapathi Sivācāriār. Excepting Appar all the Nāyaṉmārs have their names referred in these hymns.

When *Paṇṇ Isai* blossomed as what came to be known as Carnatic Music, the form of composition called *kṛti* or *kīrtana* became popular. *Pallavī*, *Anupallavī* and *Caraṇam* combine together to form a *kṛti*. The pattern of the prose in the *Caraṇam* appears to follow the *padhigam* pattern. It is to be noted that even rendering of the *caraṇams* is akin to that of the *padhigam* mode of rendering. It is of great interest to note that *kīrtana* is the form of composition of choice from Proto-Trinity of Music — Muthuttāṇḍavar, Mārimuthu Piḷḷai, and Aruṇāchala Kavirāyar followed by the Trinity of Carnatic Music, Syāma Śāstri, Tyāgarāja, and Dīkṣitar. The long traditional lineage of compositions owe their origin to Kāraikkāl Ammaiyār. The Āḻvārs, the authors of *Pāsurams* also had used the *padhigam* format in their hymns. The three

Śaiva Saints — Sambandar, Appar and Sundarar sang the *Tevārams* in the *Padhiga* pattern of Ammaiyār. The Māyāmāḷavagouḷa *rāgam* that was introduced by Kāraikkāl Ammaiyār inspired many composers to sing their first composition in it. This demonstrates the deep-rooted influence and acceptance of this *rāgam* in the domain of Carnatic Music.

This *rāgam* is now being widely used to render almost all Carnatic musical forms like — *saraḷi varisai, gītam, svarajati, varṇam, kṛti,* etc. This confirms the tremendous impact of this *rāgam* on south Indian music.

Kāraikkāl Ammaiyār — Mother of Carnatic Music

Kāraikkāl Ammaiyār is one of the 63 Śaiva Nāyaṉmārs born to a famous merchant in Kārkaikkāl. Punidavatī, as she was named, grew up in a religious environ, worshipped Lord Śiva diligently, and chanted the five letter *mantra: Namaḥ śivāya.* When she grew up she was married to Paramanāthan, a merchant in Kāraikkāl, and she continued to be a staunch Śaivite serving devotees. Once it is said that Lord Śiva came in the guise of a Śivanaḍiyār to test her and took the mango that her husband left with her for his lunch. When her husband came back and demanded the mango she prayed to Lord Śiva and a mango miraculously appeared in her hand. Her husband saw this and decided to leave her, as she was a divine being. He felt he was not fit to be her husband and he also realized that she was not meant for worldly life. Ammaiyār prayed to Lord Śiva fervently and was commanded by the Lord to proceed to Tiruvālaṅgāḍu. She immediately left for Tiruvālaṅgāḍu where she witnessed with ecstasy the eternal divine dance of the Lord. Overwhelmed with extreme delight, sweet melodies poured out of her heart, and she composed the *Tiruvālaṅgāttu Mūtha Tirupadhikam* in *Naṭṭapādai Paṇṇ Isai* and *Inthala Paṇṇ Isai.* By the immense grace of the Lord she was blessed and was placed at the feet of the Lord and attained her life's ambition. She came to be called Ammaiyār or Mother with deep reverence by the Tamils of the world. Her idol is found in Śiva temples all over south India as well as in temples overseas like Sri Lanka, Cambodia, Thailand, etc. It is to be noted that among the idols depicting the 63 Nāyaṉmārs found in the temples only Ammaiyār is in a seated posture. In the 12 Śaiva canons, *Panniru Tirumuṟai,* Ammaiyār's compositions *Arputha Tiruvanthāthi, Tiruviratai, Manimālai* and *Tiruvālangāttu Mūtha Tirupadhikam* are included in the eleventh canon. Sambandar who rendered *Tevāram* in excellent rhythmic patterns has always been depicted with cymbals in his hands. Ammaiyār's statue also depicts her with cymbals in her hands. It is also interesting to note that Ammaiyār in her 9th song refers to the ancient musical notes that are equivalent to the present day *sa, ri, ga, ma, pa, da* and *ni.* In the same context mention is also made of 12 instruments as accompaniments to the dance of Lord Śiva. From this we can ascertain and draw a conclusion that Ammaiyār not only had deep knowledge of music but also sang with rhythmic excellence like Tirujñāna Sambandar.

The Āḻvārs, the authors of the *Nālāyiram Divya Prabandham,* also had used the *padhigam* format to sing the Lord's glory. A number of scholars have drawn the conclusion that the long traditional lineage of compositions from *padhikam* to *kīrtanam* owes its origin to Ammaiyār. In course of time the nomenclature of the Tamil *paṇṇ*s changed as Carnatic *rāgams*. For example the Centhuri *paṇṇ* became Madhyamāvathi and the Paḷam Panchura *paṇṇ* as Śaṅkarābharaṇam. Likewise Ammaiyār's *Natādai Paṇṇ* was known as Gambīra Nāṭṭai *rāgam* and Indha *paṇṇ* was known as Māyāmāḷavagouḷa. In the development of Carnatic music these two *rāgams* sung by Ammaiyār have played a dominant role. It is customary for Gambīra Nāṭṭai *rāgam* to be given great importance and priority of place in performing arts and in the music traditions in temples. In temple music Gambīra Nāṭṭai has a stellar role. When the deity is brought out in procession it is accompanied by the *nādasvaram mallāri* music. The *rāgam* for *mallāri* is Gambīra Nāṭṭai. This *rāgam* creates the right musical and auspicious ambience. In temple music traditions playing this *rāgam* is strictly adhered to. Many people claim Kāraikkāl Ammaiyār as the mother of south Indian music for her tremendous contribution to the *rāga*s that are followed in Carnatic music today and also feel that adequate recognition has not been given to her contribution.

Tirupugaḻ

Tirupugaḻ means to praise the Lord. Aruṇagirināthar who composed the *Tirupugaḻ* hymns was born at Tiruvaṇṇāmalai. He was also known as *Sandha Pāvala Perumān*. The *Tirupugaḻ* hymns were unique because they had poetic lyrics, good meaning, and also rhythm (*solvaḷam, poruḷvaḷam, sandhanayam* and *thala prathara nilaigaḷ*). It is said that once a Coḷa king went to Kāśī and on his way back brought with him eight learned men to Kāñcīpuram. They were Prasādavallabha, Bhāskara Kavi, Rājanādha Kavi, Subrahmaṇya Kavi, Jadadaresa Dīkṣitar, Nīlakaṇṭa Kavi, Somanātha Dīkṣitar and Mallikārjuna Bhaṭṭar. Aruṇagirināthar was the descendent of Rājanādha Kavi. Aruṇagirināthar was born about 500 years ago (early sixteenth century). His father was Rājanādhar and mother Abhirāmbika. Aruṇagirināthar was also known as Sonādrināthar and was brought up by his uncle Somnādhar and aunt as he lost his parents when he was very young. He suffered from a chronic disease and unable to bear it he tried to commit suicide by jumping from a tower in the palace. As he attempted to jump he was supposed to have been stopped by none other than Lord Muruga Himself. Again Lord Muruga appeared before him in the guise of a sage saying *summā iru sollara* (to remain silent till the right time to come) *mouna marai upadeśam* and disappeared. Aruṇagirināthar then began his long penance and went into some kind of a trance. Again Lord Muruga appeared before him and commanded him to sing *Nam Tirupugaḻ Pāḍu* (sing in my praise). Aruṇagirināthar asked Him, "How can I? I am not a literate and do not deserve in any way to sing about you." Muruga is supposed to have touched him with His sacred spear — *Vel* — writing on his tongue the *Praṇava Mantram.* Immediately Aruṇagirināthar broke into his first hymn *Mutthai tharu* and then again went into a trance. Lord Muruga again commanded him to come over to Vāyalūr. And there he sang his second hymn *Vāyali Nagari — kanavilum nanavilum maravene.* He then began his long pilgrimage visiting several shrines of Muruga composing hymns in His praise. He went to Paḻani, Tirucendūr, Thirutthani, and several other shrines in north India like Kāśī, and also to Sri Lanka at Trincomalee, Kadirkāmam, etc. He had totally composed one thousand hymns in praise of Lord Muruga. Each hymn is dedicated to one particular temple.

The songs composed by him are compiled as follows:

1. *Tirupugaḻ*
2. *Kandar Andhādhi*
3. *Kandar Anubhūthi*
4. *Tiruvaguppu*
5. *Kandar Alaṅkāram*
6. *Vel* (spear) *Mayil* (peacock) *Seval* (cock) *Virutthaṅgal*

Some of his songs have been grouped as follows:

PAÑCA BHŪTHA STHALAṄGAḶ —

Songs composed on Lord Murugan at the following Śiva shrines:

Kāñcīpuram
Tiruvānaikkāval
Kāḷahasthi
Cidambaram
Tiruvaṇṇāmalai

ĀRUPAḌAIVĪḌU SONGS —

Songs composed on Lord Murugan at the following temples:
Tiruparankuṉṟam
Tirucendūr
Paḻaṇi
Svāmimalāi
Tirutthani
Paḻamudhir Solai

KĀÑCĪ GROUP OF SONGS —

Songs dedicated to the shrines in and around Kāñcīpuram. He has sung in praise of more than 260 Śiva shrines.

THE FIVE SABHAIS OF LORD ŚIVA —

Temples personified through the hymns [thevaram] by the Holy Trinity —

1.	Chozha Nadu (in and around Tanjore)	191
2.	Eezha Nadu (Sri Lanka)	2
3.	Pandi Nadu (in and around Madurai)	14
4.	Chera Nadu (Kerala)	1
5.	Kongu Nadu (in and around Coimbatore)	7
	Thondai Nadu (in and around Chennai, Kāñcī	32
	Nadu Nadu (Central Tamil Nadu)	22
	Thuluva Nadu (Mangalore–Karnataka)	1
	Vada Nadu (north including Andhra)	5
	Total =	**275**

SABDA VIDAṄGA STHLANGAL (SEVEN) —

These 7 temples are located in Tanjore District. *Daṅga* means Uli in Tamil (chisel) *vi* means that which cannot go through. So that which cannot be chiseled. These seven temples have the Syaṁbhūmūrti that have not been chiseled.

In all these seven temples the presiding deity Lord Tyagrāja performs seven different forms of dance. He is also addressed in different names. The dance forms have particular prescribed movements.

	Location	*Names of Deity*	*Names of Dance forms*
1.	Thiruvarur	*Veedi vidaṅgar*	Ajaba Nādanam — moving up and down, and forward and backward.
2.	Thirunalaru	*Taga vidaṅgar*	Unmatta Nādanam — Vigorous movements of the head — like a possessed person.
3.	Nagapatinam	*Sundara vidaṅgar*	Paravarakaraṅga Nādanam (like the movements of the waves)
4.	Thirukarayil	*Ādī vidaṅgar*	Kukuḍa Nādanam (movements of the hen-bird).
5.	Thirukolili	*Avanī vidaṅgar*	Bṛṅga Nādanam (movements of the bees when they collect honey from flowers.

6.	Thiruvaimur	*Nīla vidaṅgar*	Kamala Nādanam (movements of the lotus as they sway in the ponds due to gentle breeze.
7.	Thirumaraikadu	*Buvanī vidaṅgar*	Haṁsapāda Nādanam (movement of the swan as they waddle in the water.

TEMPLES WHERE ŚIVA PERFORMED HIS CELESTIAL DANCE

Cidambaram
Tiruvālaṅgāḍu
Madurai
Kāñcīpuram
Kuṟṟālam

VĪRATTĀNANGAL OF LORD ŚIVA

(8 Temples Marked with Gallantry (Valour) of Śiva).

In these temples Lord Śiva had fought and won over his enemies (evil powers) and have been sung in praise of by His devotees.

Place	Enemy
Tiru Vaḻuvūr	*gajam*
Tirukaṇḍiyūr	*brahmaśiras*
Tirukaḍavūr	Yama
Tirukovalūr	Aṅdaga
Tirupariyalūr	Thakkan
Tiruvīrkuḍi	Jalantharan
Tirūvadhigai	Thiripuram
Tirukorkai	Anmadan

Aruṇagirināthar was also known as Sandhapāvala Perumān. His songs were not only good in their poetic beauty and meaning (*Solvaḷam* and *Poruḷvaḷam*) but also in rhythmic beats (*sandhanayam, tāḷaprasthara nilaigaḷ*). The most complicated aspect in Carnatic music is the concept of *tāḷam* — beats. The *Tirupugaḻ* is mostly recommended for all musicians because the *tāḷa*s set for these hymns are very complicated and complex. Aruṇagirināthar always felt the world as form of *nādam* (sound) and *tāḷam* (rhythm). He always felt the presence of the Omnipresent as he sang his hymns with the *nāda-tāḷa.* Hence his hymns became very popular and symbolic particularly in the community singing (*bhajana sampradāyam*). Like the *Tevāram, Tirupugaḻ* is also compiled as *Tirumur̤ai*. The first six *Tirumur̤ai* contain songs dedicated to the *Arupaḍai-Vīḍu* — the six famous houses or temples of Lord Muruga namely:

Pal̤ani	near Coimbatore
Svāmimalai	near Kumbakoṇam
Tiruchendūr	near Tirunelveli
Tiruthanigai	near Arakoṇam
Tiruparankun̤ram	near Madurai
Pal̤amudhirsolai	near Madurai (above Al̤agar Malai temple)

The seventh *Tirumur̤ai* is a compilation of songs dedicated to all other Muruga shrines visited by Aruṇagirināthar.

While *paṇṇs* (*rāgams*) were prescribed for the *Tevārams,* for *Tirupugal̤* only the *sandham* (beats) was prescribed. Surprisingly some very popular *Tirupugal̤* numbers have retained the same tune for more than several centuries like *nāda bindu, bhaktiyāl yānunnai, saraṇa kamalālayathil,* etc. These songs have not been changed and have been sung in the same tune for nearly 600 years and they have authentic proof in several temples for this. The most important and unique feature of the *Tirupugal̤* is that each song has been set to a particular rhythmic pattern and with a particular tempo. If a change is made to this, the clarity of the words will be lost and so will the poetic beauty of them.

6

The Āḻvārs

Śrī Vaiṣṇavism, the oldest monotheistic religious doctrine of India having its roots in the Vedas and Upaniṣads, has passed through several stages of development. Śrī Rāmānuja expounded it as a full-fledged theological system with a strong philosophical basis. The four important phases that can be discerned in this development are the Vedic period, the period of the Itihāsas and Purāṇas, the period of the Āgamas, and the period of the Āḻvārs or the 12 Vaiṣṇava saints of south India. Of these the last phase is of special importance because the Tamil hymns of the Āḻvārs are the spontaneous outpourings of their divine experience and contain rich philosophical and theological ideas related to the three doctrines of the "Viśiṣṭādvaita Vedānta" and the Vaiṣṇava system namely, *tattva* or the "Ultimate Reality," *"hita"* or the means of its attainment and *puruṣārtha* or the supreme goal of life. The teachings of the Āḻvārs are not different from what is said in the Vedas, the Epics and the Āgamas. Their uniqueness however lies in the fact that they presented them for the first time to the common man in his spoken language (Tamil) and because of this they have been accorded an important place in the history of Vaiṣṇavism. They are worshipped at Vaiṣṇavite temple until today. Festivals are observed in Viṣṇu temples all over the south to celebrate or commemorate the birth stars of the 12 Āḻvārs.

"Āḻvār" means one who rules — or one who is deeply immersed in the Lord. It can also mean as one who rules us — meaning "one who is close to God and also rules."

These saints were always on the move, visiting temples and singing the praise of their favourite deities. All the temples they visited today speak of them, their music and their devotion. They have found a special place in the temples along with their gods and are worshipped. Today their hymns are sung as a daily ritual in many temples, on special occasions in some temples, on special festivals, on sacred months, particularly in "Mārgaḻi" (December-January).

The Āḻvārs were born in south India between the sixth and the eighth centuries of the Christian era. They were saints who devoted their entire life to the worship of Viṣṇu as the Supreme Deity. Blessed with the spiritual insight and intense love for Him they sang His glory and spent their active life in the divine service. They have bequeathed a rich heritage of sublime poetical compositions, totally comprising 4000 hymns, known as the *Nālāyira Divya Prabandham.*

In the purapadu (procession when a deity is taken out) of the Vaishnava temple, the purohits reciting the Nalayira Divya Prabhantham always lead the procession, while the purohits reciting the Vedas follow the Deity from behind.

These hymns are Tamil songs in praise of the glory of Lord Viṣṇu in all His aspects. They are intensely devotional and divine in character and represent the spontaneous outpourings of their deep love and experience of God. They have therefore gained great significance and are highly esteemed by the Vaiṣṇava preceptors or *ācāryas*. They have also sung in praise (*maṅgalāśāsanam*) of 108 Tirupatis, the famous Viṣṇu temples all over India, two of which cannot be seen as one is Vaikuṇṭam (heaven) and the other is *Tirupārkaḍal* (the sacred Ocean of Milk) that one attains after death. These hymns are sung or chanted by the Vaiṣṇavas during worship in these temples regularly as a part of their ritual and on special occasions. As devotional poems they appear to be like the devotional songs of other mystics such as *Tevāram* and the *Tiruvācakam* sung by the 63 Nāyaṉmārs (the Śaivite saints some of whom were the contemporaries of the Āḻvārs).

Dates of Āḻvārs

Traditionally we have regarded the Āḻvārs as divine incarnations and have assigned high antiquity to them ranging from 4200 BCE to 2700 BCE. Modern scholars have noted a period from fifth to ninth century CE on the basis of historical evidences. Dr N. Subba Reddiar has arrived at years of birth spread during the eighth century CE for all the Āḷvārs except Madurakavi who he believes was born in CE 800.

Divine Roots

Āḷvārs were believed to be incarnations of various facets of Lord Viṣṇu as follows:

Poygai Āḷvār	—	*śaṅkha* (conch)
Pūtattāḷvār	—	*gadā* (mace)
Pey Āḷvār	—	*nandaka* (sword)
Tirumaḷisai Āḷvār	—	*cakra* (discus)
Nammāḷvār	—	Viśvaksena (the commander of the forces of Lord Viṣṇu)
Kulaśekara Āḷvār	—	*kaustubha* (the ornament on the chest of the Lord)
Periāḷvār	—	Garuḍa (divine bird and vehicle of Viṣṇu)
Toṇḍaraḍippoḍi Āḷvār	—	*vanamālā* (garland)
Tirumaṅgai Āḷvār	—	*sārṅga* (bow)
Tiruppāṇ Āḷvār	—	*Śrivatsa* (the mole on the Lord's chest)
Madhurakavi Āḷvār	—	Chief of Viṣṇugaṇa
Āṇḍāḷ	—	Manifestation of Bhūdevī (consort of Viṣṇu)

Some of the Āḷvār are also attributed a supernatural birth and miraculous episodes in their lives. The hymns that glorify their spiritual insight contribute to a certain relevance of these stories.

A Short Note on the Āḷvārs

Poygai, Pūtattār and Pey Āzhwārs were the earliest and believed to be born on three consecutive days at Tirukkachiyur (Kāñcīpuram), Tirukaḍalmallai (Mahābalipuram) and Mylapore (Chennai) respectively. They travelled from one religious centre to another in quest of God. Each of them composed 100 hymns known as Tiruvandādi. The structure of poetry is such that the last syllable of the verse becomes the opening one of the succeeding verse. (*anta* meaning — the end and *ādi* meaning — the beginning). These are one of the earliest philosophical contributions to Vaiṣṇavism.

TIRUMAḺISAI ĀḺVĀR

Born around the same period as the other three Āḻvārs at Thirumazhisai near Śrīperumbudur, he was well known for his familiarity of Śaivism, Jainism and Buddhism. An expert *yogī*, he contributed the Hanumān Tiruvandādi (96 hymns) and Truccanda Viruttam (120 hymns).

NAMMĀḺVĀR

He was born at Tirukurugūr (Āḻvār Tirunagari) in the Tirunelveli district. Regarded as the founder-saint of Vaiṣṇavism his contribution in terms of hymns and theology is perhaps the largest among the Āḻvārs. Entranced by the vision of God he composed the beautiful *Tiruvāymoḻi* of 1102 hymns divided into 10 *pattu* (centum). His other works are *Tiruviruttam* (hymns of yearning for the Lord), *Tiruvachiriyam* (hymns of the Lord's persona) and *Periya Tiruvandādi* (of the deep love for the Lord).

MADHURAKAVI ĀḺVĀR

Believed to have been born before Nammāḻvār at Thirukolur, he was captured by the spiritual divinity of Nammāḻvār and sought him as his *guru*. Madhurakavi contributed *Kaṇṇiṇur Sirattāmbu* (11 verses) in the praise of Namm Āḻvār. The concept of *Ācārya bhakti* (reverence to the *guru*) is a doctrine in Vaiṣṇavism followed until today.

PERIĀḺVĀR

Also known as Viṣṇucitta he was born in the village of Śrīvilliputtūr and was engaged in the service of the deity at the local temple. He recited the *Tirupallāṇḍu* (12 verses) when he was overwhelmed by the sight of the Lord and his consort during a procession around the village organized by the then Pāṇḍya ruler as a sign of respect to the great saint. He glorifies Viṣṇu in the form of Kṛṣṇa in his other work *periāḻvār Tirumoḻi*. He is known to have adopted Āṇḍāḷ as a baby girl who he found in his garden.

ĀṆḌĀḶ

Āṇḍāḷ is revered as the incarnation of Bhūdevī, a consort of Viṣṇu. She was brought up by Periāḻvār in Śrīvilliputtūr and grew up with extreme love and desire to marry the Lord. The Lord is believed to have preferred the garland worn by her and Periāḻvār called his foster daughter *Sūdikoḍuttha Nāchiār*. Āṇḍāḷ contributed the *Tiruppāvai* (of 30 hymns that talk of the *vrata* (ritual) observed by the girls to attain husbands of their choice) and Nāciār Tirumoḻi (143 hymns that bring out her intense love for her Lord).

KULAŚEKHARA ĀḺVĀR

Born at Tiruvanchikuḷam, into the royal family of the Ceras from Kerala, he was preoccupied with the religious activities of the Bhāgavatas (ardent devotees of Lord Kṛṣṇa). Later he is known to have moved to Śrīraṅgam. He composed the *Perumāḷ Tirumoḻi* (105 hymns) where he pleads for the vision of God.

TOṆḌARAḌIPPOḌI ĀḺVĀR

Born in Mandangudi, he was otherwise known as Bhaktāṅghrireṇu. His devotion to the Lord Raṅganātha at Śrīraṅgam was remarkable. He called himself Toṇḍaraḍippoḍi — one who likes to smear the dust from the feet of the devotees of the Lord. *Tirumālai* (45 hymns of overcoming the bondages of human life to attain God) and *Tiruppaḷḷieḻuci* (10 verses meant to awaken the Lord in the morning from his *yoga nidrā*) were his contributions to the Vaiṣṇava philosophy.

TIRUPPĀṆ ĀḺVĀR

He was born in Uraiyur, into a low caste family of south India and was known to be a poet musician (*pāṇṇār*) deeply devoted to Raṅganātha. The story goes that the Lord himself had instructed the priest of the temple to bring *paṇṇār* into the temple and hence gained the title *munivāhana* (the one carried by a *muni*). He composed a short poem called *Amalanādipirān* (10 verses) that describes the grandeur of the various aspects of Lord Raṅganātha.

TIRUMAṄGAI ĀḺVĀR

In contrast to the other Āḻvārs he was born in a tribal family at Kuraiyalūr and was held in high regard for his archery skills and valour by the Coḷa ruler. To fulfil an expensive promise he made to his lady love — Kumudavalli, he came across the Lord and his consort in the form of a newly wedded couple whom he tried to rob. He is believed to have gained his spiritual knowledge directly from the Lord himself. Tirumaṅgai Āḻvār has contributed 6 compositions as follows:

- *Periya Tirumoḻi* (1084 hymns known for the literary grandeur)
- *Tirukkuruntakam* (20 verses that speak of the Lord's role in sustaining the world)
- *Tiruneduntāṇḍakam* (30 verses singing the agony of the separation from the Lord)
- *Tiruvelukurrirukkai* (1 poem of 47 lines of his surrender to God)
- *Siriya Tirumaḍal* (155 lines of mystic love and longing for the Lord)
- *Periya Tirumaḍal* (297 lines of mystic love and longing to be one with the Lord).

Divya Prabandham of the Āḻvārs

HOW THE DIVYA PRABANDHAMS WERE UNEARTHED

The story goes that once Nāthamuni had gone on a long pilgrimage with his family. He visited a number of places like Mathurā, Bṛndāvan, Badrī, etc. in the north and on his return via Kāśī, visited Ahobilam, Tirupati, Kāñcīpuram, Śrīraṅgam and finally came to Kumbakoṇam and prayed to Lord Śārṅgapāṇi and returned back home. One day while in a discussion at the local temple, he met some pilgrims who broke out into a beautiful song — *ārā amude, aḍiyen uḍalum ninpal anbaye . . . niṉra neḍumāle.* When Nāthamuni heard the words *ārā amude* (the nectar that one cannot stop tiring of irrespective of over intake; this nectar is none other than the Lord the poet eulogises). He was wonderstruck at the beauty of the words, and he remembered the deity when they came to the line — *seera sennel . . .. tirukuḍanthai . . . emmāne . . ..* *Tirukudanthai emmān* is the Śrī Śārṅgapāṇi the presiding deity of the Śārṅgapāṇi temple at Kumbakoṇam. He immediately knew it was none other than the temple at Kumbakoṇam and Śāraṅgpāṇi or Ārāvamudhan whom they were singing the praises of. They continued to sing more songs and Nāthamuni was awestruck at the beauty of the songs, the description of not only the deities but also the temples. Though he wanted them to go on they finally stopped singing after the ninth song. Nāthamuni walked up to them and asked them to sing more such songs. They said they did not know any more. He then decided that he would somehow get information about the other songs. He went to Tirukurugūr (Āḷvār Tirunagari), the birthplace of Nammāḷvār, and met a disciple from the lineage of Madhurakavi Āḷvār who was Nammāḷvār's disciple.

At Tirukurugūr he was advised to recite 12,000 times Madhurakavi Āḷvār's *Kanninur Siruthambu* that comprised 11 verses. He did it and then the saint Śaṭakopa appeared before Nāthamuni and revealed, with his *jñānadṛṣṭi,* all the 4000 verses to him. Thus the sacred four thousand verses were rescued for posterity. The 4000 verses of the Āḷvārs teach sublime spiritual truth contained in three *rahasya*s — *tirumantra* (*aṣṭākṣarī*), *dvaya* and *carmaślokas*. It is believed that this division is based in the order in which the Vaiṣṇava *doctrines* — *aṣṭākṣara, dvaya* and *carmaśloka* are contained in the *prabandham*s.

Nāthamuni had taught his two nephews and his disciple the "Nālāyiram" completely and with their help also composed the tunes (*rāgam*) and beats (*tāḷa*) for all the hymns. This also came to be known as *deva gānam* and *divya isai.* Since it was here that the Lord appeared before Nāthamuni and presented the verses, the place came to be called as "Kāṭṭumannār Koil" (*Kāṭṭu Mannār* — the God who showed). The temple has a separate sanctum for Nāthamuni and his birth-star Anuṣam in the month of Āni (June-July) is celebrated at the temple every year.

The *prabandham*s of the Āḷvārs can be classified thus according to Manavāḷamāmuni and his followers:

1. Poigai Āḻvār	Mudal Tiruvandādi	100 verses
2. Pūtattāḻvār	Iraṇḍām Tiruvandādi	100 verses
3. Pey Āḻvār	Mūṇḍrām Tiruvandādi	100 verses
4. Tirumaḻisai Āḻvār	Nānmukan Tiruvandādi	96 verses
	Tiruccanda Viruttam	120 verses
5. Nammāḻvār	Tiruviruttam	100 verses
	Tiruvāciriyam	7 verses
	Periya Tiruvandādi	87 verses
	Tiruvaimoḻi	1102 verses
6. Madhurakavi Āḻvār	Kaṇṇiṇur Sirattāmbu	11 verses
7. Kulaśekara Āḻvār	Perumāḷ Tirumoḻi	105 verses
8. Periāḻvār	Tiruppallāṇḍu	12 verses
	Periāḻvār Tirumoḻi	461 verses
9. Āṇḍāḷ	Thiruppāvai	30 verses
	Nācciyār Tirumoḻi	143 verses
10. Toṇḍaraḍippoḍi Āḻvār	Tiruppaḷieḻuci	10 verses
	Tirumālai	45 verses
11. Tiruppāṇ Āḻvār	Amalanādipirān	10 verses
12. Tirumaṅgai Āḻvār	Periya Tirumoḻi	1084 verses
	Tirukkuruntāṇḍakam	20 verses
	Tiruneḍuṅtāṇḍakam	30 verses
	Tiruveḻukūṟṟirukkai	1 verse
	Siriya Tirumaḍal	77 ½ verses
	Periya Tirumaḍal	148 ½ verses

There are 24 *prabandhams* of varying sizes, making a total collection of 4000 hymns, known as *Nālāyira Divyaprabandham*. Vedānta Deśika made small changes to the table by combining and splitting certain *prabandhams* and also added the *Rāmānuja Nūṟṟandādi*, a Tamil *prabhandam* of 108 hymns composed by Tiruvarangattamudanār, dedicated to Rāmānuja. The 24 *prabandhams* are in this case divided into 4 parts, *thokuthi* (collection). Nāthamuni further classified this into 2 main chapters. The word *pāsurams* means, *Suramōdu kūdiya Pā* (songs sung with a proper tune).

Isai Pā

1. Muthal Āyiram (first Thousand) — 9 *prabandhams*
2. Periya Tirumoḻi — 3 *prabandhams* (1084 hymns)
3. *Tiruvāimoḻi* — 1 *prabhandam* (1102 hymns)

Iyar Pā

Consists of 11 *prabandhams*

Besides Iyar Pā, 3 other chapters consist of *pāsurams* composed with tunes. They were meant for the purpose of *Nādhopāsanā* (prayers for the Lord). These had specified *Paṇṇ*.

The Āḻvārs describe their *Pāsurams* as *Isai Mālai* (Garland of Music). The Vaiṣṇavites consider them *Deivīga Isai* (Divine Music) and *Deva Gānam* (Music of the Gods). There are several evidences in the songs that the Āḻvārs themselves had set *rāgam* and *tāḷam* for the *Pāsurams*.

Periāḻvār

112th hymn — *Pann pāla pādi pallāṇḍu isai pā* (singing different tunes to different songs).

Āṇḍāḷ

446th hymn (*Tiruppāvai*) — *Ōngi Ulagalantha Utthaman per paadi* (singing the praise of the One who measured the World).

478th hymn (*Tiruppāvai*) — *Tūmalar tūvitoḻutu vāyināl pāḍi* (Worship through songs and flowers).

Kulaśekhara Āḻvār

707th hymn — *Kulaśekharan innisayil mevvisolliya in tamiḻmālai* (the garland of Tamil music offered in the sweet music of Kulaśekhara).

Tirumaḻisai Āḻvār

778th hymn — *Paṇṇ kaḍantha desamevu pavanasa nāthane* (tunes that reach the land of the Lord).

Toṇḍaraḍippoḍi Āḻvār

925th hymn — *Ethamil thannumai yakkam mathali yāḻ kuḻal muḻvamodu isai keḻumi gīthaḍgal pāṅinār* {offering of well-tuned songs to the accompaniments of flute, *yaḻ, muḻavu,* etc. (various instruments)}.

Tirupāṇ Āḻvār

930th hymn — *Maduramā vaṇḍu pāḍa mā mayil āḍa* (the sweet hum of the bee and the dance of the peacock).

Madhurakavi Āḻvār

936th hymn — *Kurukūr Nambi pāvin innisai pāḍi thirivane* (singing to the tune of Kurukūr Nambi).

Tirumaṅgai Āḻvār

1646th hymn — *Ariya vinnisai pāḍum nall-adiyavarkku* (for the devotee who sings rare and beautiful tunes).

Nammāḻvār

2818th hymn — *Āḍi āḍi agam karainthu isai pāḍi kaṇṇīr malgi* (dancing till the inner being dissolves and singing that brings tears).

Among the 30 *pāsuram*s composed by Āṇḍāḷ, 15 are only on musics. *Tiruvāimoḻi* composed by Nammāḻvār is believed to be the essence of *Sāmaveda* according to experts. Like *Sāmaveda, Tiruvāimoḻi* is also constructed for singing. It is said that when Periāḻvār was honoured by the Pāṇḍya king and brought to the court on an elephant, the bells around the neck of the elephant rang to the beats of the *Pallāṇḍu*. It is not an exaggeration when one says that music developed along with Vaiṣṇavism. The tradition of singing the *Pāsuram*s with actions (*abhinayam*) has been practised right from the time of Tirumaṅgai Āḻvār, who was given the title of *Nalukavi Perumān* during the eighth century. According to evidence from temples, this was known as *devagānam.* It is now practised as *Araiyar Sevai.*

Śrī Nāthamunigaḷ who has contributed a lot to Vaiṣṇavism and Tamil music has been praised by Nigamanthamahādeśikan (Vedānta Deśika) as *"kāḷam valamkuri . . . tāḷam vaḷaṅgi tamiḻ marai innissai thantha vaḷḷal"* (The great one who gave music and beats to the Tamils). The *Pāsuram*s that were previously sung as Suddhanthan without the beats was given the formatting of *tāḷam* by Nāthamuni. Madhurakavi had set the *tāḷams* only for *Tiruvāimoḻi*. Tirumaṅgai Āḻvār was supposed to have sung songs with tunes composed by him at the Śrīraṅgam temple. The temple records suggests thus. According to *Tiruvāimoḻi*, *tāḷam* is referred to as *otthu*. There are seven different *tāḷas* in the *Periya tirumoḻi* and *Tiruvāimoḻi*, the common among that is the *ādi tāḷam*. In music *śruti* is the central nerve and *layam* is its control.

There are 103 *rāgam-vakaikaḷ* (*paṇṇ*s) and 103 *tāḷa vakaikaḷ* (*otthu*) in Tamil music. Nambi Āṇḍār Nambi had formatted the *Tevārams* later according to the *paṇṇ* and the *otthu*. They say that the *paṇṇ* and the *otthu* brings out the unity in Vaiṣṇavism and Śaivism. The hymns of the Āḻvārs and the Nāyaṉmārs bring out the nuances of emotion, devotion, unity and finally the lyrical beauty of the songs that are masterpieces of Tamil literature. These savants through their hymns take us through the glorious past of spirituality, religion, history and culture of south India.

Nālāyira Divya Prabandham

The works of the Tamil devotional poets have come down to us in two great collections: the *Nālāyira Divya Prabandham* (commonly called the *Nālāyiram*) containing the hymns of the 12 Vaiṣṇava saint-poets (Āḻvārs) and the *Tirumuṟai* (of which the first seven books are known as the *Tevāram*) composed by Śaiva Saint poets (the 63 Nāyaṉmārs). It is possible that these hymns were originally sung to the ancient Indian melodic *paṇṇ* (tune). As far as *Nālāyira Divya Prabandham* is concerned *Koil-Oḷugu* a chronicle of the Śrīraṅgam temple, and *Guru-Paramparā Prabhāvam* — of which the fourteenth-century redactions are known — notice that already in the ninth century Nāthamuni from Kāṭṭumannār Koil (near Cidambaram) set the hymns of the *Divya Prabandham* to tune. It is said that in Śrīraṅgam Nāthamuni heard about an older style of performing religious music (*devagāna*) from the days of Tirumaṅgai Āḻvār (seventh century). As against the contemporary practice of singing these hymns as *viruttam* or *suddhaṅga*, i.e. in a free musical rhythm without *tāḷam,* Nāthamuni set the verses of the *Divya Prabandham* to particular melodies (*rāgam*) and in particular metres (*tāḷam*). The system of singing the verses of the *Divya Prabandham* with *rāga* and *tāḷa* by the temple minstrels at Śrīraṅgam and other temples came to be known as Araiyar. Scholars agree that the first true *bhakti* poems of Tamil literature are found in the *Paripāḍal* composed during CE 350-500. There is no doubt that these hymns were sung to particular melodies, the names of which are mentioned in the songs themselves. The fact was that these devotional hymns were addressed to the Mother Goddess and were found in the earliest Tamil literature, i.e. the Saṅgam literature. The famous epic *Silappadhikāram* (dated CE 450) mentions songs *pani* about the Goddess Durgā (*Paykāippāvai*) sung by wandering minstrels (*pāṇar*). This *pani* song may correspond to the *panika* song described in the *Nāṭyaśāstra* as a song in praise of a God to be performed in the prologue of the classical dramas and accompanied with the female dance (*lāsya*). This ancient *pani* or *panika* song is connected with the ancient *pana* ceremony. This ceremony is still performed by the Nairs in some places in Kerala as part of Kālī-worship.

Āṇḍāḷ — The Privileged Āḻvār

Periāḻvār's foster-daughter, Godā Devī's (Āṇḍāḷ) bridal mysticism inaugurated a new matrix of worship. The *Vāraṇamāyiram* poem is justly famous. Among the narratives, lyrics and other allied writings that have enriched the *bhakti* movement since the time of the Āḻvārs is the noble epic, *Āmukta Mālyada* written by Emperor Kṛṣṇadeva Rāya. The title refers to Godā Devī as (*Cūḍi Koḍu tthavaḷ*) — "the one who wore and gave." Raya had also brought in other major personalities like Periāḻvār, Yamunācārya (Āḷavandār) and Mala Dasari (Nampaḍuvān) in the annals of *bhakti* literature. Written in a sublime style that calls for a deep knowledge of Telugu to understand it, the epic is drenched in pellucid *bhakti*. This can be seen in the very opening prayer to the Rāya's favourite deity, the Lord of Tirumala. The Rāya's devotion to the Lord is paralleled by his equally intense devotion for the twelve Āḻvārs.

Āmukta Mālyada takes up the legend of Periāḻvār first. We watch him go from Śrīvillipputhūr to the Pāṇḍyan court at Madurai with his entourage. As the pilgrims proceed, they waste not a word in loose talk. Only Nārāyaṇa's name is their subject.

Traditional accounts refer to a vision Viṣṇucitta had in the city which resulted in his singing the *pallāṇḍu,* verse that opens the *Nālāyira Divya Prabandham*. Instead of translating this hymn, the Rāya, however, sings a wonderful song that deals with the ten incarnations of the Lord Kṛṣṇa including his holding up the Govardhana Hill.

One *Āsvāsa* of the epic is about Yāmunācārya, who was also known as Āḷavandār. The Rāya had made several major changes in the received tradition about this *Ācārya* whose *Catuḥ Ślokī* and *Stotra Ratna* began the wonderful concept of *Ubhaya Vedānta* and built a strong fortress to guard the flowering grove of *bhakti* nurtured by the Āḻvārs. The Rāya's version of Godā Devī's story is almost a poetic commentary on bridal mysticism. The indications in the verses of *Nācciyār Tirumoḻi* are picturized as happenings when Godā Devī undergoes the torments of waiting for the Lord to come. One of the beautiful creations of the *bhakti* movement is the *nindā stuti* (accusive verses). The Rāya uses this concept with admirable power when Godā Devī speaks to her friends about the heartless Kṛṣṇa.

The innumerable poetic conceits used by Kṛṣṇadeva Rāya to shape a grammar of *bhakti* provide shoreless enjoyment to the devotee. Godā Devī transports us to Bṛndāvan along with her and we watch the Yādava maidens on the banks of Yamunā suffering the flaming darts of love for Kṛṣṇa. It is so appropriate, for the river Yamunā happens to be the daughter of fiery Sūrya and is a sister of death-dealing Yama! Godā Devī taking her early morning baths and performing *kaiṅkarya* (duties) in the temple while reciting the *dvaya* to affirm her absolute self-surrender, is the very picture of an ideal Śrīvaiṣṇava. Kṛṣṇadeva Rāya takes us to the very pellucid pools of *bhakti* as understood in Vaiṣṇavism by retelling the story of Mala Dasari in the sixth *āsvāsa*.

The story of a Dalit singer of Tirukkuṟuṅguḍi who helped a *brahmarākṣasa* (demon) regain its original form as a brāhmaṇa has been immortalized in the Kaiśikī Ekādaśī observed by devotees. Śrīvaiṣṇavism is a religion that believes in alleviating the misery of the misguided and the downtrodden people. The Dasari had been caught by a *brahmarākṣasa,* who gave him permission to fulfil his offering of music at the Tirukkuṟuṅguḍi temple before being devoured. When the Dasari returned after having sung (what he considered to be) his last song, the dreaded spirit was taken aback. Would anyone willingly return to certain death just to keep a promise made to a demon? The repulsive spirit saluted the Dasari:

> In this wide world, among gods, demons and kings, there is none as truthful as you are. This truth is scripture. There is none equal to you. You have been swimming in the floods of music with the help of your lute's calabash shell. You have received the grace of Lord Nambi, the presiding deity of Kuṟuṅguḍi. You have heroism, knowledge, truth and devotion, to the Lord. Who can equal you?

Such is the greatness of devotion (*bhakti*) and devotees (Bhāgavatas) as revealed in *Āmukta Mālyada*. The *brahmarākṣasa* (demon) pleads with the Dasari to part with the fruits of his *bhakti* to free him from the hateful form. But the Dasari says that he would rather die than give up the fruits of *bhakti*. Alienating oneself from the fruits of one's Viṣṇu *bhakti* for saving one's life would be like exchanging camphor for salt! Ultimately, the Dasari relents and prays to the Lord Bhagavatunda Rakṣiñcu, "May the Lord save the unfortunate!" Immediately the luminous form of the brāhmaṇa issued out of the spirit. The brāhmaṇa worshipped the Dasari saying that here was a perfect image of Bhāgavata with the eightfold *lakṣana*s intact and that he was a *gāyaka sārvabhauma*. The epic poem concludes with the wedding of Godā Devī and Raṅganātha, a celebration that ensures *loka kalyāṇa,* the good of the world.

The Hundred and Eight Vaiṣṇava Shrines (Tirupatis)

These are shrines known as the *Āḻvārgaḷāl Maṅgalaśāsanam Ceydu Aruḷ Petra Sthalangaḷ* — meaning the holy shrines visited and personified by the Āḻvārs.

Maṅgalaśāsanam

Maṅgalaśāsanam is a special word denoting the wish to confer all welfare and prosperity to the Lord. Although it looks strange that the mere mortal created by the God Himself should arrogate himself to the role of blessing the Lord and protecting Him, the Supreme Being, this anomalous situation is explained as arising out of excessive love towards the Lord by two stages, being a *jñāna daśā* and by being a *prema daśā.* In the life history of Piḷḷai Uranga Villidāsar and his affection to Lord Raṅganātha or Śrīraṅgam, it is said that when the *utsava-vigraha* was taken in procession in the streets this chieftain always accompanied the Lord holding a weapon in his hand. We can find many examples in Āḻvārs *Pāsurams* and Annamayya *kīrtanams* about devotee protecting the Lord.

Viṣṇucitta's *Maṅgalaśāsanam Pallāṇḍu* is one of the famous groups of verses that are invariably rendered in all Vaiṣṇava temples till today. Parakala does *Maṅgalaśāsanam* to the deity at Tirumāliruñjolai, wherein the Āḻvār says that the deity residing in Kuḻiyūr or Uraiyūr has a body that looks like a mountain and four powerful shoulders and he is the deity of Tirumāliruñjolai. The Āḻvār uses the words *vāḻiyaro ivar* meaning "May He Live Long." Kulaśekara Āḻvār in his *Mukundamāla* verse 2 says "Let the Lord be victorious" — *jayatu jayatu*. Godā also in her *maṅgalaśāsanam* recalls episodes during various *avatāras* and says, "O Lord, who measured the three worlds with your feet, may those feet be blessed." Similarly Annamācārya in one of his songs says, *guttuna korikella olla vittae mee padapu devuniki pallāṇḍu pallāṇḍu* meaning, "O Veṅkaṭeśvara and Śrīdevī in His heart have to live long." In another song he says, "Again and again Jayamaṅgaḷam, Śubhamaṅgaḷam to the Lord of Tirumala" (*Adyathma sankīrthanalu*, vol. 1, song 448).

There are other shrines which were visited by the Āḻvārs, but do not feature in their works. These are called the Abhimāna Sthalaṅgaḷ, for example, Melkote.

There are totally 108 and are classified according to their directions and vicinity.

While 106 are accessible two are not.

Tiruppārkaḍal (107) — The Sea in which Lord Viṣṇu is supposed to be resting on the Ādiśeṣa (snake God) with his consort Goddess Lakṣmī. This is supposed to be the *avatāra sthalam* (birth place) of Lord Brahmā. A Vaiṣṇava believes that once we leave this earth the Lord Himself comes to take our mortal remains to *Tiruppārkaḍal* for His *bhakta* to see and feel His presence forever. The sea is also known as

Kṣīrāpdhi and the Lord makes His presence felt to the *bhakta*s here by taking a particular form dividing Himself as Vyūhas and is in the sleeping posture. He takes the name as Vyuha Vasudevan here and is in three forms namely — Sāṅkarsana, Pradhyumna and Aniruddha and sleeps on the mighty Ādiśeṣa with his consort Lakṣmī. It is here that He is supposed to listen to the desperate calls of His devotees who seek refuge under Him. Hence this place is also called "Kūppāḍu Ketkum Ulagu," "World where calls can be heard."

Tiruparamapadam (108) — This again is not accessible by human beings and is also known with other names such as Tirunāḍu, Vaikuṇṭam and Param.

Here the Lord makes His presence as Paramapadanathan and Paravāsudevan facing the southern side. His consort here is Periya Pirāṭṭi. According to Vaiṣṇava philosophy once our determined time in this Earth is over the Lord Himself comes and takes us to this place. To every Vaiṣṇavite this should be the objective and to achieve the goal one should be good, think good and do good. The Āḻvārs in their hymns beseech the Lord to help them reach their final destination the *parama padam* also known as "Thelivisumbuth Tirunaga."

Given Below is the list of the names of the 108 Tirupatis

S.	Temple	Deity
	Coḻa-nāṭṭu Tirupatis - 40	
1.	Tiruvaraṅgam	Sri Raṅganātha
2.	Tiru Uraiyūr	Aḻagiya Manavāḷa Perumāḷ
3.	Tiru Thañjai Māmaṇi Kovil Maṇikuṇram Thañjayali Nagar	Nīlamegha Perumāḷ Maṇikuṇdra Perumāḷ Narasiṁha
4.	Tiru Anbil	Vadivaḻagiya Nambi
5.	Tirukkarambanūr	Puruṣottaman
6.	Tiru Veḷḷarai (Vedagiri Kṣetram)	Puṇḍarīkākṣan
7.	Tiruppuḷḷam Būdanguḍi	Valvillirāman
8.	Tiruppernagar	Appakkuḍaṭṭhān, Appala Raṅganāthan
9.	Tiruvādanūr	Āndu Aḷakkum Ayyan

10.	Tiruvaḻundūr	Devādirājan
11.	Tirusirupuliyūr	Aruḷmākkadal, Jalasayana Perumāḷ
12.	Tirucceṟai	Sāranāthan
13.	Tirutalaiccaṅgāḍu Nāṇmadiyam	Nāṇmadiya Perumāḷ, Vensundar Perumāḷ
14.	Tirukuḍandai	Sārṅgapāṇi, Ārāvamudan
15.	Tirukkanḍiyūr	Haraśāpavimochana Perumāḷ
16.	Tiruviṇṇagar (Mārkaṇḍeya Kṣetram)	Oppiliappan
17.	Tirukkaṇṇapuram	Nīlamegha Perumāḷ, Sourirājan
18.	Tiruvāli Tirunagari	Lakṣmī Narasiṁhan Vedarājan
19.	Tirunāgai	Nīlamegha Perumāḷ
20.	Tirunāṟaiyūr	Tirunāṟaiyūr Nambi
21.	Tirunandipura Viṇṇagaram	Jagannāthan
22.	Tiruvindalūr	Parimaḷa Raṅganāthan
23.	Tiruccitrakūṭam (Tillai)	Govindarājan
24.	Tirukāḻiccirāma Viṇṇagaram	Tiruvikraman
25.	Tirukūḍalūr	Vaiyyamkāttha Perumāḷ, Jagatrakṣakan
26.	Tirukkaṇṇaṅkuḍi	Lokanāthan Shyāmaḷameni Perumāḷ
27.	Tirukkaṇṇamaṅgai	Bhaktavatsala Perumāḷ
28.	Tirukkavitthalam	Gajendra Varadan
29.	Tiruveḷḷiankuḍi	Kolavalli Rāman
30.	Tirumaṇimāḍa Kovil	Nara Nārāyaṇan Nandā Viḷakku Perumāḷ
31.	Tiruvaikuṇṭha Viṇṇagaram Tamaraikaṇṇuḍaiyappiran	Vaikuṇṭhanāthan
32.	Tiruarimeya Viṇṇagaram	Kudamāḍukūthan
33.	Tirutthevanār Thogai	Deivanāyakan
34.	Tiruvaṇpuruṣottamam	Puruṣotaman
35.	Tiru Semponssei Kovil	Peraruḷāḷan
36.	Tirutteṟṟi Ambalam	Sengaṇmāl, Raṅganāthan, Śrīlakṣmīraṅgar
37.	Tirumaṇikkūḍam	Varadarājan
38.	Tirukkāvaḷampāḍi	Rājagopālan with Rukmiṇī and Satyabhāmā

39.	Tiruveḷḷakkuḷam	Śrīnivāsan, Kaṇṇan, Nārāyaṇan
40.	Tirupārthan Paḷḷi	Thamaraiyāl Kelvan

Pāṇḍiya-nāṭṭu Tirupati — 18

41.	Tirumāliruñjolai	Aḻagar Māliruñjolai Nambi
42.	Tirukoṣṭiyūr	Uragaellanaiyan
43.	Tirumeyyam	Satyagirināthan
44.	Tiruppullāṇi	Kalyāṇa Jagannāthan
45.	Tiruthaṇkāl	Niṉrā Nārāyaṇan
46.	Tirumogūr	Kāḷamegha Perumāḷ
47.	Tirukūḍal	Kūḍalaḻgar
48.	Śrivilliputhūr	Vaṭapatraśāyī Raṅgamannār
49.	Tirukurugūr	Ādināthan Polindu Niṉru Pirān
50.	Tirutholaivilli Maṅgalam	Devappirān
51.	Tiruccīvaramaṅgai	Vānamāmalai Thotādrināthan
52.	Tiruppuḷiṅguḍi	Kāychinavendan
53.	Tirupperai	Makara Nedunkuḻaikkādan
54.	Tiruvaikuṇṭham	Śrī Vaikuṇṭha Nāthan
55.	Tiruvaraguṇamaṅgai	Vijayāśana Perumāḷ
56.	Tirukuḷanthai	Śrīnivāsan
57.	Tirukkuṟuṅguḍi	Niṉra Nambi Kuṟunguḍi Nambi
58.	Tirukkoḷūr	Vaithamānidhi

Malai-nāṭṭu Tirupatis (Kerala) — 13

59.	Tiruvananthapuram	Anantapadmanābhan
60.	Tiruvaṇparisāram	Tirukkuraḷappan Tiruvāḻmārban
61.	Tirukkāṭkarai	Kātkaraiappan
62.	Tirumūḻikalam	Tirumūḻikkalanāthan Śrīsūkthinātha Perumāḷ
63.	Tiruppuliyūr	Māyappirān
64.	Tiruccenkunṟūr	Imayavarappan
65.	Tirunāvāi	Nāvāi Mukundan, Nārāyaṇan
66.	Tiruvallavāḻ (Thiruvallā)	Kolappirān Śrī Vallabhan
67.	Tiruvaṇvaṇḍūr	Pāmbaṇaiappan, Kamalanāthan
68.	Tiruvāṭṭāṟu	Ādikeśava Perumāḷ

69.	Tiruvittuvakkoḍu (Tiruvichikkoḍu)	Uyyavanda Perumāḷ Abhayapradan
70.	Tirukkaḍitthānam	Amṛta Nārāyaṇan
71.	Tiruvāṟaṇviḷai (Āranmuḷa)	Tirukkuṟaḷappan Śeṣāśanar

Nadu-nāṭṭu Tirupati — 2

72.	Tiruvahīndrapuram	Deivanāyakan
73.	Tirukkovalūr (Gopalapuram)	Trivikraman

Toṇḍai-nāṭṭu Tirupati — 22

74.	Tirukacchi (Kāñcīpuram)	Varadarāja Perumāḷ
75.	Aṣṭabhujakaram (Kāñcīpuram)	Ādikeśava Perumāḷ
76.	Tiruthaṇkā (Kāñcīpuram)	Dīpaprakāśar
77.	Tiruveḷukai (Kāñcīpuram)	Aḻagiyasiṅgar
78.	Tiruppādagam (Kāñcīpuram)	Pāṇḍava Dūtan
79.	Tirunīragam (Kāñcīpuram)	Jagadīsa Perumāḷ
80.	Tirunilāthiṅgaḷ Thunḍam (Kāñcīpuram)	Candracūḍa Perumāḷ
81.	Tiru Ūragam (Kāñcīpuram)	Trivikraman
82.	Tiruvehkā (Kāñcīpuram)	Sonnavaṇṇamseida Perumāḷ
83.	Tirukkāragam (Kāñcīpuram)	Karuṇākara Perumāḷ
84.	Tirukkārvānam (Kāñcīpuram)	Kaḷvar Perumāḷ
85.	Tirukkaḷvanūr (Kāñcīpuram)	Ādivarāha Perumāḷ
86.	Tiruppavaḻavaṇṇan (Kāñcīpuram)	Pavaḻavaṇṇan
87.	Tiruparameśvara Viṇṇagaram (Kāñcīpuram Vaikuṇṭha Perumāḷ Temple)	Paramapada Nāthan
88.	Tiruputkuḻi	Vijayarāghava Perumāḷ
89.	Tiruninṟavūr (near Chennai)	Bhaktavatsala Perumāḷ
90.	Tiruvaḷḷūr (near Chennai)	Vīrarāghava Perumāḷ
91.	Tirunīrmalai (near Chennai)	Nīla Mugil Vaṇṇan
92.	Tiruviḍavendhai (near Chennai)	Lakṣmī-Varāha Perumāḷ
93.	Tirukaḍalmallai (Mahābalipuram)	Sthalaśayana Perumāḷ

94.	Tiruvallikkeṇi (Chennai)	Pārthasārathi Perumāḷ
95.	Tirukadigai (Sholingapuram)	Yoga Narasiṁha
	Vada-nāṭṭu Tirupati — 11	
96.	Tiruveṅkaṭam (Tirupati)	Govindarāja Perumāḷ
	Tirumalai	Thiruveṅkaṭamuḍaiyān, Śrīnivāsan, Veṅkaṭācalapati
	Tiruchānūr	Thāyār — Alarmelmaṅgai
97.	Tirusiṅgaveḷkunṟam (Ahobilam)	Ahobila Nṛsiṁha
98.	Tiru Ayoddhi (Ayodhyā)	Śrīrāma, Cakravartī Tirumagan
99.	Thirunaimiśāraṇyam	Devarājan, Śrīhari
100.	Tirusaḷagrām (Śālagrāma)	Śrī Mūrthi
101.	Tiru Badrikāśrama (Badrīnāth)	Badrī Nārāyaṇan
102.	Tirukkaṇḍaṅkadinagar (Devaprayāg)	Nīlamegha Perumāḷ, Puruṣottaman
103.	Tiruppiridhi (Nandaprayāg, Joshimath)	Paramapuruṣan
104.	Tirudvarakai (Dwārakā)	Kalyāṇa Nārāyaṇan, Dvārakādhīśan
105.	Tiruvaḍamadurai (Mathurā)	Govardhaneśa, Bālakṛṣṇa
106.	Tiruvāipāḍi (Gokul)	Navamohana Kṛṣṇa
107.	Tiru Pārkaḍal (Kṣīrābdi Vyūham)	Kṣīrābdi Nāthan
108.	Tiru Parama padam	Paramapada Nāthan

There are two important sects in Vaiṣṇavism.

Vaḍakalai — (Northerners) more of Sanskrit influence.

Tenkalai — (Southerners) more of Tamil influence.

Though there are a lot of differences (more than 100) between the two, the most important one is that they both follow different teachers or *ācārya*s.

Vedānta Deśikan — The *ācārya* for the Vaḍakalais, has composed the *Godhā sthuthi* an invocatory for the *Tiruppāvai* that is sung in all Vaḍakalai temples during Mārgaḻi month.

Maṇavāḷa Māmunigaḷ — The *ācārya* for the Tenkalais.

The 108 Tirupatis are also divided into the Vaḍakalai temples and the Tenkalai temples.

The Vaiṣṇavite sign (the *nāmam*) that adorns the forehead of the gods is different. The Vaiṣṇavites wear the *nāmam* or the traditional sign drawn with white lines on either side called the *Tirumaṇṇ* and with a central red line called the *Śrīcūrṇam*. While the Vaḍakalai's sign will be in a "U" shape, the sign of the Tenkalais will be in the shape of "Y". We will find these signs in the temples, on the *gopurams*, on the walls and of course on the forehead of the deities to identify whether the temple follows the Vaḍakalai *sampradāya* (tradition) or the Tenkalai *sampradāya*. Even the temple elephants will have this sign adorning their foreheads!

Both Maṇavāḷa Māmunigaḷ and Vedānta Deśikan find a special and significant place in the temple and during festivals will be given all the honours given to a guru. Their birth anniversary is celebrated in the respective temples in a big way. All music rituals conclude with a mention of these *Ācārya*s like — "Manavāḷamuniye poṯṟṟi." Very traditional and conservative Vaiṣṇavites will have this sign drawn at twelve places on their body, like the forhead, chest, arms, hands, belly etc. each signifying an Āḻvār.

Śrī Rāmānuja (CE 1017–1137)

Śrī Rāmānuja was one of the greatest philosophers and geniuses of his times. Born at Sriperumbudur, near Chennai, he is considered the *ācārya* (teacher) for all Vaiṣṇavites. He was also called Bhāṣyakāra, Uḍayavar, Ethiraj and Emperumān. He wrote the *Vedavyāsarin Brahmasutrathukku Vishishtadvaitaparam Urai* (A commentary on the *Brahmasūtra* written by Veda-Vyāsa) and hence gained the title — Bhāṣyakāra. He took over the administration of Śrī Raṅganātha temple and brought about several changes in its functioning. This earned him the title of Uḍayavar. He died at the age of 120 at Śrīraṅgam and his embalmed body is believed to be kept in the temple in a separate sanctum known as the Uḍayavar Sannidhi. He was considered to be a revolutionary and had disciples among all castes. Every morning, when he went to bathe in the river Kāverī his disciple Kūrattāḻvān would lead him by hand to the water. Uraṅgāvilli, another disciple who was supposed to be an untouchable would help him out of water.

Most of his doctrines were based on the values in *Nālāyira Divya Prabandham*. Śrī Rāmānuja's philosophy is as follows:

A MAN HAS SIX ENEMIES

1.	*Āśreyaṇam*	—	Ego, for example, expecting something in return (Toṇḍaraḍippoḍi Āḻvār, Hymn 30)
2.	*Śravaṇam*	—	Questioning God (Toṇḍaraḍippoḍi Āḻvār, Hymn 9)
3.	*Anubhavam*	—	Aspiring for things beyond your reach
4.	*Svarūpam*	—	To be independent of God (Periāḻvār, Hymn 6)
5.	*Bharatvam*	—	To compare God with anything mortal or immortal (Tirumaḻisai Āḻvār, Tiruccaṇḍa Viruttam, Hymn 18).
6.	*Prāpti Virodhī*	—	To be or be associated with an aethist (Toṇḍaraḍippoḍi Āḻvār, Tirumālai, hymn 16).

If the above six enemies are conquered and the 10 commandments mentioned below are followed, one is sure to attain *parama-pada*.

The ten doctrines prescribed by Śrī Rāmānuja are as follows:

1. *Pūrṇa Śaraṇāgati* — Complete surrender and unquestioned faith to the Lord (Kulaśekhara Āḻvār, Perumāḷ Tirumoḻi).
2. Once one has surrendered himself to God, he should see all the good and the bad in his life as a result of the past.
3. One should never do any deed expecting *mokṣa* (salvation) (Toṇḍaraḍipoḍi Āḻvār, Tirumālai, Hymn 2).
4. Learn, practise and then preach the *Śrī Bhāṣyam* to the Vaiṣṇavites who you think worthy.
5. In case of not being able to do the fourth, learn, practise and preach Nammāḻvār's Tirumoḻi 2-2 and 4).
6. In case of not being able to follow four and five, learn, practise

and preach the essence of the *Mahābhārata, Rāmāyaṇa* and the *Śrīmad Bhāgavatam*.

7. Visit all the 108 *Divya Deśams*, serve God and help Vaiṣṇavas.
8. Build at least a hut in Śrīraṅgam, Kāñcīpuram, Śrī Veṅkaṭam or Tirunārāyaṇapuram to stay and pray to the Lord at these places.
9. Shift all your burdens to the Lord and your *ācārya* (*guru*).
10. By observing all the aspects of Vaiṣṇava philosophy, forgo one's ego, be compassionate to all living beings and be a role model of a true Vaiṣṇavite. (*Kamba Rāmāyaṇam* — Bālakāṇḍam — Anaithu Uyir Onṟu).

7

Temple of Lord Veṅkaṭeśvara — Tirumala

Āḻvārs' fascination for the Deity of Tirumala

Of the twelve Āḻvār mystics, Kulaśekhara carries the special honorific of "Perumāḷ." Perumāḷ signifies *mahā-puruṣa* which is the integral and specific cognomen (*rūdhī-vācyam*) of Śrīman Nārāyaṇa.

The Āḻvār savants were those who were "immersed" in the tide of God-awareness, and have severally dedicated benedictional hymns (*maṅgalaśāsana Pāsurams*) to one or the other or several of the *divya-deśam* shrines. To put it differently, *divya-deśam* shrines are sacred centres that have variously received adoration from different Āḻvārs. However, it is Kulaśekara alone who has the distinction of having his name for a part in the layout of the very sanctum sanctorum of every divya-deśam shrine. The stone-step in the sanctum is the *Kulaśekharan paḍi* which secures the consecrated arch deity within the holy of holies, and where the visiting devotee (*sevārthī*) halts and looks at the Lord. The relevant text is found in the decade of verses dedicated to the Lord of Tiruveṅkaṭam in the Āḻvār's *prabandham* known as *Perumāḷ Tirumoḻi*. The great (Sanskrit) work of hagiology, *Prapannāmṛtam* of Anantācārya, describes this *prabandham* as *Veda śikhārtha garbam,* the *Upaniṣad* itself.

Identity of the Lord in Tirumalai and in Śrīraṅgam

In the Śrī Vaiṣṇava *sampradāyam,* four shrines are specially adored principally, for the unique services rendered therein by Śrī Rāmānujācārya. The shrines are the ones at Śrīraṅgam (known as "Koyil"), Tiruveṅkaṭam (known as "Tirumalai" or Srisailam), Kāñcīpuram Hastigiri (known as "Perumāḷ Koyil") and Melkoṭe (known as Tirunārāyaṇa Puram). Of these, the Lords of Śrīraṅgam (known as Periya Perumāḷ) and of Tirumalai (referred to simply as *Appan*) are identified with each other in the post-Āḻvār *rahasya* literature nurtured by the *ācāryas*. This inner tradition is based on the affirmation of Tiruppāṇ Āḻvār, "The Lord who reclines on the (Ananta) serpent in Śrīraṅgam is verily the one that stands in benign stance over the lofty northern Veṅkaṭa hills where the monkeys leap and roam about and where He is hymned by the celestials."

The similarity, and frequent simultaneity, of descriptions of Tirumālai and Śrīraṅgam through the *Divya Prabandham* of the Āḻvār saints is quite striking. Kulaśekara's name is established for the sanctum step in Tirumalai, and it is he who has also marked out the innermost pair of pillars (*Tirumaṇattūṇ* or *Āmodastambham*) of the sanctum of Śrīraṅga-vimānam. Bhuthath Āḻvār says, "Veṅkaṭam, the very hill we adore!" This sounds a note complementary to Āḻvār Tirumaṅgai's declaration, "Śrīraṅgam the favoured repose (*Śayanam*) of the Lord of the milk-ocean (*kṣīrābdhi-nātha*)!"

Āḻvār Saints and Tirumalai

Āṇḍāḷ — Godā known to Telugu classical literature as *Āmukta Mālyada,* has dedicated surpassingly beautiful hymns to *Tirumalai Tiruveṅkaṭam,* but she is not addressed as "Āḻvār" as she is regarded as the Divinity of Mother Earth. Madhurakavi Āḻvār is also not counted among the Āḻvārs as his single decadis of verses is dedicated not to the Lord but to his *ācārya* Śrī Ṣaṭakopa Nammāḻvār; he declares he knows no deity other than Ṣaṭakopa.

Of the ten Āḻvār saints, nine have adored the Lord of Tiruveṅkaṭam hills in their *Divya Prabandhams*. Their mystic experience is alike, their adoration issues in the same language and diction, but their phrasing is personal to them. Their adoration of the unexcelled visual beauty of Lord Śrī Veṅkaṭeśvara (Appan) often comes out together with their joyful description of the ravishing beauties of the vast Veṅkaṭam hill range itself. This is also accompanied by vivid verbal cameos of the instinctive behaviour of the animals that inhabit and create episodes out of the rich endowments of these hills. The Āḻvārs, to one man, prize the coolness of the slopes, the pellucid water cascading down its high slopes, high rising bamboo clusters that seem to drum at the sky, the numerous crystal pools that dot the generous hillscape, the fantastic array and heady aroma of honey-rich flowers, the soothing drone of swarming beetles, and the like.

Their *Pāsurams* (in the *Divya Prabandham*) in praise of the presiding deity Lord Veṅkaṭeśvara are chanted every day in the temple as a part of the music tradition while performing the daily religious rituals and the festivals right through the year.

Kulaśekara Āḻvār and his Prabandham

Kulaśekara Āḻvār was born into royalty in Tiruvañchikkalam in Kerala and his daughter, known simply as Cerakulavalli, is said to have attained wedlock with Lord Śrīraṅganātha Himself. A shrine is dedicated to her in the Śrīraṅgam temple, and Lord Śrīraṅganātha is seated with her on the Śrī Rāmanavamī day for an *abhiṣekam* together. The Āḻvār lived a life of fulfilment and devotion and spent his last days in Brahmadeśam — Mannārkoyil situated to the west of Āḻvār Tirunagari.

The Āḻvār's *prabandham, Perumāḷ Tirumoḻi,* consists of ten decades of hymns, of which one decade (the fourth) is entirely dedicated to Tirumalai. The principal theme-content of this decade is the celebration of the unsuspected gift of being born, the great potentials of "being," and the ultimate beatitude of perennial God-awareness. In his edition of the *Divya Prabandham,* S. Krishnaswami Aiyangar has provided a succinct capsule of the sequential message of each decade of *Perumāḷ Tirumoḻi*. In the first two verses, the Āḻvār savours how, by the grace of the Lord, he came into the spiritually receptive state of *Bhagavad Bhāgavata Anukūlyam,* that is, being inclined to serve the Lord and simultaneously questing for the fraternity of the Lord's devotees. In the third verse, he has decisively renounced the company of the materialists (*dehātma abhimāni*) and the sensualists (*viṣaya-pravaṇa*). Despite this manner of spiritual coming of age, the Āḻvār is apprehensive that the Lord may remain hidden for him for the reason that the devotee has not been fully liberated from hankering after the many lures of power and pelf in this world or the world beyond. In the fourth (Tirumalai) verse, the Āḻvār comes out with affirmation after affirmation that worldly glory holds no fascination whatsoever for him and that he would be fulfilled if only the Lord would grant him a toe-hold in any form or capacity on his sacred *Tiruveṅkaṭam* hill. The Āḻvār's insights are best appreciated by an actual reading of this Tirumālai verse, which is offered here in translation.

The name used is *koneri* which is the exact Tamil equivalent of Svāmi Puṣkariṇī. The *Varāha Purāṇa* section on Veṅkaṭacalam gives the etymology as — *vyutpattiḥ kathitā yasyāḥ tīrthānām svāminī yataḥ, svāmi puṣkariṇī tyeva* . . .. Since it is the principal pond there, it is the Svāmi Puṣkariṇī. This finds corroboration in several texts in other Purāṇas.

The Tirumalai Lord Beautiful

The *Mahā Nārāyaṇa Upaniṣad* delineates the five manifestations of the Maker in the famous verse.

It is evident that the *arcā-vigraham* forms the passionate core of the practice of the Śrī Vaiṣṇava religion. The given Tirumalai *prabandham* of Kulaśekara Āḻvār owes its heightened lyricism to the saint's ecstatic adoration of the physical beauty of the Lord of Tirumalai.

An elegant delineation of the Āḻvār's worship of Tirumalai (Veṅkaṭeśa-samādhi' as the *Varāha Purāṇa* captivatingly puts it) is available in the writings of Kāñcī Śrī Prativādi-bhayaṅkaram Annaṅgarācārya. The yearning expressed by the Āḻvār (verse 1) to dwell as a heron beside the Svāmi Puṣkariṇī is his way of channelling the celestial river Virajā itself on to this earth. His seeking to be even a fish (verse 2) in a Tirumalai pool seems an improvement over the previous prayer to be a bird, for the bird may take wings and easily migrate away from Tirumalai, whereas the fish in a pool would stay on in the sacred hill and would live while the water is there. The life-sustaining water is the metaphor for the Lord's compassion. (The *Bhaviṣyottara Purāṇam* carries a strident declaration — *tatra sthitānām jantūnām bhāgyam bhāgyam ahonmām*! The various creatures that inhabit the Veṅkaṭam hills are veritably a blessing for mankind!

One verse shows an apprehension that existence as a fish is so fragile, whereas the Āḻvār wants to live here and now, and has no desire but to be in Tirumalai only. He applies to be a temple servant (*paricāraka*) to carry the ceremonial mouth rinsing golden salver of the Lord as it would get him easy entry into the sanctum! This could well be the yearning of millions of people who throng Tirumalai even today and fall under the spell of Veṅkaṭeśvara's visual beauty!

The next thought of the Āḻvār (verse 5) shows him to be very worldly-wise. The service as a temple servant has its own uncertainties, and the Āḻvār would no way accept dismissal from the holy hill of Veṅkaṭam. In the "*Sampradāyam,*' Śrīraṅgam is known as the *bhoga maṇḍapam*, Kāñcīpuram as the *tyāga maṇḍapam*, Melkoṭe Tirunārāyaṇapuram as *jñāna maṇḍapam*, and Tirumalai has the unique name of *puṣpa maṇḍapam*. This gives the Āḻvār the idea that he could ask to be raised as a *campaka* tree on the hill, and he could all the time remain in active contact with the Lord through the *campaka* blossoms offered to Him.

On second thoughts, the Āḻvār is apprehensive that a highly coveted tree like the *campaka* could be eyed by someone and removed from Tirumalai, even as Śrī Kṛṣṇa translocated to his capital Dvārakā the *kalpaka* tree from the world of Indra, in order to please his spouse Satyabhāmā. Accordingly, he seeks (verse 5) rather to be a clump of grass-weed on this very hill so that no one would grab and remove him away from Tirumalai hills.

This is the culmination of the Āḻvār's prayers to the Lord of Tirumalai!

History of Tirupati

Śrī Nammāḻvār's firm faith is that the Supreme Being has of His own choice and for the spiritual benefit of mortals settled Himself on the Veṅgaḍam Hill and therefore the hill itself is a hallowed spot for mankind. It is also mentioned that Śrī Nammāḻvār alone has given his mystic reason for His manifestation as an Idol. That statement should not be taken to mean that the other Āḻvārs have not expressed the same belief. They have said the same thing but not in the manner that

Śrī Nammāḻvār has done. This is necessary to show that from the earliest times Veṅgaḍam has been considered to be the most hallowed spot on earth for worshippers of Śrī Viṣṇu and that the Idol on the hill has been taken to be self-manifest *Para-Brahman* to make it possible for *bhakta*s to do the *arcā* form of worship for obtaining salvation without resorting to the more arduous methods which were extensively practised in the previous ages.

Preamble

As a preliminary to a correct appreciation of the Āḻvār's *prabandham*s with reference to Veṅgaḍam a few points have to be borne in mind. The hill is referred to as Veṅgaḍam and not by any other name except in two stanzas of Peyāḻvār's third *Tiruvandādi* (nos. 63 and 75) where the term Tirumala is used. The genuineness of these two stanzas is open to doubt and will be discussed later. The other names with which we are acquainted, viz. Śeṣādri, Śeṣacalam, Veṅkaṭādri, Vṛṣādri, Vṛṣacalam, etc. do not appear to have been known to the Āḻvārs. These seem to have been in use even in the fourteenth century CE. They became more common after the compilation of the book *Veṅkaṭācala Māhātmyam* about the end of the fifteenth century CE. Even a cursory reading of the *prabandham*s will show that the Āḻvārs were well versed in the Purāṇas and that they frequently refer to incidents connected with the different *avatāras* of Śrī Viṣṇu. But there is not a single reference in the *prabandham*s to any of the anecdotes mentioned in the *Brahmāṇḍa* and other Purāṇas mentioned in the *Veṅkaṭacala Māhātmyam* that assign a reason for the manifestation of Viṣṇu on the Veṅgaḍam Hill.

None of the numerous rivulets and waterfalls on the hill is mentioned by name in the *prabandhams*. They are collectively mentioned as the cool and swift flowing tortuous torrents of the hill streams. Anecdotes connected with the sanctity of each waterfall or stream seem to be of later origin. The Āḻvārs do not mention the existence of any village or of any other place of worship on the hill or nearby in the plains. It was either that none existed or that they were too insignificant to be mentioned. Even the Deity Śrī Varāhasvāmi has not been mentioned by any of the Āḻvārs; nor Tiruchānūr and the

Deities therein; nor Tirupati. The names of kings are not given by them (except by Tirumaṅgai, the last of the Āḻvārs). They do not refer to their compeers or contemporary great men. Tirumaḻisai Āḻvār plainly states "My tongue will not sing a human being." Poygai Āḻvār says that he will approach only God's feet, will sing every day only His praise, will place flowers only at His feet (the feet of the one who has the *cakram* in His hand) "what care I about what happens to me." None of the early Āḻvārs has described even cursorily the form and the features of the image, the divine ornaments depicted thereon and the divine weapons borne. We have to draw the inference that they attached little importance to these. But they were all staunch Viṣṇu *bhakta*s and their faith in Nārāyaṇa as the Supreme Being was unwavering. They attached great importance to concentration of all the senses on the image during worship, whether that image was a painting or sculpture or metal casting. The image should be to the best taste of the worshipper, should be identified as Nārāyaṇa and treated in every respect as God Himself.

There are however a few verses of Poygai Āḻvār's and one of Periāḻvār that may raise a doubt whether after all these two Āḻvārs were not as much votaries of Śiva as they were of Viṣṇu. The verses of Poygai Āḻvār are nos. 5, 74 and 98. If they are read along with verses 7, 11, 15, 28, 46, 52, 67, 75 there will be no reason to doubt that the Āḻvār was a devoted *bhakta* of Śrī Viṣṇu alone. The former makes a bare statement of the fact that Śiva and Viṣṇu have each distinctive functions and appurtenances. Thus (verse 5) one is called Hara and the other Nārāyaṇa, one rides the bull and the other flies on the eagle; one has given us his "Nūl" or Āgama and the other the Vedas; one resides on the hill (Kailāsa) and the other on the ocean; one works destruction and the other gives protection; one has the trident in his hand and the other the *cakram* and lastly one is of the hue of flaming fire and the other of the colour of the sky (5). Again verse 74 says, one rides the bull and the other the eagle, one burnt to ashes the Tripuram and the other opened the breast of Hiraṇya; one smears his body white with ashes and the other is bright sky blue in colour; one shares his body with his spouse and the other keeps his consort on a flower over his chest; one has long matted hair (*jaṭā*) and the other wears a high peaked crown; one wears the Gaṅgā on his head and the other receives the waters safely on his feet. Verse 98 says that although the golden-hued Śiva (Puṇṇiyan) with the matted locks of hair and Neḍumāl (Viṣṇu) who strode the earth may be considered by us to have two different bodies, one has his abode only within the body of the other. The precise relationship between the two is given by the Āḻvār in verses (15 and 28). The first and foremost beings in creation (in the manifested universe) are three and of these the highest is the one who manifested himself on the primeval waters (Mur-nīr vaṇṇan). Without His grace the good offices of the others will be of no avail for salvation (verse 15): O thou of the dark hue! in thine hands are the right winded *Śaṅkham* and the *Cakram* (Nemi); She who is seated on the flower is on your body (chest), (Brahmā) who gave the four Vedas is in your navel and he who destroyed the three castles (Tripura) has his residence in your body (verse 28). Verse 11 says that the Āḻvār's mouth would not praise any other Deity, nor his hands worship another. In verse 46 reference is made to the Purāṇic account that Śiva had to get his sin of nipping off one of the heads of Brahmā absolved only by the grace of Viṣṇu. In verse 52 we are told that the eight Dikpālas, the Ekādaśa Rudras, the Dvādaśa Ādityas and the matchless two (Brahmā and Śiva) daily worship Tirumāl (Viṣṇu) with flowers gathered with their own hands. Verse 67 says that all rivers direct their courses to the ocean; the flower turns its face to the rising Sun; life looks to Yama (Dharman); so also True knowledge seeks the Lord of Padmāvatī. Verse 75 says that by prayerful meditation of Tirumāl all evil spells and incantations vanish and so also the oppressive effects of all bad *karmas* are destroyed; weakness of old age not felt and the way to salvation is assured.

It will be clear from a reading of the verses quoted above that Poygai Āḻvār being an out and out Nārāyaṇa *bhakta* has only given a reply to those who in his days entertained the notion that Śiva and Viṣṇu are only different aspects of the one Supreme being. He flourished in days when the relative merits of the ritualistic worship of Śiva and Viṣṇu were being seriously discussed and also the philosophy on which such worship was based. Even the Āgamas recognized the worship of the Trimūrtis and Dvimūrtis and temples were constructed accordingly.

Bhūdath Āḻvār's (second) *Tiruvandādi* gives no room for doubt in the matter. In verse 17 he says that Śiva who wears the moon on the matted locks of his head waited on (Māl) Viṣṇu and got his sin expiated. Periyāḻvār commences his (Third) *Tiruvandādi* with a description of the beatific vision of Śrī Devī and Nārāyaṇa in dazzling golden colour, the *śaṅkham* and *cakram* in the hands, and worships his feet (III. T.A. 1 and 2). He restates his conviction in the last verse (III. T.A. 100) by stating that we depend only on the one who bears the *cakram* in his hand for our salvation.

There is however one verse (III.63) which describes the form of Śrī Veṅkaṭeśa as a composite one of Viṣṇu and Śiva. This verse will be duly considered a little later in this section of the chapter while dealing with what each of the Āḻvārs has said about Veṅgaḍam and its presiding Deity.

Tirumaḻisai Āḻvār's views given in his *Nānmukhan Tiruvandādi* are more emphatic than the views of his predecessors. Poygai Āḻvār stated the Purāṇic version that Śrī Devī, Brahmā and Śiva all have their abode in the body of the Supreme Being, Nārāyaṇa. But in what order they emerge during creation is not mentioned. Tirumaḻisai however commences his *Tiruvandādi* with the unequivocal statement that "Nārāyaṇa created the four-faced one (Brahmā) and the four-faced one from out of his forehead created Śaṅkara (Śiva). I am commissioned to let the world know this great truth through this *Andādi* of mine. Take every bit of what is said herein as tested truth" (Nan. T. 1). With reference to the Trimūrtis he says that all those who have become *devas* and from among them the three who stand out as the foremost, in fact they are what all they appear to us to be only because they represent Neḍumāl. All the learning of those who do not realise this truth is rubbish *kadai* (Nan. Tiru. 54). We infer from this that in the view of this Āḻvār sincere and consistent *upāsanā* or worship of any Deity is worship offered to Nārāyaṇa because it ultimately leads the worshipper to become a Nārāyaṇa *bhakta*. The Āḻvārs were all out and out Nārāyaṇa *bhaktas* because their spiritual evolution had reached that stage. The early Āḻvārs have given in their works greater importance to the direct offer of individual daily worship than to resorting to temples for attending the worship offered there. The number of places of temple worship seems also to have been very limited in those days.

An analysis of the number of verses devoted by them in praise of the presiding Deity in temples will now be presented. It will be seen therefrom how greatly Tiruveṅgaḍam loomed large in their eyes in comparison with other places.

References by the Early Āḻvārs to Veṅgaḍam and to the Other Places of Public Worship

Poygai Āḻvār's *Mudal Tiruvandādi* consists of one hundred verses. Five temples only are referred to in eleven verses. Eight out of the eleven verses are exclusively in praise of Veṅgaḍam. Tiruvarangam or Śrīraṅgam is referred to in verse 6; and Tirukkovalur in v. 86. In the eleventh one (v. 77) four places (Veṅgaḍam, Viṇṇagar, Vehka and Kovil) are sung in one lot to illustrate the different postures of images for worship, viz. the standing, the sitting, the walking and the reposing.

Bhūdath Āḻvār's second *Tiruvandādi* also consists of one hundred verses. Twelve temples are referred to in seventeen verses. Seven verses out of the seventeen are devoted exclusively in praise of *Veṅgaḍam*. Śrīraṅgam is referred to in v. 88; Pāḍagam in v. 94; Kacchi (Attiyūr) in v. 95 and 96; Tirukkoṭṭiyūr in v. 87; Tirukkuḍandai in v. 97; and Ṭirumāl-iruñjolai in v. 48. The other places, viz. Tañjai, Taṅkal, Velai, Māmallai and Kovil occur in combination with Veṅgaḍam, Śrīraṅgam, Tirmaliruñjolai, Tirukkuḍandai and Tirukkoṭṭiyūr in verses 28, 46, 54 and 70. It will be seen that Veṅgaḍam has been largely sung exclusively as well as in combination with other places.

Periāḻvār's Third *Tiruvandādi* also consists of one hundred verses. Twelve temples are referred to in nineteen verses. Ten verses out of the nineteen are exclusively devoted in praise of Veṅgaḍam. In five more verses it is sung in conjunction with other places. Tiruvallikkeṇi is sung exclusively in verse 16 and Aṣṭabhujam in v. 99. In v. 62 Śrīraṅgam, Tirukkoṭṭiyūr, Vekha, Tirukkuḍandai and Katigam

(Sholingūr) are sung together; in v. 64 Vehka, Veḷukkai and Kacchi are sung together and in v. 30 Pāḍagam shares with Veṅgaḍam.

Tirumaḻisai Āḻvār's *Nānmukhan Tiruvandādi* consists of ninety-six verses only and his *Thiruchchanda viruttam* one hundred and twenty verses. The total numbers of his verses are two hundred and sixteen. Thirteen temples are sung in twenty-six verses (seventeen in the *Tiruvandādi* and nine in *Tiruccaṇḍa viruttam*). Fourteen verses out of the twenty-six are exclusively in praise of Veṅgaḍam. Śrīraṅgam, exclusively in v. 3, 30, 60, of *N.T.A.* and v. 49, 55 of *T. Viruttam;* Tirukkuḍandai exclusively in *T.V.* 56, 61, 62, Tiruvallikkeṇi in *N.T.A.* 35, and Kapisthalam in *N.T.A.* 50. In *N.T.A.* 36 and 34, Śrīraṅgam, Vehka, Tiruvallūr, Tiruppernagar and Tiruvanbil occur in combination. In *T.V.* 63, 64 Pāḍagam and Ūragam are exclusively sung.

In the final analysis out of a total contribution of 517 verses by the four Āḻvārs, seventy-three verses only refer to temples (or places of public worship). Out of the seventy-three verses thirty-nine are exclusively in praise of Veṅgaḍam and its presiding Deity. In nine more it occurs in conjunction with other places. Śrīraṅgam is exclusively sung in seven verses only. Our Deity is invariably referred to as Veṅgaḍattān or Veṅgaḍattu-meyyan and not by any of the other names with which we are now familiar (Śrī Veṅkaṭeśvara, Śrīnivāsa, Śeṣācalapati, etc.). They likewise call Raṅganātha, as Arangattu-meyyan and the Deity in Tirukkoṭṭiyūr, Tirukkoṭṭiyūr-meyyan. The Āḻvārs do not describe the features of any *mūrti* nor do they state if there were any attendant deities.

It will be plain from the above analysis that to the early Āḻvārs Veṅgaḍam was the foremost place of Viṣṇu worship. That they considered the *mūrti* to be the self-manifest image of the Supreme Being Nārāyaṇa will be clear from their verses. A clear exposition of this from their songs is necessary to set at rest the vague impression in the minds of some people that at some period in the remote past the image represented a form of Śiva or Śrī Subrahmaṇya although positive proof of it is not till now forthcoming and that Śrī Rāmānuja by some device converted the image into one of Viṣṇu. The early Āḻvārs flourished at least six centuries before Rāmānuja and *bhaktas* have to be told what these Āḻvārs considered the deity to represent and to which deity Veṅgaḍam has been considered the hallowed spot.

Tirumala Tirupati Temple

As per our tradition, Tirumala, the abode of Lord Veṅkaṭeśvara is one the holiest shrines in India. It is the foremost of the eight *svayamvyakta divya kṣetras*. The oldest Tamil text Tolkāppiyam refers to it as Veṅkiḍam.

Many a saint and composers have composed songs and sung in praise of the Lord. These include the Āḻvārs of Dakṣiṇadeśa, the Haridāsas of Karnartaka, Annamācārya and many others. Śrī Rāmānuja, the foremost of the Śrī Vaiṣṇavite Ācāryas, is said to have crawled all the way to the holy shrine. He deigned to set foot on the holy hills, which he considered as an embodiment of Lord Śeṣa. The worship at Tirumala shrine systematised by the *ācārya* then continues till today unchanged.

Situated in the Chittoor district in southern Andhra Pradesh, Tirumala-Tirupati is the abode of the legendary Lord of the Seven Hills. Tirupati is one of the most famous shrines in the country where an uninterrupted worship of the Lord has been carried out for over thirteen centuries. Even today, Tirupati draws enormous crowds throughout the year. The *pratimā maṇḍapam* has the statue of Śrī Kṛṣṇadeva Rāya, the Vijaynagar emperor, and his two consorts. Then there is the *tulābhāram*, the scales upon which materials for offerings are weighed. The peculiar aspect of this scale is that the offerings are offered in proportion to the weight of the devotee. The next spot, a little inside the temple, is the *tirumalanāyaka maṇḍapam*, which is replete with beautiful carvings. The gold plated *dhvajastambham* in a *maṇḍapam* follows this. The inner *gopuram* has a small but beautiful shrine of Śrī Varadarājasvāmi. The *baṅgaruvakiḷi* (the Golden Gate) has Lord Garuḍa with wings spread wide. Just in the step are the *dvārapālakas* (sentries) on either side of the *baṅgaruvakiḷi*, the entrance to the sanctum sanctorum. Inside the sanctum is the reverence and awe inspiring Lord Veṅkaṭeśvara. The temple has always received royal patronage. It is said that the Pallava queen Samavai consecrated the first silver image of the Lord on these hills in CE 614. The area was called Tirumalai and was situated across seven hills — the reason why Veṅkaṭeśvara came to be referred to as Eḻumalai or the Lord of Seven Hills. Some say evidence of this pilgrimage centre can be found even earlier in the Saṅgam poetry. Apart from the Pallavas, the Coḷas and the Pāṇḍyas also generously laid open their treasuries to this temple. However, its most liberal donors were the Vijayanagar rulers. As testimony to their munificence, there are bronze statues of the emperor Śrī Kr̥ṣṇadeva Rāya and his consorts installed at the portals of the temple. Even the Marāṭhā general, Raghojī Bhonsle, visited the temple in those days and set up a permanent administration at the temple for the conduct of daily worship. A number of valuables — jewels, emeralds and diamonds — presented by him are still preserved in a box named after him. However, legend has another tale to tell. It is said that there was a huge anthill at Tirupati. A farmer heard the voice from heavens asking him to feed the ants. When the king came to know of this, he ordered that milk be fed to the ants.

His compassion resulted in the liquid uncovering a brilliant idol of Lord Veṅkaṭeśvara hidden beneath the anthill. Each day pilgrims in thousands throng the temple. They wait patiently in serpentine queues for hours, offer cash and jewellery and tonsure their heads in fulfilment of their vows. It is their ultimate destination, an experience of a lifetime of inexplicable contentment, which leaves them with a strong wish to return again. The view of the deity profusely ornamented from tip to toe is in itself awe-inspiring. The idol of Śrī Veṅkaṭeśvara has attributes of both Viṣṇu the preserver and Śiva the destroyer — two of the three aspects of the Hindu Trinity. Before entering the temple, devotees have to take a dip in the Puṣkariṇī (tank), the waters of which are considered sacred and highly praised in the Purāṇas. Once inside the temple, you are in a different world. Devotees overflowing with *bhakti* (devotion), with prayer on their lips, move in single file with hands held high in salutation. The day starts with the *suprabhāta darśanam* (waking up) and ends with the *ekānta sevā* going to sleep) when the Lord is put to bed in a velvet mattress spread over a swing cot suspended by gold chains.

Festivals at Tirumala

It is believed that Śrī Veṅkaṭeśvara enjoys festival (*utsavams*) and therefore every moment in Tirumala is considered a festive occasion. The most important festival is the *Brahmotsavam*, which is celebrated for 9 days. The details are discussed as under:

BRAHMOTSAVAM CELEBRATIONS

DAY 1

On the first day, *dhvajārohaṇa* is conducted by hoisting the *garuḍa-dhvaja* (flag with the emblem of a black Garuḍa), near the Śrīvari Ālaya Dhvajastambham.

A spectacular procession of Lord Veṅkaṭeśvara on the *Pedda Śeṣavāhana* is taken around the four streets of the main temple from 2200 hrs till midnight.

The meaning of *Śeṣa* is "to serve." Ādi Śeṣa is a thousand-headed serpent, on whom Lord Śrī Mahā Viṣṇu rests in his abode, Vaikuṇṭham.

Tirumala Hills, the abode of Lord Śrī Veṅkaṭeśvara, is believed to be the manifestation of Ādi Śeṣa. In commemoration of this event, the Lord is carried in a procession around the streets of Tirumala on the Śeṣavāhana (vehicle shaped like Ādi Śeṣa) during the first two days of *Brahmotsavam* (Pedda Śeṣavāhana and Cinna Śeṣavāhana).

DAY 2

On the second day, the Lord is taken around the streets of the temple on the Cinna Śeṣavāhana in the morning.

In the night, the deities are taken to the *uyala maṇḍapam* for the *ūñjal sevā*. They are then taken around the streets of Tirumala on the Haṁsavāhana.

Haṁsa or swan means "pure." *Haṁsa* is believed to have a high intellectual capability, and can distinguish the good from the bad. In addition, *haṁsa* is visually appealing. It is for these reasons that Lord Brahmā uses *haṁsa* not only as his vehicle, but also to chant the Vedas (the Vedas are believed to have emanated from the soul of Viṣṇu).

DAY 3

On the morning of the third day, the deities are carried on the *siṁhavāhana*.

Siṁha (lion) is a symbol of regality and power. According to the *Bhagavad-Gītā*, the Lord is the *siṁha* among animals (*mṛgānāṁca mṛgendroham*). The Lord is also called Hari (which in turn means *siṁha*) and Hari sits on *siṁha*. In other words, we have the phenomenon of the Lord sitting on Himself.

It is also believed that the Lord assumed the form of Narasiṁha (half man and half lion) to kill the demon Hiraṇyakaśipu. Therefore, Lord Veṅkaṭeśvara uses the *siṁha* as his vehicle on the third day of *Brahmotsavam*.

In the night, *ūñjal sevā* is conducted. The deities then ride in the *mutayalapandiri vāhana*, which is decorated with a pearl canopy. *Mutyam* (pearl) is a symbol of purity and royalty.

DAY 4

On the fourth day, the deities are carried in a *kalpavṛkṣa vāhana* in the morning.

Kalpavṛkṣam is the celestial tree that is believed to grant boons and fulfil devotees' wishes. The vehicle shaped like the *kalpavṛkṣam* signifies that the Lord grants boons and fulfils the wishes of his devotees.

In the night, after the *ūñjal sevā*, the deities are carried in a *sarvabhūpāla vāhana*.

Sarvabhūpāla means "all the kings of Mother Earth." According to the Hindu religion, kings, like Lord Viṣṇu, should always protect their people (*na viṣṇuhu pṛthivī patiḥ*).

To thank Lord Viṣṇu for his ideals and pray to him, the kings take the form of the *sarvabhūpāla vāhana* on the fourth day of *Brahmotsavam*.

DAY 5

On the fifth day, *Mohinī Avatārotsavam* is celebrated to commemorate the Lord's incarnation as Mohinī, in the morning.

According to legend, the *devatā*s and the demons performed *kṣīrasāgara-mathanam* that resulted in *amṛta* (nectar which when consumed grants immortality) and other sacred objects. The *devatās* and the demons fought for possession of the *amṛta*. Lord Viṣṇu then assumed the form of Mohinī (a beautiful woman) and procured the *amṛta* for the *devatās*.

The Lord is dressed like Mohinī, and He is taken in a procession in a *pālakī* (palanquin). Lord Kṛṣṇa is also taken in the same procession. This is to celebrate the assistance rendered by Lord Viṣṇu to the *devatās* during *kṣīrasāgara-mathanam*.

After the *ūñjal sevā* in the night, the Lord and his consorts are seated on *garuḍavāhana*. Lord is decorated with *mahākānti, sahasranāmamālā* that day.

According to the ancient Hindu texts, Garuḍa, the king of birds, is a replica of the Vedas (*vedātma vihageśvara*), while Lord Viṣṇu is the God of the Vedas. Therefore, the Lord sees Himself in Garuḍa. In the Vaiṣṇava Purāṇas, Garuḍa is also called *Periyatiruvaḍi*, meaning the first devotee.

Therefore, Lord Veṅkaṭeśvara selected Garuḍa as his vehicle for the most important day of the *Brahmotsavam*. Garuḍa *vāhana* is the greatest of all the *vāhanas*. A large number of pilgrims visit the temple on this day.

DAY 6

On the morning of the sixth day, the deities are carried on a beautifully-decorated *Hanumad vāhana*.

Hanumān was one of the greatest devotees of Śrī Rāma, an incarnation of Lord Viṣṇu. Hanumān served the Lord so faithfully that even the Lord could not thank Hanumān enough. Devotees believe that they are indeed blessed if they catch a glimpse of the Lord on *Hanumad vāhana*.

Ūñjal sevā is not performed on the sixth day. Instead, *Vasantotsavam* (spring festival) is celebrated.

In the night, the Lord is mounted on the *gaja vāhana*. *Gaja* (elephant) is also called the *sāmājam* (born from *Sāmaveda*). It symbolizes wealth (*gajaṁtam aiśvaryam*). It also symbolizes Airāvata — the vehicle of

Devendra, the Lord of the Devas in Hindu mythology. It also can be attributed to the elephant in Gajendramokṣam (story from the *Mahābhāgavatapurāṇa*), which is saved from a crocodile by Lord Viṣṇu.

Therefore, the Lord is taken in a procession seated on a *gaja vāhana* during *Brahmotsavam*.

DAY 7

On the morning of the seventh day, the Lord rides on *Sūryaprabha vāhana* (Sun chariot). Sūrya (the Sun), the son of Aditi, is another form of Lord Viṣṇu (Sūrya Nārāyaṇa).

Hindu mythology supports the heliocentric theory, and believes that Lord Viṣṇu is the centre of the universe (*dhyassada Savitṛmaṇḍala madhyavartī*). To symbolize this, Lord Veṅkaṭeśvara uses the Sūryaprabha (light of the sun) *vāhana*.

After the *ūñjal sevā* in the night, the Lord is taken in the *Candraprabha vāhana* (moon-shaped vehicle) around the brightly-lit streets of Tirumala.

Candra means the moon, which is considered cool and pleasant. According to Hindu mythology, Candra is the commander of the mind (*candramā manaso jātaḥ*). He is also the king of *auṣadha* (medicine).

It is believed that riding in the *candraprabha vāhana* is a soothing experience for the Lord. The Lord's contentment will bring peace to devotees' minds and result in a good crop.

DAY 8

On the penultimate day, *Rathotsavam* is celebrated, in which the Lord is seated in a *ratham* (chariot) and taken in a procession in the morning.

It is believed that those who witness *Rathotsavam* will not be reborn (*rathostam keśavam dṛṣṭvā punarjanma na vidyate*).

The idols of Dāruka (the charioteer of Lord Śrī Kṛṣṇa) and the four horses (Śaibyam, Sugrīvam, Meghapuṣpam and Valahakam) are placed before the decorated idols of the Lord and his consorts. This symbolizes that the Lord's charioteer is driving the chariot.

Devotees, who chant *Govinda-Govinda* . . . pull the chariot along! This is the only opportunity that devotees get to be of service to the Lord during *Brahmotsavam.*

After the *ūñjal sevā* in the night, the deities are taken in the *aśva* (horse) *vāhana.*

Horses formed one of the four wings (*ratha, gaja, turaga* and *pada*) of the military forces in ancient times. *Aśvam*, a symbol of energy, means "one who runs fast."

Lord Veṅkaṭeśvara travels on a horse when he goes for *paruveṭa.* According to Hindu mythology, the horse was born along with Śrī Mahālakṣmī, Airāvata elephant and *amṛtam* during Kṣīrasāgara-manthanam.

DAY 9

On the last day, *pālakī sevā* and *cakrasnāna mahotsavam* in the morning and *dhvajārohaṇam* are performed in the evening.

The processional images are anointed with oil, turmeric powder and other auspicious ingredients and *abhiṣekam* is performed. *Sudarśana cakram* is given a bath in the Svāmi Puṣkariṇī. The Garuḍa flag is then lowered.

During the entire festival there are a lot of music rituals particularly a lot of *nādasvaram* and singing and chanting of the *Divya Prabandham* and also singing of Annamayya's songs. The hills echo the music and the chantings.

Padmāvatī Temple at Tirucānūr near Tirupati

This town is host to the ancient temple dedicated to Padmāvatī, the consort of Śrī Veṅkaṭeśvara who resides at Tirumala-Tirupati, one of the most popular pilgrimage resorts in India. A visit to Tirumala is considered incomplete without a visit to Tirucānūr. Goddess Padmāvatī is glorified as the queen of the Universe. She represents the Lord's *saṅkalpa* (will). The divine mother feels concerned for the miserable plight of her children and tries to save them by appealing to the Lord's forgiveness and compassion. Padmāvatī who is the divine incarnation of Mahālakṣmī, the consort of Śrīman Nārāyaṇa, is known as *Ākāra traya sampanna*. In order to emancipate the *jīva*s she has three important functions:

TIRUCĀNŪR

Here Devī Padmāvatī in all her bridal glory is worshipped. It is customary to worship the Goddess here after *darśana* of Lord Veṅkaṭeśvara at Tirumala. The deities of Lord Kṛṣṇa and Veṅkaṭacalapati are enshrined on the *prākāram*. Nearby, there is a Śiva temple dedicated to Śrī Parāsareśvara. Tirucānūr is about 5 km from Tirupati. The temple of Alarmelu Maṅgai is situated here. She is the consort of Lord Veṅkaṭacālāpati. She is also known as Padmāvatī Thāyār, as she is believed to have been born out of a lotus flower. There is a legend that soon after the marriage, the Lord and his consort fell out, because of a feud that ensued between them. The spirit of the legend is even today preserved in the form of *pūjā* prevalent in the shrines. While Vaikhānasa form of worship is done for Veṅkaṭeśvara, on the hills, the Pañcarātra is observed for his consort at the foot of the hills.

Śrī Padmāvatī is seated in *padmāsana*, holding a lotus in both of her upper hands. Her lower hands are in poses of *abhaya* (fearlessness), and *varada* (benediction). Also in this temple are the deities of Śrī Kṛṣṇa, Balarāma, Sundarārāja Svāmi, and Sūrya-nārāyaṇa Svāmi. It is traditional to first worship Śrī Kṛṣṇa and then to have *darśana* of Śrī Padmāvatī.

Once a year there is a large festival that celebrates the marriage of Lord Veṅkaṭeśvara to Padmāvatī Devī. Padmāvatī Devī arrives at Tirumala on the back of a splendid elephant decorated with *tilaka* of solid gold as Lord Śrī Veṅkaṭeśvara comes out to meet her.

The main festival, *Brahmotsavam*, is in November/December. The ninth day of this festival is the appearance day of Śrī Padmāvatī. On this day Lord Śrī Veṅkaṭeśvara presents his consort birthday gifts, which are brought from Tirumala on a magnificently decorated elephant, covered with jewels and pearls.

Vedānta Deśika describes the Mother Goddess as Dayā Devī, being the embodiment of compassion.

She is the mediatory; She wards off the sins of those who approach her and enhances the good qualities of fallen souls making them fit to approach the Lord. The sacred town of Tirucānūr popularly known as Alamelumaṅgāpuram had acquired considerable importance during the time of Pallavas and Coḷas. This region came under the influence of Vaiṣṇavism as early as the eighth century. There was an important Vaiṣṇava settlement at Tirucānūr by the beginning of the ninth century. Though Tirumala and Śrī Veṅkaṭeśvara were better known by this time, the hill continued to be inaccessible. The Vaiṣṇavas of Tirucānūr established a Tirumantra Salai and propagated the teachings of Śrī Rāmānuja and the Āḷvārs. They also constructed a temple dedicated to Lord Veṅkaṭeśvara. Thus the temple — Tirivelan Kovil — became the proxy temple of Lord Veṅkaṭeśvara at Tirumala and attracted a large number of devotees. When the Coḷa suzerainty was extended to this region, they constructed a temple for Śiva, named after Parameśvara. After the decline of the Coḷa power, many local chieftains rose to independence. The Yādava Rāyas who were the most powerful among these petty chieftains constructed a temple dedicated to Aḷagiya Perumāḷor Śrī Kṛṣṇa. During the halcyon days of Vijayanagar rule, Vaiṣṇavism exercised considerable influence and power. It also received unprecedented patronage from the emperors. In the sixteenth century a temple for Śrī Varadarāja was built at Tirucānūr. Thanks to the missionary zeal and unalloyed devotion of the Vaiṣṇava devotees, a temple for Goddess Padmāvatī came up at Tirucānūr during this period.

The shrine resembles the temple of Govindarājasvāmi at Tirupati in many aspects. It consists of a *garbhagṛha* and an *antarāla* with a pillared verandah on three sides and the *mukha maṇḍapa* on the north. The *garbhagṛha* is square in design. The outside of the south wall of the sanctum santorum is relieved by three pilasters, *śālakoṣṭha* and three pilasters. The *pradakṣiṇa* round the *garbhagṛha* and *antarāla* contains a row of four pillars each in the south-west and north. The temple also has *Kalyāṇa maṇḍapa* and a *mahāmaṇḍapa* connected by another *maṇḍapa* with an entrance in the east. A shrine for Viśvaksena is situated at the southern edge of the floor of the *mukha maṇḍapa*. At the northern edge of the *mukha maṇḍapa* is a shrine dedicated to Śrī Rāmānuja. The image of the *ācāryas* is flanked by the idols of Tirumaṅgai Āḻvār and Cakrattāḻvār on either side. The temple complex also contains Śrī Aḻagiyaperumāḷ temple and Śrī Varadarāja temple. A unique temple for Śrī Sūrya Nārāyaṇasvāmi is situated on the bank of the Padmasarovara.

FESTIVALS

The graceful and enchanting presence of Goddess is a blissful experience to a devotee who visits Tirucānūr. He is drawn like a magnet by her unparalleled beauty. *Teeppotsavam* and *Brahmotsavam* are celebrated here with great fervor. The float festival conducted in June-July is an important festival at Tirucānūr. Hundreds of devotees visit the temple to worship the Goddess splendidly attired and seated on the floats during the 3-day long festival. However the most exquisite festival celebrated at Tirucānūr is the *Bṛahmothsavam*. It is undoubtedly a resplendent festival that provides an opportunity to the devotee to worship the mother to his heart's content. *Dhvajārohaṇam* takes place in November/December. It is conducted according to *Pāñcarātra Āgama* in an impressive manner. On the fifth day *gaja vāhana sevā*, on the next day *garuḍa sevā* and on the eighth day *Ratotsavam* are observed. Generally in all other temples, *Brahmotsavam* almost closes with the car festival (*Ratotsavam*) though *avabhṛta* takes place the next day. In Alamelumaṅgāpuram the day after the car festival is known as *pañcamī tīrtham*. It occurs on *pañcamī* in the bright fortnight.

Tirucānūr Pañcamī

On the previous day of *pañcamī* special arrangements are being made for *pūjā* and in the morning of the grand occasion, *padi*, consising of *tulasī*, turmeric paste, ochre dress and *pāyasam* is taken around the streets of Tirumala temple with all customary honours. Later it is taken in procession in the important streets in Tirupati. It is then taken on elephant with all honours to Tirucānūr. Meanwhile, the Goddess is taken around the temple streets in a taste-fully decorated palanquin. On reaching the temple special *pūjās* and *cūrṇābhiṣekam* are offered. The deity is then taken along with *Sudarśana cakra* to the eight-pillared *maṇḍapa* on the bank of Padmasarovara. The temple authorities receive the *padi* from Tirumala with the due honours on the outskirts of the village. *Sthāpana tirumañjanam* is performed at the *maṇḍapam* and the *Cakra snānam* takes place. Thousands of devotees take bath in the *sarovara* on this auspicious occasion to get their sins washed off. In the evening the special *āsthānam* of Śrī Padmāvatī Devī takes place in the *gangundra maṇḍapam*. From there the deity is taken in procession to the temple. At night again after *tiruvīdhi utsavam, dhvajārohaṇam* takes place marking the end of this magnificent festival.

Annual Festivals

1. Śrī Padmāvatī Thāyar Teppotsavam (float festival)
2. Śrī Padmāvatī Ammavari Kārtika Brahmotsavam
3. Vasantotsavam (Ubhayadār Utsavam)
4. Navarātrī festival (Ubhayadār Utsavam)

Daily Programme

5.00 a.m.–5.30 a.m.	*Suprabhātam*
5.30 a.m.–6.00 a.m.	*Sahasranāma arcanā*
6.00 a.m.–6.30 a.m.	First Bell
6.30 a.m.–11.30 a.m.	*Sarva darśanam*
11.30 a.m.–12.30 p.m.	*Śuddhi* and Second Bell
12.30 p.m.–6.00 p.m.	*Sarva darśanam*
6.00 p.m.–7. 00 p.m.	*Śuddhi* and 3rd Bell
7.30 p.m.–8.45 p.m.	*Sarva Darśanam*
8.45 p.m.–9 p.m.	*Śuddhi* and preparation for *ekānta sevā*
9 p.m.	*Ekānta sevā*

Friday Special programme

5.00 a.m.–5.30 a.m.	*Suprabhātam*
5.30 a.m.–6.00 a.m.	*Sahasranāma Arcanā*
6.00 a.m.-6.30 a.m.	First Bell

6.30 a.m.–8.30 a.m.	*Sarva darśanam*
8.30 a.m.-9.00 a.m.	Preparation for *abhiṣekam*
9.00 a.m.–10.00 a.m.	*abhiṣekam*
10.00 a.m.–11.00 a.m.	*Alaṁkāram* and 2nd bell
5.00 p.m.–5.30 p.m.	*Śuddhi* and *Alaṁkāram*
5.00 p.m.–8.00 p.m.	*Sarva darśanam*
6.30 p.m.–8.00 p.m.	*ūñjal sevā*
8.45 p.m.–9.45 p.m.	*Sarva darśanam*
9.45 p.m.–10.00 p.m.	*Śuddhi* and preparation for *ekānta sevā*
10.00 p.m.	*Ekantha sevā*

The music rituals at this temple are just as in Govindarāja temple. The *nādasvaram* is played five times a day. There is procession on Friday evenings in the four streets around the temple when the *utsava vigraham* is taken around with grand celebration preceded by *nādasvarams* followed by Veda Goṣam and singing of *Pāsurams*. Every evening many sing at the *ūñjal utsavam*. The songs vary from Annamācārya *padas* to devotional songs of other composers. There is also *upanyāsam* in the evenings on special occasions. There is a hereditary group of *nādasvaram* players who are appointed by the *devasthānam*. The *mukha vīṇā* playing in the *ekānta sevā* stopped owing to lack of players.

Pāñcarātra

THE CONTENTS OF THE PĀÑCARĀTRA

Pāñcarātra treats several topics like any other system of thought. It is necessary to find out whether this treatment accords well with the sense of the name *pāñcarātra*. This is to be ascertained from the *pāñcaratra* texts themselves. Here arises a problem regarding the period when the texts were composed. It must be admitted at first that the tenets and doctrines are earlier in origin and it's only at a later period that the need must have arisen to record them in writing. It is learnt from the *Mahābhārata* that the Sāṁkhya and Yoga principles formed the basis of *pāñcarātra* for development. Nārāyaṇa was treated as the ultimate reality. *Vyūha* doctrine was admitted. It is also known from the *pāñcarātra* texts which could be treated earlier in origin that the metaphysics, cosmology, social life, code of conduct, daily routine and initiation for worship received a detailed treatment in these texts. Lord Veṅkaṭeśvara the presiding deity of Tirumala is acknowledged to be the most perfect *arcā* aspect of Śrīman Nārāyaṇa the inconceivable primeval deity.

While the Vedas, several Āgamas, Purāṇas, Itihāsas, Kāvyas and Stotras in Sanskrit sing Lord Veṅkaṭeśvara's auspicious qualities, the *Prabandham* of the Āḻvārs rapturously praise the glorious grandeur of this great Lord in Tamil. The 12 Āḻvārs who flourished between the sixth and eighth centuries maintained *bhakti* as the great and perhaps the most plausible way to salvation. They propagated the glory of the Lord in an inimitable style and extolled the *vaibhava* mode of the Supreme Being.

The *Nālāyira Divya Prabandham* of the Āḻvārs is rightly called the Draviḍa Veda as it contains the essence of the Vedas. Like all savants and saints who have tried to take spirituality to the masses the Āḻvārs laid stress on the devotional aspect of religion and relied upon the popular local language for spreading the message of the Sanātana Dharma. The *Divya Prabandham* is given a unique honour in the daily rituals performed at Tirumala. Among the 108 *divya deśa*s that are famous with the voice of Āḻvārs hymns, three *divya deśa*s, viz. Koil-Śrīraṅgam, Tirumala and Perumāḷ Kovil-Kāñcīpuram have claimed great importance. In this the centrally placed *divya deśa* is Tirumala. This is called the Śrī Viṣṇu Kṣetram and the presiding deity Śrī Viṣṇu is called Veṅkaṭeśvara and this is much praised in the Vedas, Purāṇas, Itihāsas, Śrī Pāñcarātra and Vaikhānasa Āgama. Āḻvārs also have praised Him. In this temple *Nitya Tiruvārādhāna Utsavams* etc. are conducted according to Śrī Vaikānasa Āgama. Śrī Veṅkaṭācala Mahātmyam speaks of the glory of Malayappa Svāmi in 12,000 verses. Paṇḍits recite *Śrī Veṅkaṭācala Mahātmyam* in Tirumala. Although the aforesaid tradition of Śrī Vaiṣṇava Sampradāya is in existence, the tradition is not complete without the reciting of Āḻvār's hymns. The traditions of *ācaryas* like Ramanuja's are being practised in Tirumala temple even today. There is a clear evidence to show that the tradition of reciting Āḻvārs' hymns was in existence even before the time of Rāmānuja in Tirumala temple. There is a saying in *Ārāyira paḍi, gurum parampara prabhāva* that during the first visit to Tirumala Rāmānuja worshipped Āḻvārs at the foot of the hills (Alipiri). In Tirumala Oḻugu also, there is a saying that Periya Tirumala Nambi and Anantāḻvān requested Tiruvaraṅgaperumāḷ, Araiyar of Śrīraṅgam when he visited Tirumala, to recite the hymns of Āḻvārs in *deva gāna* during *Adhyayana Utsavam,* that is the next day of his visit.

Occasions for Recitation of Āḻvār Hymns in the Presence of Veṅkaṭeśvara Suprabhāta Sevā

There is a saying that originally all through the year in the early morning after opening the temple the recitation of Toṇḍaraḍipoḍi Āḻvār's Tirupaḷḷi Eḻucci was in existence. When Manavāḷa Mahāmuni visited the temple his disciple Prathivāthi Bhayaṅkaram Annan at his *ācārya*'s order did *suprabhāta, stotram, prapatti* and *maṅgaḷam* on Śrīnivāsa. Having inspired with these *stotras* Manavāḷa Mahāmuni ordered the recitation of Tirupaḷḷi Eḻucci during Mārgaḻi-Dhanur month, and in all the other months the four *stotras* namely *suprabhāta, stotram, prapatti* and *maṅgaḷam* have to be recited at the time of opening of the temple in the morning.

Daily Thomāla Sevā

Everyday during Thomāla Sevā, Śrīnivāsa hears the hymns of Āḻvārs as follows:

Daily Toṇḍaraḍipoḍi Āḻvār's Tirupaḷḷi Eḻucci and Āṇḍāḷ's Tiruppāvai are recited. After offering food to the deity, there will be *Tiruppāvai Sāthumurai.* In the evening Tomāla Sevā, *Tirupallāṇḍu,* Pūcūḍal, Kāpiḍal, Semmiyoṅgu of Periāḻvār's hymns *Vinnīla melappu* of Āṇḍāḷ, *Thāye Thandhai, Vadamāruthidai* and *Eḻai Eethalān* of Tirumaṅgai Āḻvār, *Oḻvil kālam Ulagamuṇḍa Peruvāya, Kāngulam kāgalum, Aḻi yeḻa* of Nammāḻvār, Tiruppān Āḻvār's *Amalanādhipiran* and Madhurakavi Āḻvār's *Kanninum Chiru Thambhu,* in total 15 decad are being recited.

During *tiruvārādhanā* both in the morning and evening Periya Jīyar or Chinna Jīyar or Ekaṅgi gives *tulasī* to *arcaka* and recites *prabandhams* by doing *Ālavaṭṭha kaiṅkaryam*. During *Sātumurai arcaka* performs *pūjā* at the feet of the Lord with *tulasī* given by Periya Jīyar. Such a tradition and custom used to be held for all Mūlavar and Utsavar Deities during *Sātumurai*. Lastly after *Sātumurai* the *Tirupaḷḷāṇḍu* will be recited and ending the *Sātumurai* saying *Vāḻi Tiru Nāmam* of Manavāḷa Mahāmuni. Then *tīrtham*, Śrī Saṭhāri and *prasādam* will be given to all devotees who are inside the temple. The word *thoṭṭamālā* (garden garland) and *thoḷmālā* (upper hand garland) changed as Thomāla. There are two reasons for calling this as Thomāla Sevā:

1. Tirumala is famous for the name *puṣpa maṇḍapam*.
2. At the end of *Tiruvārādhanā* garland is being given or adorned to the Lord.

Pūlaṅgi Sevā

During Thursdays' Pūlaṅgi Thomala Sevā, Tirumaṅgai Āḻvār's *Vada marudhidhai Onnodu Unnadhu* will be recited.

Friday Tirumañjana Sevā

During Friday *mūla* Virāṭ Tirumañjanam, Periāḻvārs *Venni Alaindha* and *Pinnai Mālanai* are recited and after Tirumañjanam Āṅḍāḷ's *Nāciyār Tirumoḻi* will be sung. Then Tirumaṅgai Āḻvār's *Siṟiya Tirumaḍal* also will be recited. After offering *prasādam Nāciyar Tirumoḻi Sāthumurai* will be held. During Fridays there will be three Thomāla Sevās.

Kalyāṇa Utsavam

During daily *Kalyāṇa Utsavam* there is a custom of rolling the coconuts as bride and bridegroom do in our traditional wedding ceremonies and at that time Āṇḍāḷ's *Vāraṇamāyiram* will be recited. The traditional wedding tunes are played in the *nādasvaram*.

Monthly Rohiṇī Utsavam

For every Rohiṇī, Kaṇṇan Svāmi will go around the Māḍā streets. At that time, *Periāḻvār Tirumoḻi* will be recited.

Monthly Tiruvātirai Sevāi

Tiruvādira is the birth star of Śrī Rāmānuja. Śrīvaru and Rāmānuja visit the Māḍā streets during every Tiruvātirai and Rāmānuja *Nūṟṟandhādhi* of Amudhanār will be recited and *Sātumurai* will be performed at the entrance of the temple. On the occasion of *Anadhyayanam, Upsadeśarathnamāla* of Manavāḷa Mahāmuni will be recited.

Monthly Punarvasu Utsavam

For every Punarvasu when Cakravartī Tirumagan (Śrī Rāma) visits, *Perumāḷ Tirumoḻi* is recited in Māḍā streets and *Sātumurai* will be done at the entrance of the *gopuram* on each occasion.

Monthly Śrāvaṇa Utsavam

Every month on Śrāvaṇa day, when Malayappā Svāmi visits outside the temple, Mudal *Tiruvandhādhi* of Poygai Āḻvār will be recited. When the deity comes back to the temple, at the entrance of *gopuram,* Sātumurai Pallāṇḍu and Vāḻi Tirunāmam will find a place.

Nitya Utsavam

There is a 40-day *nitya Utsava* to Śrī Malayappā Svāmi from Ugādi, the Telugu New Year, which is held in evenings. Śrī Malayappā Svāmi goes around the temple and at that time *Ciriya Tirumaḍal* will be recited.

Śrī Jayanti Utsavam

On the night of Śrī Jayanti celebrations, Dvādaśa Tiruvārādhanam (12 times *pūjā*) will be performed to Ugra Śrīnivāsa. After Tirumañjanam to Kaṇṇan Svāmi on that day, Periāḻvār's hymns will be recited.

Vasantotsavam

On the third day of Malayappā Svāmi's *Vasantotsavam,* Varāha-perumāḷ's Adhyayana Utsavam is performed. While performing Sātumurai of Manavāḷa Māmunigaḷ at the Rāmānuja shrine, recitation of some hymns and *Sātumurai* will be held.

Pavitrotsavam

During the 3-day *Pavitrotsavam* to Malayappa Svāmi recitation of three Āṇḍāl's, and three Āḻvārs Pāsurams — Poygai Āḻvār, Bhoodath Āḻvār and Periya Āḻvār — and Sātumurai is held. In the presence of Rāmānuja the Iyalpaḍi will be distributed.

Kārtikai Dīpotsavam

During Kārtikai Dīpam the three hymns of Poigai, Bhūtham and Periāḻvār *prabandhams* like *Vayyam tagali, Anbe tagali, Tirukanden* respectively will be recited by jiyār Svāmihal while the *arcakas* perform *hāratīs* to Mūlavirāṭ Śrī Vari. It is appropriate to recite these hymns as Mudal Āḻvārs have seen the Lord through these hymns of lamps. During Kārtikai month after Tirukārtikai Dīpam both in the morning and evening *Thomala Sevā Upadeśaratnamālā* and *Tiruvāimoḻi Nūṟṟandhādhi* of Manavāḷa Mahāmuni will be recited.

Dhanur Māsa Sevā

During Mārgaḻi month, *Tirupaḷḷieḻucci* will be recited when opening the temple in the early morning and then during Dhanur Māsa Thomāla Sevā, *Tiruppāvai* is sung. In the morning Thomāla Sevā *Tiruvāimoḻi Nūṟṟandhādhi* will be recited. During Friday's Thomāla Sevā after *tirumañjanam,* there is no recitation of *Nātchiyār Tirumoḻi* and *Ciriya Tirumaḍal. Upadeśaratnamālā* will be recited during the Thomāla Sevā and after *naivedhyam,* Sātumurai will be held. There is no Anadhyayanam during Dhanur Māsa and *Tiruppāvai* is recited only in early mornings. *Upadeśaratnamālā* only will be recited during the morning Thomāla Sevā. But in the evening *Nityānusandhānam* will be recited.

Other Deities Utsavams

During Annual Birthday of Aḻagiya Singar, Meyan Veṅgaḍam, Varāha Perumāḷ, *Tirupallāṇḍu, Kanninum Sirutthāmbhu, Koiltiruvāimoḻi, Rāmānuja Nūtrandhadhi,* and *Upadeśaratnamālā* will be recited and Sāthumurai will be offered.

Purattāsi Brahmotsavam

During *Purattāsi Brahmotsavam,* the following hymns of Āḻvārs are recited as noted against each *vāhanam.* It should be noted that on the day of *dhvajārohaṇam* there is no recitation of *Divya Prabandham* in the morning.

Day	Time	Vāhanam	Āḻvārs Hymn
1st day	Morning	Dhvajārohaṇam	—
1st day	Evening	Śeṣavāhanam	*Mudal Tiruvandādhi*
2nd day	Morning	Cinna Śeṣavāhanam	*Iraṅḍām Tiruvandhādhi*
2nd day	Evening	Haṁsavāhanam	*Iraṅḍām Tiruvandhādhi*
3rd day	Morning	Siṁhavāhanam	*Mūṇḍrām Tiruvandhādhi*
3rd day	Evening	Muthu paṇḍala	*Mūndram Tiruvandhādhi*
4th day	Morning	Kalpa Vṛkṣam	*Nānmugan Tiruvandhādhi*
4th day	Evening	Sarvabhūpālam	*Nānmugan Tiruvandhādhi*
5th day	Morning	Nātchiyar Pallāku Tirukolam	*Tiruviruttham*
5th day	Evening	Garuḍotsavam	*Tiruviruthaṁ*
6th day	Morning	Hanumata Vāhanam	*Periya Tiruvandhādhi*
6th day	Evening	Vasantotsavam	No recitation
6th day	Night	Gajavāhanam	*Periya Tiruvandhādhi*

During the above six days Periāḻvār's hymns also will be recited along with those hymns stated above.

7th day	Morning	Sūryaprabha	*Periya Tirumoḻi*
7th day	Evening	Candraprabha	*Periya Tirumoḻi*
8th day	Morning	Ratotsavam	*Periya Tirumoḻi*

At the feet of *ratha* (car) Saathumurai will be held by reciting Periāḻvār's hymns and Tirumaṅgai Āḻvār's hymns. During this *utsavam, Periya Tirumaḍal* and *Siṟiya Tirumaḍal* also will be recited.

8th day	Morning	Ratotsavam	*Periya Tirumoḻi*
8th day	Evening	Horse Vāhanam	*Nācciyār Tirumoḻi*
9th day	Morning	Pallaku	*Perumāḷ Tirumoḻi*

At the *cūrṇābhiṣekam,* ninth day morning, *Tiruccanḍa Viruthaṁ* of

Tirumaḻisai Āḻvār will be recited and at the end, Madhurakavi Āḻvār's *Kaṇṇinuṇ Siṟutāmbu* will be recited.

For the *cakrāsana* of the Svāmi Puṣkariṇī *Tiruneḍuntāṇḍakam* of Tirumaṅgai Āḻvār will be recited. At the Svāmi Puṣkariṇī in the Varāhasvāmi temple, Tirumañjanam for Malayappa Svāmi, Ubhaya Nacciyār and Cakrattāḻvār will be held. Then *tīrtham* will be distributed. At the end of Tiruvārādhanā, *Tiruppaḷḷieḻucci, Tirupaḷḷāṇḍu, Tiruppāvai, Kaṇṇinuṇsiṟuttāmbu, Koil Tiruvāimoḻi, Rāmānuja Nūtrandhādhi* and *Upadeśaratnamālā* will be recited and Sāthumurai will be performed. On the eighth day of *Ratotsavam* at the feet of the car and on ninth day at Varāha Svāmi temple *Sāthumurai* and *Vāḻi Tirunāmam* will be recited. According to Tirumala Oḻugu on the ninth day night at the *dhvajārohaṇa, Rāmānuja Nūṟṟandhādhi* and *Upadeśarathnamālā* and on the tenth day *dvādaśa Ārādhanā, Tiruvāimoḻi* used to be recited. This tradition is dispensed with now. But this will be done on the Śrī Jayanti day for Ugra Śrīnivāsa as stated above. Only *Kovil Tiruvāimoḻi* will be recited. We don't know the reason for this. During *Brahmotsavam* except on the eighth and ninth day all other days in both sessions after coming from *vāhana* and at the entrance of the temple, *Sāthumurai* will be held at Śrī Rāmānuja temple. *Iyal Sāthu* and *vāḻi Tirunāmam* will be recited. Even during Navarātri Brahmotsavam this kind of recitation of hymns will be there.

During Brahmotsavam on Śrāvaṇam Tīrtha *vāri* night *utsavam* afer *Rāmānuja Nūṟandhadhi Sāthumurai*, Śrīvari will be seated in the mirror palace near *dvārapālakā*s facing Śrī Rāmānuja who is presiding in the north and *naivedhyam* will be held.

Adhyayana Utsavam

Adhyayana Utsavam is held for 23 days in Tirumala usually from the night of *amāvasyā* preceding Vaikuṇṭha Ekādaśī in Dhanur Māsa. After evening Thomāla Sevā and *naivedhyam* Malayappa Svāmi with his consorts will be placed in Thirumāmaṇi *maṇḍapa* facing east in the *divya siṁhāsanam*. In view of non-existence of Nammāḻvār's *vigraha* in Tirumala, Śrī Senāpati Āḻvār will be seated facing south near the *siṁhāsanam*. Śrī Rāmānuja also will be seated south in that *maṇḍapa*.

After *naivedhya*, Jīyar Svāmi and *adhyāpakas* recite the first and last hymns in each *Andādi* from *Mudal Tiruvandhādhi* to *Tiruviruttham*.

Pagal Pattu

Day	Morning	Night
1st day	Recitation of *Iyrapa* in full	*Tirupaḷḷāṇḍu*
	Periyāḻvār Tirumoḻi	*Vannamadangal*
2nd day	*Periyāḻvār Tirumoḻi*	*Senniyongu*
3rd day	Remaining hymns in *Periyāḻvār Tirumoḻi*	*Vinnela melapu*
4th day	*Tiruppāvai Nācciyar Tirumoḻi*	*Oneru Selvadhu*
5th day	*Perumāḷ Tirumoḻi* to *Kaṇṇinuṇ Siṟuttāmbhu*	*Vedinen vādi 'thāye thandai* and *Peria tirumoḻi*
6th day	1st and 2nd centum of *Periya Tirumoḻi*	*Vaḍamarudhidhai*
7th day	3rd and 4th centum in *Periya Tirumoḻi*	*Paṇḍai Nanmarai*
8th day	5th and 6th centum in *Periya Tirumoḻi*	*Thelliyīr*
9th day	8th and 9th centum in *Periya Tirumoḻi*	*Kādil kadippittu*
10th day	10th and 11th centum	*Tirukurunthāṇḍakam*
	in *Periya Tirumoḻi*	*Tiruneḍunthāṇḍkam* and *Sāthumurai* in *Periāḻvār Tirumoḻi*, *Periya Tirumoḻi* and *Tiruneḍuṇthāṇḍakam*

Erāpatthu

Evening session — By beginning *Tirupallāṇḍu* each decad from *Tiruvaimoḻi* will be recited and on tenth night *Sāthumurai* will be held. The next day/night *Kaṇṇinuṇ Siṟuttāmbhu* will be recited separately. The next night *Rāmānuja Nūtrandhādhi* and *Upadeśaratnamālā* and in Sāthumurai, *Iyal Sāththu*, *Vāḻi Tirunāmam* will be recited. This will be the ending of Adhyayana Utsavam. Hence Malayappa Svāmi will have Adhyayana Utsavam for 23 days. Reciting *Kovil Tiruvāimoḻi* will do the next day for Varāha Svāmi Adhyayana Utsavam. On the Erapatthu Sāthumurai and the next day *Rāmānuja Nūṟandhādhi Sāthumurai.* After *Sāthumurai* Rāmānuja is believed to go round from *tirumāmaṇi maṇḍap* and stand before the *mūla virāṭ* near the *dvārapālakas* in *Garuḍa maṇḍapam.* The *arcaka* will bring *parivaṭṭam,* garlands, Śeṣa *vastram,* etc. from *mūla virāṭ* and all these are adorned to Śrī Rāmānuja and Śaṭṭāri will be placed on him. As Rāmānuja quoted Jīyār Svāmi recites *Kundramendhi, Akālekellin Oḻivil kālam, Paḷḷāṇḍu, Ādiyomodam,* 1st *cūrṇa* of *gadya.* There will be recitation of *Thanian* and *Vāḻi Tirunāmam* both at the beginning and ending. Śaṭṭāri will be placed for *goṣṭī.* It is said in *Tirumala oḻugu* that as Śrī Rāmānuja did this *Maṅgalaśāsanam mūla virāṭ* has attained greater importance. In this way *maṅgalaśāsana* will be held for 3 days. On all 3 days after *maṅgalaśāsanam* Rāmānuja again goes around the temple inside. At that time, *stotra pāṭham* like *dāti pañcakam,* Yatirāja *viṁśati goṣṭī* will be held. After reaching his *sannidhi, tīrtham, pādukā, anantāḻvan, prasādam* will be distributed. There will be a 10-day *utsava* to Śrī Rāmānuja. During that period, *Nālāyira Divya Prabandhams* will be recited. In the evening round up on all 10 days Śrī Rāmānuja will accompany Śrī Malapayya Svāmi. In the mornings of all 10 days Malayappa Svāmi Śaṭṭāri will go round along with Śrī Rāmānuja. In the mornings *Vīdhi Utsavam* and at noon *Āsthāna* the first 3000 hymns of *Āḻvārs Iyarpa,* etc. will be recited. In the night *Āsthāna Tiruvāimoḻi* is recited. In the morning Vīdhi Utsava after Iyal sathu at the entrance of *gopuram* while going round *vimānam* the recitation of *Dhāthi Pañcakam* and *Yatirāja Viṁśati* will be held on all 10 days. After reaching Sannidhi Iyal Satthu, Iyal Pāḍi and distribution will be there. In the evenings *Vīdhi Utsava Siṟiya Tirumaḍal* will be recited and on Sāthumurai day (Rāmānuja Jayanti) in the presence of Malayappa Svāmi at Rāmānuja temple entrance, *Tiruvāimoḻi Sāthumurai* will be held. Whenever *goṣṭī* comes along with the deity in *Vīdhi Utsavam* Śrī Sāttari will be placed to *goṣṭī* at the end of Iyal, at the entrance of the *gopuram.*

Śrī Govindarāja Svāmi Temple

Śrī Govindarāja Svāmi Temple Tirupati is a part of the Tirupati Tirumala Devasthānam. This is a big temple. It has a seven-storey *gopuram*, built in 1628. There are carvings depicting scenes from the *Rāmāyaṇa* and Lord Kṛṣṇa's pastimes on the second *gopuram*. This huge temple is located in the foothills of the Tirumala at Tirupati. This temple follows the same Vaiṣṇavite tradition as the Tirumala Veṅkaṭeśvara Temple.

Tirupaḷḷieḻcci and *Tiruppāvai* are recited in the morning and in the evening Thomāla Sevā when *Nityānusandhānam* is recited. The method of *Iyal* recitation *Iyal Sathu* at Rāmānuja shrine and *Iyal padi* distributions will be held during Govindarāja, Śrī Rāma and Tiruchānūr Alamelu Mangai Thāyar Brahmotsavam as followed in Tirumala. In Tiruchānūr, Brahmotsavam falls in Anadhyayana, *Upadeśaratnamālā, Tiruvāimoḻi, Nūṟandhādhi* will be recited. On every month on Śrī Govindarāja Svāmi's Star Uttara, Vīdhi Utsavam is done during which *Andhādhi*s are recited in order. On *pūrṇimā* nights, Pūlaṅgi Sevā is done and *Perumāḷ Tirumoḻi* is recited. On Phālguna Uttara day in the morning *Nāciyār Tirumoḻi* and in the night, *Perumāḷ Tirumoḻi* is recited. Anandhyayana Utsava for Śrī Govindarāja Svāmi is held from the *amāvasyā* day as is held in Tirumala. But this starts on the next *amāvasyā* of Tirumala Adhyayana Utsava Amāvasyā. The presence of 10 Āḻvārs and *ācārya*s like Śrī Rāmānuja and Kūrattāḻvān add lustre at the *maṇḍapam*. During the festivals of Pagal Patthu, Irāpatthu, Sāthumurai's, *Kaṇṇinuṇ Siṟuttāmbu* and *Rāmānuja Nūṟandhādhi* days, Tirumaṅgai Āḻvār, Nammāḻvār, Madhurakavi and Śrī Rāmānuja respectively will have *maṅgalaśāsana* (special rituals) at Śrī Govindarāja Svāmi temple's *sanctum sanctorum*. Then as practised in Tirumala, *Dhāti Pañcaka Parāṅkuśa Aṣṭaka* and *Yatirāja Viṁśati stotra*s will be recited. During Irāpatthu Sāthumurai Nammāḻvār will go round the streets in the evening along with Govindarāja Svāmi. In the streets both Śrī Govindarāja Svāmi and Nammāḻvār will face each other leaving a small gap. Nammāḻvār will separate from Svāmi, facing north, looking at the hills. Hymns of Nammāḻvār will be recited and *maṅgalaśāsana* will be held. Then along with Govindarāja Svāmi he will go around the streets. After *maṅgalaśāsanam* Nammāḻvār joins Śrī Govindarāja Svāmi and the *Stotra Ratnam* will be recited. In the night at Tirumāmaṇi *maṇḍapam*, Nammāḻvār will pray at the feet of Śrī Govindarāja Svāmi.

In Tirupati there are two Nammāḻvār idols, they are called Inside Nammāḻvār and Outside Nammāḻvār. During Adhyayana Utsavam outside Nammāḻvār will pray at the feet of Govindarāja Svāmi. This outside Nammāḻvār will hear the recitation of his own hymns along with other hymns during the 10-day *utsavam*. Inside Nammāḻvār on Sāthumurai day will have Tirumañjanam along with Śrī Govindarāja Svāmi. At that time, *Kovil Tiruvāimoḻi* will be recited and Sāthumurai will be conducted. There are also two idols of Periāḻvār. The outside Periāḻvār on the Sāthumurai day along with Śrī Govindarāja Svāmi will hear the hymns of *Tiruppāvai, Tiruvāimoḻi* and Sāthumurai. The 10-day *utsavam* is not observed for the other Āḻvārs. Like monthly Tirunakṣatram, one day Sāthumurai is held. Since Senai Mudaliār is beside Govindarāja Svāmi, Parivaṭṭam garlands and Śrī Sattāri will be offered to Senai Mudaliār. This honour is not for other Āḻvārs and *ācārya*s. On Sudarśana Āḻvār Sāthumurai after Vīdhi Ula Utsavam of Govindarāja Svāmi, *Koil Tiruvāimoḻi Sāthumurai* will be held. For the Sāthumurai of Kūrattāḻvān, Govindarāja Svāmi will be present. There is no Vīdhi Utsavam. However, *Koil Tiruvāimoḻi* will be recited.

There will be a 7-day *utsavam* for Godess Puṇḍarīkavalli Thāyar ending on Phālgunī Uttara. 10-day Utsavam will be conducted for Āṇḍāḷ, Periāḻvār, Tirumaṅgai Āḻvār, Madhurakavi Āḻvār with Ananthāḻvān and Vedānta Deśika. On Sāthumurai day in the morning itself Govindarāja Svāmi visits their temples followed by Tirumañjanam, *Tiruppāvai* Sāthumurai will be held. There will be Vīdhi Utsavam in the evening. On the same night *Tiruvāimoḻi* will be recited and Sāthumurai will be held for the above Āḻvār *ācārya*s. *Tiruvāimoḻi* and their hymns will be recited. For Vedānta Deśika, 4000 hymns will be recited. Except Puṇḍarīkavallī Thāyar and Āṇḍāḷ, for others in Govindarāja Svāmi Mūlavar Sannidhi after *Tiruvāimoḻi Sāthumurai, maṅgalaśāsanam* will be conducted. For Vedānta Deśika there is no *maṅgalaśāsanam*. There will be a 10-day *utsavam* for Rāmānuja and Maṇavāḷa Māmunigaḷ. On Sāthumurai day Govindarāja Svāmi visits their temples in the evening. *Dhinācārya Yatirāja Viṁśati* and *Stotra Ratnam* will be recited in the Vīdhi Utsavam. After reaching the temple, Naivedhanam and *Tiruvāimoḻi* Sāthumurai will be held. During

Rāmānuja's 10-day *utsavam* both morning and evening 4000 hymns will be recited and on reaching Sannidhi Iyal Sathu, Iyal Pādi also will be there. For Mānavāḷa Māmuni the recitation of 4000 hymns takes place in the temple itself. On Sāthumurai days Govindarāja Svāmi with Maṇavāḷa Māmuni will have Vīdhi Utsavam in the night. For Rāmānuja on all 10 days both morning and evening 4000 hymns will be recited and Iyal Sathu and Iyal Paadi will be there. For Maṇavāḷa Māmuni 4000 hymns will be recited on Sāthumurai day/night only. Maṇavāḷa Māmuni will accompany Govindarāja Svāmi in the Vīdhi Utsavam. For Rāmānuja on Sāthumurai day both morning and evening Govindarāja Svāmi Vimana Pradakṣiṇa Dhāti Pañcaka and Yatirāja Viṁśati *goṣṭī* will be held. On Maṇavāḷa Māmuni Sāthumurai and after Tiruvāimoḻi Sāthumurai both sessions, *Dhinācārya, Yatirāja Viṁśati* will be recited. On Vedānta Deśika Sāthumurai Aippasi Śrāvaṇa Vaḍagalai people will recite Deśika *stotras* in Vīdhi and in the Deśika's temple. On Śrī Kṛṣṇa Jayanti day, *Periāḻvār Tirumoḻi* will be recited for Lord Kṛṣṇa. On Śrī Rāmanavami day, for the idol of Śrī Rāma enshrined in Govindarāja Svāmi temple and Śrī Rāma temple Perumāḷ *Tirumoḻi* will be recited. In Tirukacci Nambi temple, which is under the control of Beri Cettiars during 10-day *utsavam, Tiruvāimoḻi* is recited and on Sāthumurai the temple deity Śrī Devarāja Svāmi accompanying Tirukacci Nambi will have Vīdhi Utsavam. It is the privilege enjoyed by Peddha Jīyār Svāmi as head of *adhyāpakas* to begin Śrī Śaileṣa Daya Patram and recite Āḻvārs hymns in all temples at Tirumala, Tirupati and Tirucānūr.

In the absence of Peddha Jīyār, Chinna Jīyār Svāmi or his nominee Ekāṅgī Śrī Vaiṣṇava will act on behalf of Peddha Jīyār. This responsibility also is taken care of by Peddha Jīyār through Vadakalai Ekāṅgī Śrī Vaiṣṇava in Vedānta Deśika temple. In that temple, instead of *Śrī Śaileṣa Dayā Pātram, Thanian Rāmānuja Dayā Pātram* will be recited by Vaḍakalai Ekāṅgī. Apart from the privilege of *adhyāpakas* headship to Peddha Jīyār; he has also two more prestigious privileges *dharma kartha* and *attāni sevakam,* which means giving Tirumañjana Tīrtham.

Music Rituals at Govindarāja Svāmi Temple

Daily the *nādasvaram vidvāns* who are appointed by the *devasthānams* play regularly from the morning *Suprabhātam* till the *Ekānta Sevā* in the night. The *rāgams* are prescribed as morning and evening *rāgams* and they tend to change as per the *vidvān*'s proficiency.

During the Vīdhi Ulā along with Pāri Nāyanam and Suddha Maddhalam the Sannidhi Ḍol is also played. Sannidhi Ḍol is the instrument which looks similar to the *nādasvaram* but without holes in the body and is usually used to announce the "Purappāḍu."

Previously, there were generations of players for the *nādasvaram* but unfortunately in recent times the hereditary chart is not followed for the *nādasvaram vidvans* or the *mukha vīṇā* players. *Mukha vīṇā* was played until seven years ago and due to the lack of players the playing of *mukha vīṇa* stopped at this temple.

For the Tepotsavam and Ratotsavam, concerts both vocal and instrumental are held in this temple. The Tirumala Tirupati Devasthānam usually organizes this. In the Govindarāja Svāmi temple during every ritual the singing of hymns of Āḻvārs is a regular custom. The temple priests appointed by the *devasthānam* are trained well in the *Pāsurams* and the Sāthumurais and there is a constant uplift in the standard of recitation owing to the growing consciousness towards the learning process.

In this temple there are two main shrines. In the northern shrine is Śrī Govindarāja, who is Lord Viṣṇu lying on Ananta. He is considered to be Lord Veṅkaṭeśvara's brother. The other main shrine has deities of Śrī Pārthasārathi (Kṛṣṇa as the charioteer of Arjuna), Rukmiṇī and Satyabhāmā (Kṛṣṇa's wives).

Parts of the inner shrine date back to the ninth and tenth centuries. The original temple had Śrī Pārthasārathi on the main altar. Śrī Rāmānuja added the Śrī Govindarāja deity around 1130. To the left, as one enters the first *gopuram* (gate) of the temple, is a temple dedicated to Lakṣmī. She is seated on a lotus in her four-armed form, holding a lotus in each of her upper hands, while her other two hands are in poses of *abhaya* (fearlessness), and *varada* (benediction). Situated above the door of this temple there is a carving of Lakṣmī holding a lotus in her hand.

Near the first *gopuram* there is a shrine dedicated to Vedānta Deśika. There is also a memorial for three of the Āḻvār devotees — Tirumaḻisai Āḻvār, Nammāḻvār, and Kurattaḻvār — near the *vāhana-maṇḍapa*, and another nearby shrine is dedicated to Śrī Rāmānuja. On the left of the second entrance is a Kūrma deity, Lord Viṣṇu as a tortoise.

8

Comparison between the Works of Āḻvārs and Nāyaṉmārs

THE two main streams of Indian music that prevails and flourishes in India are — Hindustani and Carnatic music. Carnatic music has been nurtured and developed mainly in south India. It owes its origin to the ancient Tamils. It was the *Paṇṇisai* of the ancient Tamils that dates back to over 2000 years, that later blossomed and flourished as Carnatic music.

When *Paṇṇisai* blossomed as what came to be known as Carnatic music, the form of composition called *kṛti* became popular. The composer of Tirupugaḻ Saint Aruṇagirināthar of the fifteenth century is aptly praised as *Canta Pāvala Perumān* (Lord of rhythmic lyrics) for the excellence of setting compositions to intricate rhythmic patterns.

Among the Nāyaṉmārs three most important Nāyaṉmārs were Appar, Sambandar and Sundarar who lived even before Saint Aruṇagirināthar who has composed the *Tirupugaḻ*. These three composed the *Tevārams* and pioneered the *"bhakti* movement" in the seventh, eighth and ninth centuries. These composers have also been identified in the long history of south Indian music and have been given due recognition.

The Āḻvārs, the composers of *Tiru Pāsurams* also used the *padhigam* format to sing the glory of the Lord. This is confirmed by Periāḻvār's *pāsuram* that speaks of the devotees singing the ten songs to music.

mālai pathum paṇṇ inbam vatrap pāḍum bhaktar

— 3.1-10

Saint Māṇikkavācagar had also sought to follow the *padhikam* form.

This can be seen from his *Koviltirupadiham, Tirukaḻukkunra Padiham* and *Acchopadiham*. It is the traditional practice to render all the ten songs of the *padhikam* in the same pattern.

When *Paṇṇisai* blossomed as to what came to be known as Carnatic music, the form of composition called *kṛti* or *kīrtana* became popular. *Pallavī, Anupallavī* and *Caraṇam* combined together to form a *kṛti*. The pattern of the prose in the *Caraṇam* appears to follow the *Padiham* pattern. It is to be noted that even rendering of the *Caraṇams* is akin to that of the *Padiham* mode of rendering. It is of great interest to note that *kīrtana* is the form of composition of choice from Proto-Trinity of Music — Muthuthāṇḍavar, Mārimuthu Piḷḷai, and Arunāchala Kavirāyar — followed by the Trinity of Carnatic music Śyāma Śāstrī, Tyāgarāja, and Dīkṣitar. The long traditional lineage of compositions owe their origin to Kāraikkal Ammaiyār. The Āḻvārs, the authors of *Pāsurams* also had used the *Padiham* format in their hymns. The three Śaiva Saints — Sambandar, Appar and Sundarar sang the *Tevarams* in the *Padiha* pattern of Ammaiyār. The *Māyāmāḷavagouḷa rāgam* that was introduced by Kāraikkal Ammaiyār inspired many composers to sing their first composition in it. This demonstrates the deep-rooted influence and acceptance of this *rāgam* in the domain of Carnatic music.

This *rāgam* is now being widely used to render almost all Carnatic musical forms like *saraḷi varisai, gītam, svarajati, varṇam, kṛti,* etc. This confirms the tremendous impact of this *rāgam* on south Indian music.

Kāraikkal Ammaiyār, the Śaivite poet (Nāyaṉmār), is also called as the mother of south Indian music for her contribution towards Carnatic music. Also in most of the temples the *rāgams* set to tune by these saints remain the same, and sung as an offering to the deity in the same tradition, as they are meant to be sung.

Āḻvārs and Nāyaṉmārs appeared in the south Indian society at a crucial time when the Hindu philosophy and values were on their way down. They brought forth a change in the thought process and the lives of the people with utmost passion, lyrical and musical beauty in their songs. While the Nāyaṉmārs conveyed determination and philosophy, the Āḻvārs captured the minds of the common man through the human emotions and aesthetic appeal in their songs. Godly pleasures, philosophical thoughts, self-realization and the hardships of life were brought together with poetic language and musical appeal in their songs. To them, even art was a form of religion. They saw their beloved gods as temples, as places, as the world and its beings, as a father, mother, child, friend and lover. Their songs ask the devotee to take both happiness and sorrow in the same stride to attain eternal bliss. We see them now as *avatāra*s (re-incarnations) of god or enlightned souls who educated the common man on the philosophy of life. They brought about a complete change in the cultural backdrop and history of society.

9

Contribution of Devadāsīs to Temple Music Tradition

THE Āgamic tradition and the *bhakti* movement gave a ritual and religious orientation to the arts. With the emergence of temples, many arts found their way into them. Music and dance were considered auspicious and therefore they were performed to invoke gods. These arts, suffused with aesthetic and religious sense, were depicted on the walls of temples to please gods. "*Śivavilāsam,*" the *Maṇipravāḷa* work of Damodara Cākyār, says that gods took their seats in the temple after having seen the dances of the *devadāsī*s in the Kandiyar temple at Kerala. The *devadāsī*s of the medieval period were repositories of music and dance. They performed these arts in temple rituals and festivals. Perhaps they also served as models to the sculptors and painters who have depicted them in beautiful scenes and images. Having been directly involved in the fine arts, the *devadāsī*s have enriched the tradition of fine arts.

As music and dance played a significant role in temple worship, the *devadāsī*s were expected to have mastery over them. The initiates received strict training in them even from their early childhood. Music masters, both vocal and instrumental and dance masters were appointed for this purpose. Sometimes *pāṇar*s (music masters) were appointed to impart training to them. In a few temples *ulvaccar* (drummers) trained them in the art of dancing. Aged grandmothers called *thāikillavi*s (mother grandmothers) trained them in music (vocal). Under their guidance some of them flowered as composers, songstresses, instrumentalists, and reciters of devotional hymns. A stone panel (plate 10) from the Naṭarāja temple at Cidambaram, depicts probably one such training in music. It has two figures, a male probably the instrumentalist and a female, a *devadāsī* receiving the training. Sambandar had popularized 23 *paṇṇ*s (what are today known as *rāgams*) and they were taken from him and were being sung in all the temples in the divine presence every day during the several times of worship. This singing ensured the continuance of the music through the centuries, seem to be eleven, when they were taken up by the Coḷa emperor Rājaraja Coḷa who created special endowments for the perpetuation of the singing in temples. He constructed 400 houses for the dancers, brought together to Tanjāvūr from almost all the Śiva shrines throughout Tamil Nadu, and more houses for the instrument players. Their instrument acquired a new name, *nādasvaram* and the *pāṇars*, who were the practitioners of music and dance from the Saṅgam period but had got neglected during a period of about 300 years before Sambandar, had now a new royal recognition and patronage. Society also recognized them in their rebirth as the melakkārar and they came to have definite cultural place in the domestic festivals of the temples. The Āgamas and the *bhakti* literature specify the time and place and the kind of the music and place and the kind of music and dance to be performed in ritual worship.

The tradition of the *devadāsī*, as a person who assumed an important role in society due to the socio-religious functions she performed can be traced from the time of the Saṅgam age poetry and literature as in *Maṇimekalai*. These were women dedicated to the temples for the service of the Lord. The function of the devadāsī seems beyond her appearance as part of the temple and its rituals during the Pallava period (5th-9th centuries CE). They were classified as *devadāsī*, *rājadāsī*, and *alaṁkāradāsī* and in the Vaiṣṇava temples they were known as *devadāsī* and *viṣṇudāsī*. The *devadāsī* had the privilege of entering the *sanctum sanctorum* of the temple and performing the *dīpārādhanā* every day. She also had to necessarily undergo the *Śiva-dīkṣā*. Though they were essentially kept in the temple for performing dance and singing they were also there for certain rituals done every morning. They had to come into the temple early in the morning after a bath in the river and carry a silver pot (*kuḍam*) on which a lamp would be placed. The *devadāsī* would collect this *kuḍam* from the priest after it was lit and take the lamp to the deity. It was she who opened the doors of the *sanctum sanctorum* every morning. She would sing for the deity as the early morning *pūjā* started. She would sing and mime (*abhinaya*) when the 16 rituals (*upacāra*s) were performed. In Puḍukkoṭai and Tiruvārūr this ritual was known as *Kaikāṭumurai;* they also sang special formatted songs while the *naivedyam* (food for the Lord) was offered. Though they were mostly dancers, for a number of religious rituals they always sang hymns from the *Tevāram*. In the Tanjāvūr temple they also danced for the *Tevāram*s.

Their day would begin with the singing of the *Tirupaḷḷieḻuci,* songs to wake up the Lord and go till the night concluding with the *ardha-jāma pūjā* in the night.

There are several inscriptions about the *devadāsī*s in many temples particularly about their dance performances and some of the items mentioned are the *navasaṅdhi nṛtyam, Kavuthuvam* (Kavuthuvams were dedicated for each and every deity like Gaṇeśa Kavuthuvam). When a *devadāsī* attached to a particular temple died, all the temple rituals would be stopped until the rituals of her death were completed. The fire to light the pyre of the dead *devadāsī* was also taken from the lamp of the presiding deity. The God was believed to be in mourning until all the rituals for the dead person were performed. Those thirteen days the presiding deity was left without the usual religious rituals. Such was the honour given to these *devadāsī*s.

Their dances were performed daily during the *pūjā*s. *The Mānasāra* specifies the time of music and dance in worshipping a deity. According to it, instrumental music and dance are to be performed by the *devadāsī*s after the *dhenu-mudrā* (a hand pose indicating the udder of a cow) of the ceremonious rites. In the Śrīraṅgam temple, the recitation of the *avadariya gītam* of the *Sāmaveda* was followed by the performance of the arts. The last item of the sequence was dance by the *Emperumānaḍiyār* (*devadāsī* of the Viṣṇu temples). As soon as the *arcaka* gave the signal lead, the *devadāsī* of the temple performed the dance, taking the Lord as her husband. According to *Tiruvārūr Purāṇam*, the *devadāsī* of the Śiva temple performed music and dance during the daily worship. An inscription of the time of Koḍal Ravi stipulates that music (both vocal and instrumental) and dance were to be performed during the daily worship. Musical forms such as *gāndhāra, ṣaḍava, nattaraka, kauśika* and *pañjama* are to be recited in the early morning, midday, afternoon, evening and midnight respectively. As part of daily worship (*nityotsava*), the *devadāsī*s of the Tiruvārūr temple produced the melodious music, while they danced and sang. Abdu Razaak, the Arab traveller to the court of the Vijayanagar ruler Devarāya II, says, "in the temple (*bednur*) night and day, after prayers accepted by God, they sing and play musical instruments, enjoy concerts, and give feasts. They danced in the *ardhamaṇḍapa* (sacred hall), *mahāmaṇḍapa* (big hall) and the *nāṭyamaṇḍapa* (dance hall) when the deity was taken out in a procession; they danced the *sandhinṛtya* in the evening. The small-scale daily procession (*nityotsava*) was also followed in almost all the temples where the song and the dance by the *devadāsī*s played an important part every day. A small *pada*, a *jāvaḷi* or any song on the presiding deity would be performed by the *devadāsī*s. Both in Tiruvārūr and Pudukkoṭṭai the *devadāsī*s used to imitate the ritual actions of the priest during the *dīpārādhanā* for the benefit of the devotees who could never enter the *sanctum sanctorum*. The terms used for this imitation was known as *śuddha nṛtyam* (pure dance) and *kaikkāṭum murai* (display of hands). This practice was carefully adhered to in most of the temples until CE 1947. For instance, the following table states dances performed at the Tirucendūr temple

Time	Music	Instrument	Dance
Morning	Gāndhāra	*Sacaputa*	Bhujaṅgatrāsitam
Noon	Sigamara	*Kumba*	Lalitam
Evening	Pañjama	*Siṁhavādya*	Kamalavartitam
Midnight	Kauśiga	*Pañcavādyam*	Svastikam
Other times		*Pañcavādya*	Sandyānṛtta

Cultural-historical evidence points to her as a phenomenon possessing meaning at all levels of society throughout historical times.

The temple and royal court together were responsible for maintaining socio-cultural harmony within the society. The heroic strength and valour of the king found its divine bliss from the generous support the temples received from its royal patrons. It is found during the Vijayanagara period (CE 1336–1565) that the king, being especially susceptible to "inauspicious" forces was almost "protected" by *devadāsīs* through their performances of rituals in the temples. It is therefore to the temple and later to the royal court that the *devadāsīs* owed their allegiance.

10

Music Traditions in the Temples of Tamil Nadu

THE ancient history of our music witnessed the perception of the fundamental concepts of governing this art and the best music of the age found expression in the services of God. Music is a holy art in India. From time immemorial, to the Hindus, worship to God had to be only through music. Otherwise they felt that it was like a lifeless body without a soul or spirit. Hence music, dance drama, etc. were formatted, or prescribed to be sung, before the gods everyday in the temples. These arts were not considered as mere symbols of entertainment in the temples but the temples also served as the promoters and institutions of all these arts that were considered sacred. Temples also served as educational institutions for those students who came to learn the Vedas, Āgamas and other sciences like astronomy, medicine, etc. Likewise all fine arts like music, dance, sculpture, etc. were not only taught but also preserved for thousands of years and the temples served as archives.

The kings of those days took a keen interest in preserving these arts and made sure that all these artistes were treated with due honours. Care was taken for their housing and food, in short the entire wellbeing of these artistes and their families to ensure that their art was preserved for the generations to come. These artistes were recognized as the *āsthāna vidvān*s (musicians attached to that particular temple) of the temple and were paid monthly salary along with perks like free housing and free land (agricultural). Such lands owned by them (given by the government) were known as *Vīṇāi Kāṇi* (land given for the *vīṇā* artiste), *Meḷakāra Kāṇi* (land given for the percussion player), *Nāṭya Kāṇi* (for the dancer), and so on.

On of the greatest rulers of Tanjāvūr, Rājarāja Coḷa had allotted lands for all the artistes attached to the temples like the — Koṭṭi Matthaḷam, Uḍukai, Vangiyam (flute) Naḍanamāḍar (dancing women), Oduvārs (those who recited *Tevāram*) and these details have been inscribed in the temple of Tanjāvūr. In the year CE 1343 the king Tirubhuvana Cakravarti Rājarāja Nārāyaṇa Sambuvarayan had allotted lands to those people who sang hymns in the temples. In the year CE 1015 Rājendra Coḷa I had ordered that those who sang the *Tiruvaimoḻi* in the temple be given free food thrice a day life long. In the year 1085 Kulottuṅga Coḷa had allotted free land to the singers who sang the *Tirupaḷḷieḻuci, Tiruvaimoḻi,* etc. in the temples. Similarly we have evidence in the temple of Tindivanam (through the inscriptions) that the *vīṇā* player was allotted free land. All these only go to show the importance given to these arts and how and why the kings patronized these artistes.

Some of the art forms were considered very sacred and it was rare or not allowed to be presented outside the temples. They were strictly dedicated only to gods and hence, were not allowed to be performed outside the temple. The *Kouthuvams, Śuddha Nṛtyam, Bhujaṅgatrāsita Nṛttyam, Kuravanji* (dance forms) are some of them. Similarly in the *Nādasvaram* (known as *Peruvangiyam* in olden days) items like the *Mallāri, Ratthi, Echarika* could be played only in temples for the enjoyment of the gods.

The *nādasvaram* is one of the oldest instruments in south India (Tamil Nadu) and is supposed to be the most sacred and important instrument played for the gods in the temples everyday. It could be heard from a long distance and alerted the devotees about the prayer time in the temple. Though it is considered the oldest, there is no reference to this instrument in ancient Tamil literature, probably because it had a different name.

The temples observed and followed a strict tradition to play this instrument — for daily *pūjā*s and during festivals. The *rāga*s to be played every morning, every afternoon, every evening, during night, etc. were specified and followed. Similarly, the accompanying instruments (mainly percussion) also had to follow a routine pattern that was set up for the playing in the temples for each and every *pūjā*.

Mallāri

Whenever the main (presiding) God or Goddess came out of the *sanctum sanctorum* to go in a procession around the temple (be it inside or outside) the *mallāri* was played. This was an indicator to the devotees even far away from the temple that the God was outside and he or she could come for worship. This going around is known as (*purappaadu*). There is no song in *mallāri*; it is only the beats (*taṭakāra*). There are different types of *mallāri* played for different occasions. The *Tīrtha Mallāri* is played when water is brought from the nearby river for the Lord's holy bath, *Taḷigai Mallāri* when *naivedyam* is brought for the deity from the temple kitchen. *Periya* (big) *mallāri* when the deity is on the *vāhana* (carrier) for the *vīdhi* procession (outside the four streets of the temple). Some were known by the *tāḷam* or beats like the *Tirupuṭai Mallāri* (the *tirupuṭai tāḷa*) with seven counts, the *Ther Mallāri* (the temple car) and all the other *mallāri*s were known as *cinna* (small) *mallāri*. Whatever *mallāri* it is the *rāga* to be played to the *mallāri* beat has to be only *Gambira Nāṭai Rāga*. As this *rāga* depicts valour and bravery and is played at a fast tempo this *rāga* was strictly adhered to by the players. Sadly over the years the artistes have started playing other *rāga*s and have even started playing it in wedding processions, etc.

Ratthi

When the deity is taken in a procession in or outside the temple, *Ratthi* is to be followed after the *mallāri*. *Ratthi* comprises *layam* (beats) and has to be played on the *nādasvaram*. It does not contain lyrics but is an intricately woven set of beats (highly technical and scientific) to any *rāga*. The *tāḷa* recommended is *miśra cāpu* followed by *tisra jāti* and then in *sarva lagu*. The *Ratthi* is generally a challenge to the artistes and a pleasure to the listener. When the deity reaches the southern entrance the *Pallavī* begins. There can be *sāhityam* (lyrics) or it may comprise only *suraprastāram* and can be in any *tāḷa* or *rāga* or even in *Rāgamālika* (a combination of nine *rāgas*). Once the deity reaches the main entrance of the temple, *padams* or even *Tevāram* can be played.

The order (tradition) was that no songs should be played while the deity was out of the *sanctum sanctorum*. And this was a tradition that was strictly adhered to for many centuries. The tradition that only *rāgas* — *mallāri* (*ālāpana*) and *svaras* (*layams*) — *Ratthi* had to be played when the deity went on his rounds encouraged the artistes to go deeply into the nuances of the *rāgas* and gave them a lot of scope to exhibit and explore their creativity.

But this system of playing the *Mallāri* followed by *Ratthi* is almost out in all the temples now. The other traditions are also dying a slow death. Today it is very difficult to find a *nādasvaram* artiste who can play the *Ratthi*.

Once the deity comes back from the daily rounds (procession) there will be a *Dīpārādhanā* at the entrance of the temple or at some *maṇḍapam* inside the temple. At this stage a *devadāsī* employed in the temple would bring a lamp on an urn and show it to the God. Mostly this *devadāsī* would also sing a *padam* or a hymn while doing this ritual. She would go thrice around the Deity with the lamp. This ritual was to ward off any evil eye on the deity. During this ritual the *nādasvaram* and the percussion group would follow the *devadāsī*. After the first round she would stop for a few minutes. At this juncture, only the *nādasvram* would be played. But when she went around the deity, only the *Thavil* is played with the *tāḷam* (instrument). Much later, when the *devadāsī* system stopped, this ritual of taking the lamp around the deity — was done by the temple *arcaka* (priest). The singing of the hymn or the *padam* then went over to the *nādasvaram* artiste who played it on the instrument. This tradition of going around the deity with the Muḷavu was called as the *Taṭṭicuṟṟu* or *Taṭṭamchutrru* in the Śaivite temples and was known as the *Tiruvandhikāppu* in the Vaiṣṇavite temples. In Tiruvārūr, and Vaithīśvaran temples they have *maṇḍapams* specially built for this purpose and are today known as the *Taṭṭicutṟṟu maṇḍapam*. Once this ritual of going around with the lamp was over the deity would be all set to go and settle down in his seat. At this stage the *Eccharika* would be played. And this song had to be only in the *rāga* that was played for the *Taṭṭicutṟṟu*. This ritual is known as the *Padi-etṟṟam* (climbing up) and is still followed in temples like the Tiruvaḻundūr-Parimelaḻaghar temple (Vaiṣṇavite). This is done during evenings and the singers are still known by the old name *Pāḍuvār*.

During night some music rituals had to be followed. While the deity was taken to His bed the *Cinna Mallāri* had to be played. This had to be followed by *padams*, *lālī* (lullaby) and *ūñjal* (swing) songs. During the olden days the *devadāsī*s were the privileged ones to sing these songs before the deity. During the days of the temple festivals after the Deity had rested the *mallāri* was played again. This was to inform the people that the festival was still on and that the Deity would be again taken out for a procession outside the temple the next day too.

During the festivities connected to the temple tank float (*Teppotsavam*) the deity is accompanied by the *mallāri*, and starts the float in the tank on reaching the *Teppam*. The float should then be followed by the *oḍapāṭṭukal* (boat songs) in the first round, in the second round there would be dance, and in the third round the *Oduvār*s will sing hymns from the *Tirumuṟai*. This was the formated tradition that was followed for a very long time in all the temples, and the difference was only the slight changes between the Vaiṣṇavite and the Śaivite traditions.

In the Śaiva temple festivals, on the eighth day, the presiding deity will be taken around the four streets of the temple asking for alms. On this particular day there will be no *mallāri* at all. Instead there would be a music ritual known as *Oḍakūru* which would be played by the *Periyameḷam* (big *melam*). For this songs composed by the *siddha*s conveying the meaning (philosophy) that the human body is bound to die would be played. They say that what was known as *uḍalkūru* (*uḍal*=body; *kūru*=part) over the years became *Oḍakūru* and the *rāga* for this was always in *Nādanāmakriya* and the *tālam* was *miśra cāpu*. This was a tradition only followed in the Śaiva temples.

11

Vocal Music

MUSIC was both vocal and instrumental. Though *gānam* (vocal) and *vādyam* (instrumental) are parts of the *gītam* (music), each one was distinctly spoken of in Rājarāja Coḷa I's inscription of Tanjāvūr. Singing of devotional hymns was one of the duties of the *devadāsī*s. On all auspicious occasions, they recited the devotional songs with *svara* (melody). During daily worship, they recited certain hymns from the Vedas or from the Tamil Vedas (*Tevāram*, *Tiruvācakam*, and *Nālayira Divya Prabandham*). The act of reciting the sacred Tamil hymns was called *Viṇṇappippār* or *Pāḍuvār* (reciters). Truvaliamudanar says that temple girls sang the praise of the Lord of Tillai in mellifluous voice. The *Periyapurāṇam,* tells that Paravai Nacciyar used to dance to the accompaniment of sweet music in the Tiruvārūr temple. In the Śiva Temples the *devadāsī*s sang the *Tevāram* hymn of Sambandar beginning with *veyru toil pangan vitamunda kanthan. . . .* In the Devadānam Temple in Sethūr a *cinnamela* (musical troupe with a few instruments) performance was conducted daily between evening and midnight. At that time the *devadāsī*s sang a song beginning with *sami samukhamadanil lili solumam. . . .* They sang the famous eight *śloka*s on Tyāgarāja in the Tiruvārūr temple. During the reign of Parakesari Vikrama Coḷa, provisions were made for reciting the "Tiruccalal" every day. The hymns begin with "*pusuvadu venniur . . .* and end with *iyalpanan chalalo. . . .*

Like the *devadāsī*s of the Śiva temples, the *Emperumānaḍiyār* of the Viṣṇu temple also recited the *Pāsuram*s (hymns) in praise of Lord Viṣṇu. A record from Tekal registers show that two dancing girls were employed for reciting the *Tirupallāṇḍu* hymns of Periyāḻvār in the temple. *Tiruvāimoḻi* hymns of Nammāḻvār were also sung in a few temples. The hymn beginning with *tokkup palandisaithuk kavari seivar elaiyare* . . . was popular among the *devadāsī*s. The *Tiruppāvai* hymns of Āṇḍāḷ were also recited with devotion and dedication.

Hymns were also recited during divine processions. When the idol of Māṇikkavācagar was taken out in the procession, it is believed that the saint heard the singing of Tiruvempāvai hymns in its graceful form and the hymns sung in another temple when the God Karanai Viṭankar was taken out in procession. It is on record that the right to sing certain verses of the *Tiruvempāvai* was sold by the temple authorities to some *devadāsī*s. This shows how the divine art of music was made a commodity and sold out to *devadāsī*s who had the money to buy it. It indicates a kind of degeneracy that had already set in the temple administration.

Temple festivals were occasions of music performances. Tradition holds that the *devadāsī*s of the Tiruvānaikka temple jointly recited some hymns of the *Tiruvempāvai* in the festival month of Mārgaḷi (December–January). Mohanānkī, a *devadāsī* of that temple recited the *Tiruvempāvai* hymns beginning with *unkaiyir pillai yunakke yadaikkalamen* . . . . The song refers to their vow taken during the month of observance to serve the devotees of Lord Śiva only. Similarly a song was sung in the *Teppat-Tiruviḷa* (float-festival) of the Tiruvānmiyūr temple. It was regularly sung in the month of Paṅguni (March-April) sixteen days after the *Brahmotsava* (grand festivals). Sitting inside the car they recited the song beginning with *ithenna karanamnanunthisar enra perku*. . . . When the idol of the temple of Tirukkalimeḍu was taken to inner *prākāra* (circumambulatory pathway) after the procession during the festival days, a song beginning with *kamalāsana kamalasena*. . . . was sung by the *devadāsī*s.

The *Tirupaḷḷieḷuci* (waking up the Lord early in the morning) was done by the *devadāsī* with the song *Melukolopu*. During the *Sāyaratchai pūjā* (evening *pūjā*) participation of the *devadāsī*s was considered very important, as this was the time when the maximum number of devotees attended the temple. The *maṅgala āratī* would be performed for the deities at this time by the *devadāsī*s who would also simultaneously sing *maṅgalam* songs. Similarly lullabies (*lālī*) and swing songs (*ūñjal*) were sung by the *devadāsī*s after the deities were carried to their chamber (*paḷḷi-arai*) daily.

Sarva Vādyam

In *sarva vādyam* the general practice was to sing eight different pieces of music ranging from vocal exercises. However the number of offerings could be extended according to the ritual occasion. In some temples the total amount of instrumental, vocal and dance compositions reached the number seventy- two. The Tiruttani tradition dictated that the priest should introduce each vocal offering with the *avatārika ślokam — jaya vijaya digvaya bhava . . .* — Long live, be victorious.

Community Singing

Community singing was in vogue even in the Saṅgam age. Only Tamil songs were sung in groups in the temples once in a week or so. Slowly, songs in other languages were also sung and the community singing (*kūṭṭisai vaḻipāḍu*) came to be known as *bhajanai. Bhajana*s are songs sung in praise of the gods or goddesses filled with *bhakti* and happened during the early fifteenth century. There was no discrimination of age and sex for people joining this *bhajana* singing. The group would go around the temple from one sanctum to the other singing songs in praise of gods and goddesses. Sometimes they would also sit in the *maṇḍapam* singing songs during the month of Mārgaḻi (December-January) all over Tamil Nadu when the *Tiruvempāvai utsavam* would be held. The group singers would get up early in the morning, collecting people from different streets or meeting points, all the time singing and finally end up at the temples. These groups usually had instruments like *tālam, gañjira* and harmonium.

In those days the traditions in vogue other than the *Tevāram*s and *Pāsuram*s were the *bhajana, nāma kīrtana,* and the *aṣṭapadī*s. The *pañca-mahāpuruṣa*s (five great men) of the *bhajana* style were Sadāśiva Brahmendra, Sadguru Bhodendra Svāmi, Śrīdhara Veṅkaṭeśa Ārya, Nārāyaṇa Tīrtha and Marudānallūr Sadguru Svāmi. Kṣetrajña's *padam*s have also enriched and contributed immensely to devotional music.

With the advent of Marāṭhā rule, due to the influence of great saints, Māraṭhī *kīrtana* was introduced in Tanjāvūr. This was one of the prime reasons for Tanjāvūr becoming an important centre for devotional music. When Samartha Rāmadāsa established his Muṭṭ in 1663 at Tanjāvūr, he also laid a strong foundation for *kīrtana* singing at temples.

Kīrtana singing is one of the forms of *navavidha bhakti* (nine types of devotion). This means singing the glory of God by praising Him. With the development of the *bhakti* movement in the seventh and eighth centuries in south India, the great Coḷa kings, who were devotees of Lord Śiva, studded the land with temples and endowed them richly with land and wealth for the perpetual conduct of religious worship. The temple was not only a place of worship but also became a cultural centre patronizing *Oduvār*s, *Araiyar*s, dancers, instrumentalists, musicians, sculptors and painters. The singing of *Tevāram* hymns (composed by Nāyaṉmārs), *Tirupallāṇḍu*, *Tiruvāimoḻi*, and *Divya Prabandham* (composed by Āḻvārs) performance of *Kuravañci Nāṭakam*, musical plays and dance forms are all an integral part of the daily ritual at the temples.

Contemporary Devotional Music in Temples

The earliest musicology text to deal with the musical practices, the *Bṛhaddeśī* written by Mataṅga in the seventh or eighth century CE, contains valuable information on contemporary devotional music devoted to various deities and composed in Sanskrit and in one of the old vernaculars like Tamil, Telugu, Bengali, etc. Among the songs mentioned by Palkuriki Somanātha (Telugu) the following (*deśī*) songs are of special interest:

The *Prabhāta padamu* (*melukopu*) to wake up the God, the *Parvata padamu* songs sung at the sacred hills at Tirupati, Śrīśailam, etc., the *Gobi padamu* sung by the young unmarried girls to God during Danurmāsa (December–January — Mārghaḻi in Tamil), the *Veṉṉila-padamu* sung before the deity in the moonlight and the *Guṇavarṇana-padamu* sung in praise of the virtues of the gods. With the spreading of the *bhakti* cult all over India in the period of the twelfth to the sixteenth century the popular (*deśī*) forms of music came to be replaced by the traditional (*mārga*) ones. Today we only know the ancient forms of music through the definitions of its obsolete compositions in the Sanskrit treatises form before the sixteenth century. Popular (*deśī*) songs in simpler *tāḷam* and written in the popular poetical metres (*ovi, dohā, caupāī, tripadī, ṣaṭpadī*, etc.) are already described in the eighth century *Bṛhaddeśī* which became the vehicle of devotional music. In the thirteenth century a characteristic form of Vaiṣṇava *bhakti* developed in Maharashtra. This Varakari pilgrimage cult was based on the principles of Kṛṣṇa *bhakti* as described in the *Bhāgavata Purāṇa.* In Paṇḍaripur, Lord Kṛṣṇa came to be worshipped as *Paṇḍarinātha Viṭṭhala.* The initiator of this type of *bhakti* was Jñānadeva (1275-96). Later Nāmadeva (1270–1350) and a host of disciples joined him in his pilgrimages. Their *kīrtana* singing resulted in collections *(gāthā)* of thousands of *abhaṅga* hymns. Songs of a certain Nāmadeva are included in the sacred book of the Sikhs, the *Ādi-Grantha* or *Guru-Grantha.* According to some inscriptions of the Coḷas these two (Nāmadeva) are one and the same person.

Though the Varakari cult is generally Vaiṣṇava in character, one can trace in it elements of Śaivism and Śaktism. The Varakari pilgrims may have been quite different in spiritual lineage and social class. In their pilgrimage to Paṇḍaripur they all met and sang together (*saṁkīrtana*) the hymns of their favourite God Viṭṭhala. It became a custom among Marāṭhī *bhakta* to make a pilgrimage to Paṇḍaripur twice a year and hold private religious meetings in the house of an important member of the community on every *Ekādaśī* (the eleventh day of every fortnight starting from the new moon and full moon). During these pilgrimages and meetings the musical repertoire contained a number of *abhaṅga*s composed by Tukārām and other poets and always concluded with the *āratī abhaṅga* (the presentation of lit camphor and other scented materials) in front of the images of the gods Viṭṭhala and Viṭobhā. The lyrical-type of *abhaṅga*s are prayer songs and laud Lord Viṭṭhala. In south India the Nāyaṉmārs and Āḻvārs had already developed the less strict auxiliary metres *pavinam-talicai, tuṟai,* and *viruttam* in their musical poetry. These poetical metres became very popular not only in Tamil, but also in Telugu, Kannada and Malayalam. According to a musicologist S. Subramaniam the musical poetical metres *talicai, tuṟai,* and *viruttam* of the *Tevāram* and the *Divya Prabandham* were originally part of the ancient Tamil metres of the *Paripāḍal* and the *Kalipā* that had developed into independent verses. The development of devotional music in the north-eastern parts of India cannot be understood without a closer examination of the *Gīta-Govinda* of Jayadeva. Composed towards the end of the twelfth century in Bengal, this work that reconciled old and new religious ideas and amalgamated old and new styles of poetry and music, was soon regarded as a classic all over India. Its performance became part of the regular programme in Vaiṣṇava temples, particularly in Kerala.

From the tenth century onwards devotion, that had already reached great heights in the south, also developed in other parts of India. But the important pilgrimage route from south to the north and vice versa ran along the Eastern Coast. Great philosophers from the south such as Rāmānuja, Viṣṇusvāmi, Nimbārka and Madhva followed this route, when travelling to the north. It is not surprising that these religious leaders not only carried their philosophical ideas but also their devotional songs. They continued the tradition of the Āḻvārs. Their ancestor teacher Nāthamuni had compiled the great body of the devotional hymns, the *Divya Prabandham* or the *Nālayira Divya Prabandham* (four thousand divine works). Therefore we assume that they taught some of these hymns to their disciples in the north. Though the original music of the *Gīta-Govinda* is lost we may assume that Jayadeva was inspired by the popular, devotional music of his days, since the *rāgams* he prescribes for his songs are all contemporary *rāgams*. During the years he lived as an ascetic, he may have listened to the songs of the wandering *yogī* from the north and the pilgrims from the south, who were on their way to Mathurā (Kṛṣṇa's birth place) and Purī (in Orissa) and its famous pilgrimage centres near the Jagannātha temple, where Jayadeva may have lived for some time. The *Gīta-Govinda* which reconciled older and contemporary styles or rather traditional and popular styles of poetry and music, was not only regarded as a great work of personal devotion (*bhakti*) but it was also integrated in temple ceremonies (rituals). The *Gīta-Govinda* as a literary work composed in sets of songs was not only limited in Vaiṣṇava circles but also the Śaiva composers who were interested in its literary and musical form. The *Śivagīti* of Ramapanivida is not dedicated to Śiva, as the title might suggest, but composed in praise of the mother Goddess Ambā of Melakāvu Bhagavatī temple at Mukhola near Ponnāni. The general style of this work is descriptive. The *Śivagīti* must have originally been sung at the steps (*sopāna*) of the Muktisthala temple during the *pūjā*.

Tāṇḍava Kṛṣṇācārya, a wandering saint from Tamil Nadu, composed Telugu hymns (*kṛti*s) in praise of Varāha-Lakṣmī Narasiṁha, the incarnation of Viṣṇu as a boar, in the Siṁhacalam temple (northern part of Andhra Pradesh). From the musical point of view we may distinguish in the less complex *kṛti*s the following varieties:

The *Nāmāvaḷī Kīrtana* and the two types of *Divyanāma Kīrtana*. The text of a *Nāmāvalī Kīrtana* mainly consists of names and epithets of a god, "a string of names" (*nāmāvaḷī*). It is set to a few simple musical phrases sung by the lead singer and repeated by the congregation to the rhythmic accompaniment of small cymbals or bells. The *Nāmāvaḷī* is often followed by a plain simple phrase (*puṇḍarīka*) consisting of a few regular words sung by the lead singer, to which the chorus of devotees answers with exclamations like *jaya, jaya* (hail, hail). The *puṇḍarīka* often functions as the starting signal for a ceremonial act in the *bhajana* sessions or temple services. The simple *Nāmāvalī Kīrtana* lends itself very well for being sung on the way, when during a religious temple festival (*utsava*) a group of devotees is moving from one sacred place to another. This practice was already known in the ancient days. References to it can be found in the works of the Āḷvārs. Reciting the names of a God (*nāmārcanā*) as a part of the temple ritual is also a very old practice. The singing of a thousand sacred names (*sahasranāmārcanā*) usually takes place during the offering of clothes, flowers, and sandal, following the bathing of the idol (*abhiṣeka*). In Sanskrit (*stotra*) literature we can find numerous examples of hymns consisting of names only as for example *Viṣṇu-Sahasranāmastotra*. It is chanted as a tradition (ritual) in Vaiṣṇavite temples almost everyday in the evening. In the older musicological works we may find descriptions of particular types of compositions, such as the *Viruda-Karaṇa,* in which the epithets (*viruda*) were the predominant text element. Today, the *Nāmāvaḷī* is not only sung in temple processions and religious ceremonies but also is a part of the well-known religious discourses, called *Hari-Kathā*. A *Divyanāma Saṁkīrtana* can be sung on the way like the *Nāmāvaḷī,* for example, during the great *utsava* (festival) at Tiruvaiyārū (in the Tañjāvūr dist.), when seven sacred places are visited by a grand procession in which several groups of devotees take part. It is said that the great composer Tyāgarāja himself, whose *Divyanāma Kīrtana*s remind us of the older *bhajana* style, led a *bhajana* party in this festival (ritual). However, the *Divyanāma Kīrtana*s are specially meant to be sung during part of a congregation meeting which is called *Divyanāma Saṁkīrtanam,* when the lamp is taken from the main shrine of the temple and brought out to the hall. The devotees then walk around the lamp, which symbolizes the deity, and sing their songs of praise named after this ceremony. Śrī Annamācārya, the famous fifth-century composer of Andhra Pradesh, has also composed a lot of such hymns that are sung at the Tirupati temple and other temples in Andhra. Annamācārya dedicated most of his songs to Lord Veṅkaṭeśvara of Tirupati. The *Śṛṅgāra-Kīrtana* describes the various aspects of the love relationship between a god and His consort (Veṅkaṭeśa and Alamelumanga), Rāma and Sītā, Narasiṁha and Lakṣmī.). It expresses in a mystic way the composer's feelings of devotion towards his God, and may have served as a model for the devotional songs of the sixteenth-century Andhra composer Kṣetrayya and other *pada* composers. The references to religious ceremonies (rituals) in the texts of some of Annamācārya's songs suggest that they were meant to be sung during the festivals held in the temples at different times of the day. The following traditional (rituals) songs of Annamācārya were sung during the following ceremonies:

Melukolopu	a song to wake up the deity in the morning
Nalugu	a song for ablution
Keluvu	a song in praise of the God residing in

	the court
Uregimpu	a song to praise the God, when he is carried in a procession
Aragimpu or *Naivediyam*	a song to be sung during the offering of various ablutions
Pavalimpu or *Ekantaseva*	a song which is sung, when the God and His Consort are brought to their chamber (sanctum)

It seems that in the days of Annamācārya the number of daily services (music traditions/rituals) in the Tirupati Tirumala temple were limited. T.K.T. Vijayaraghavācārya, historian, states that before CE 1434, the year when the early morning ceremony (*uṣākālam* or *aruṇodaya*) was introduced in this temple, there was probably one daily *pūjā* service, performed at daytime. This scholar also thinks that the extension of the ritual and the introduction of morning hymns such as the Sanskrit *Suprabhātam* composed by Prativādibhayaṅkaram Aṇṇan towards the end of the fourth century, was influenced by the fact that the image of the Lord Śrī Raṅganātha from Śrīraṅgam had been given shelter in Tirumala from 1330 to 1360, a period when the Śrīraṅgam temple was threatened by the Muslim invaders. Priests who went from Śrīraṅgam to Tirupati may have brought their ritualistic practices that were richer in music and dance. Sri T.K.T. Vijayaraghavācārya also suggests that Annamācārya's songs were sung in the Tirumala-Tirupati temple for the first time only in the sixteenth century during the reign of the Vijayanagar emperor Kṛṣṇadeva Raya. Annamācārya may have composed all his songs as a personal *bhakti* in moments of religious ecstasy. They were probably written by his son Pedda Tirumalācārya and his grandson Cinna Tirumalācārya who themselves have also composed thousands of *kīrtanas*. The latter wrote a Telugu version of his grandfather's treatise on composing devotional songs, called *Saṁkīrtalakṣaṇa*, and organized regular singing of *kīrtanas* by the devotees. He is therefore regarded as the father of the south Indian *bhajana* tradition. The thirteenth-century philosopher Madhva (Ānanda Tīrtha) whose Dvaita system is considered to be the theological basis of this religious movement, made his birth place Uḍupi (in south

Karnataka), a centre of *bhakti* after he had installed a Kṛṣṇa idol in the temple. In this type of devotion there is no trace of the bridal mysticism of the north Indian *bhakti*. It is pure devotion to Viṣṇu-Kṛṣṇa.

In Madhva's twelve laudatory hymns in Sanskrit (*Dvādaśa- Stotra*) that have come down to us we find the beginnings of this cult of devotional singing. Some of these hymns are like the song in the older *Prabhandha* style of musical composition. In the hands of Purandaradāsa (1484–1564), the great Haridāsa, who is regarded as the father of Karnatic Music, the *kīrtana*, called *devarnama*s assumed a mature, almost classical form. Its standardized structure — *pallavī, anupallavī*, and the three *caraṇa*s — served as a vehicle for all kinds of devotional music. Some of his ceremonial songs were used as *Melukolopu* to wake up the deity in the morning. Some of his hymns were also suited for choral rendering (a salutation to the deity in group).

Music Discourses — Kālakṣepam

Telling stories from epics like *Rāmāyaṇa* and *Bhāgavatam* were a part of temple rituals especially during festivals like the Navarātrī, Rāma Navamī, Kṛṣṇa Jayanti, etc. and auspicious months like Mārgaḻi when priests well versed in the epics would narrate stories relevant to the festivals or occasions. Each day one chapter would be covered. To make it more interesting the story telling would always have a number of songs in between with some instruments accompanying the narrator. The *kalākṣepam* artiste had to be a good singer, with a good stage presence, witty, and have good voice modulation because here and there he would have to do a lot of dialogue delivery. He should be proficient in Sanskrit, Telugu, Tamil, Kannada and also Marāṭhī, as he should be able to sing songs. This art form was very popular in Maharashtra and was introduced by the Maraṭha kings of Tanjāvūr (particularly, Sarabhojī).

Here again there was a formatted way of narrating that continues to this day. The narrator begins with a brief introduction or summary of the story. For this he always prepares well in advance as this enables him to retain in mind the story that he would present that day. This introduction is called *nirūpaṇam*. After this he presents what is known as the *pañcapat.* This is presentation of five *urupaḍīs* — five small *kṛtis*. And from here he will continue with the story. The other *urupaḍīs* (varieties) that he presents during the discourse are the following: *Āryam; Ślokam; Pathyam; Vṛtam; Abhaṅga; Dora; Ovi; Nāmāvalī; Lāvaṇī; Sadhi; Dhindi; Tillana;* and *maṅgaḷam.*

In some temples they also had story telling — *Kadai Solludal.* Stories from Purāṇas, epics, even folklore, etc. would be told by learned men in simple language. During the Mārgaḷi month most of the Vaiṣṇavite temples had *upanyāsam,* discourse on the *sārāṁśam* (summary) of each day's *Tirupāvai* for thirty days. This would conclude with Āṇḍāḷ Kalyāṇam that would be on the day after Poṅgal celebrated in Tamil Nadu as *kanu* or *kāṇum* Poṅgal. The *upanyāsam* would begin with the story of Āṇḍāḷ and on the thirtieth day her wedding would be celebrated with the Lord Raṅganātha in a grand manner. This trend is still on and even in cities like Chennai we find that there is always a good crowd to attend these discourses. These days, these discourses are also conducted in English.

Bhāgavatameḷa

This dance form was introduced in Tanjāvūr district during the reign of Acyutappa Nāyaka by dancers who were brahmins by birth and had migrated from Andhra. Because the regular dancers in temples were *devadāsīs*, this art form performed by the *paṇḍits* came to be known as *Bhāgavatameḷa*. The unique feature about this dance was that the performers were all men. This art form was performed in Telugu language and these artistes were not appointed in temples as permanent artistes. They were still given adequate financial support from the kings. This art form flourished in the temples of five towns namely Melaṭṭūr, Sāliyamaṅgaḷam, Sūlamaṅgaḷam, Ūtthukāḍu, and Teperumānallūr. These performances started in the evening and would go on till the early hours in the morning. The themes were mostly based on *Prahlādacaritram, Rāmāyaṇa* and *Mahābhārata*. These dance-dramas were classical in nature and had tunes and *tālams* set according to the *rasa* (moods) of the characters and the dialogues. This dying art form presently takes place only at Melaṭṭūr and Sāliyamaṅgalam outside the temples on a stage erected for this purpose in the months of Chittirai and Vaikāsi (April & May). The Narasiṁha mask used at Sāliyamaṅgalam is more than 400 years old and is preserved with religious sanctity and brought out every year during Navarātri (for worshipping) and Vaikāsi (when the performer wears it). Tyāgarāja's *Naukācaritra* was inspired by the *Bhāgavatameḷa.*

Folk Music as a part of Temple Rituals

Folk music played a dominant role in villages as an offering for the local village deity. Similar to the *Bhāgavatameḷa,* a street play like Terukūthu was performed. The themes were taken from mythology and folklore of Tamil Nadu. An art form that had only male performers singing and dancing, it was conducted all through the night. Mostly percussive instruments like *Koṁbu, Elathalam, Kaichelambu, Paṁpai* and *Nādasvaram,* (*Urumi*) were used.

A community called "Iruḷas" living near Singi follow a traditional ritual called *Kannipoṅgal* to this day. This is observed on the night of Poṅgal. A number of percussion instruments are played the whole night. The fervour does not stop until one of the women is said to be possessed by the Goddess.

At the Maṭṭapaḷḷi Narasiṁha Temple, in Andhra Pradesh, the wandering community of Laṁbadīs sing songs for the Goddess Señculakṣmī, the consort of the presiding deity every Friday. They gather at the temple and after bathing at the Godāvarī nearby, sing in praise of the Goddess until morning.

12

Instrumental Music

INSTRUMENTAL music was very popular in the temples. Indigenous evidences show that many instruments were played to produce melodious music. Saints Appār, Sambandar and Sundarar gave a list of various instruments played during daily worship (rituals) and festivals. The number of instruments depended on the prosperity and popularity of the temples concerned. The temples of Tanjavūr, Tiruvārūr, Konerirājapuram, Tiruviḍaimarudūr and Tirunelveli had many musical instruments. Instruments such as *calari, kokkari, matthalam, iḍakkai, takkai, tannumai yāḻ, kuḻal, uḍukkai, tāḷam, vīṇai*, and *muḻavu* are recorded in history. Small temples with meagre income had a few instruments such as the *tāḷam, matthalam, iḍakkai* and *kuḻal*.

The best specimen is preserved in a sculpture of the Bhūloganāthar temple at Māyavaram. One of the pillars of the *mahāmaṇḍapa* in the temple contains the figure of a *matthalam* player. Above the player is inscribed as "*matthalam perumāḷ* (*Pl.* 11) he is playing on the matthalam, and his legs show some rhythmic movements." According to Sri Sundarar, *kuḻal* and *muḻavu* were played while the *devadāsī*s danced. Generally the drum, the hand drum and the cymbals were played to keep the rhythm of the dance. Some wealthy temples had troupes of female musicians and instrumentalists. Such a party generally consisted of the vocal musician, instrumentalists and the drummers. The big musical group consisted of many instruments, which also gave place to violin, clarinet, flute and *mukavīnai*. Sometimes more wind instruments were added to attract devotees to the temple. Thus they preserved the musical traditions in the temples in those days. The songs and music of the *devadāsī*s have always evoked feelings of praise in those days as they performed their arts with devotion and dedication.

Their songs moved the feelings and emotions of the devotees. By performing these arts, the *devadāsī*s of medieval period aroused a sense of love for preserving the arts from extinction.

Beginning of the Nādasvaram tradition

It is no exaggeration to say that the *nādasvaram* has vastly contributed to the development of south Indian culture. The term *peru-vaṅgiyam* in the ancient period is considered to refer to the *nādasvaram*. Here, *vaṅgiyam* means the *kuḻal* (flute). The epithet *peru* (big) does not refer to its size but refers to the largeness of its sound.

There are many conventions and the traditions relating to the playing of the *nādasvaram* on various temple occasions. It should be remembered that it is only the traditions and conventions that have helped to preserve the culture through the centuries. Conventions have a lot of significance, values and meaning. And this meaning has helped us to enable life. During the reign of emperor Rājarāja Coḷa I there was a severe drought in Tanjāvūr. Those were the days when Rājarāja Coḷa is believed to have visited Tiruvārūr temple once in a week from Tanjāvūr through a secret passage. (built underground leading from Tanjāvūr temple to Tiruvārūr temple). The king performed many *yajña*s and *pūjā*s in vain. His minister then suggested that the *nādasvaram* players from Tiruvārūr should be brought to Tanjāvūr to play in the palace beseeching the rain gods. The *nādasvaram* players came to the palace the very next day from Tiruvārūr and played for many hours. The king, who was listening to them in rapt attention, later got up angrily and walked away because there was no rain. But when his minister went out he found that it was raining heavily outside and the city was in spate and the people were rushing to the palace to take refuge. The minister taken by surprise, called the king and pointed out to the miracle caused by the divine instrument. The king bowed down to the artistes in all humility and expressed then and there that the *nādasvaram* had the divinity to invoke gods and hence must be played in all the existing temples and also the ones that would be built later. The king also passed a resolution saying that the *nādasvaram* artistes would be given a special place in the society and also provided them with houses, land, etc.

Any temple ritual is accompanied with the *nādasvaram* music. Beginning from the opening of the temple in the early morning to the closing of the temple at mid-night, there is a *nādasvaram* play for every ritual. There is an unwritten rule specifying the music for the hour of the day and for that particular day. This has been in force for more than ten centuries, so much so that when people listened to the music from their houses along the streets of the temple, they at once knew what was going on in the temple. The *nādasvaram* is very loud and reaches a long distance. So, though one may not be listening particularly to the music, it falls on his ears and reminds him that a particular activity is going on in the temple.

The music at day-break is *Tirupaḷḷieḻuci,* in *Bhūpāḷam rāgam* in all the temples. The very structure of this *rāgam* is most thrilling. The *rāgam* is formed to represent the lotus flower that gently opens its petals to welcome the rays of the slowly ascending morning sun. It is a great wonder how this *rāgam* was conceived in this manner and so shaped. Only those who have enjoyed the *Bhūpāḷa rāgam* can imagine in their mind's eye the beauty of the gentle opening of the petals of the lotus flower. *Bhūpāḷam* is the *puranirmai-paṇṇ* of the *Tevāram* and going a few centuries earlier in time, it was known as the *paṇṇ-nothiram* in the Saṅgam anthology *Paripāḍal*. This *paṇṇ*, through its various names as *nothiram* and *puranirmai* and *bhūpāḷa rāgam* from the second century CE to the twentieth century, indicates to us in the most astonishing manner how the great culture of the Tamil people had been harmoniously continuing over the long period.

Revagupti, bowli, etc. follow *bhūpāḷam* in the temples. On this occasion, in the morning *ārādhanā-bilahari, dhanyasi, malayarutham,* etc. are played. At the time of the midday *ārādhana*, the most soothing *rāgams madhyamavatī* (*senduruṭṭi- paṇṇ*), *suruṭṭi* and *devagāndhārī* are played. During the evening *pūjā, pūrvi kalyāṇī, kedāra gouḷā, śaṅkarābharaṇam* are played and during the night *ārādhanā, aṭāṇa, ānanda bhairavī, yadukula kambhojī, bhairavī, nilāmbarī,* etc. are played.

When the deity is taken out in procession, along the temple inner corridors or its outer main streets, *mallāri* is played for lifting the deity and placing the *mūrti* (deity) on the *mañjam* (couch). *Mallāri* is a majestic *rāgam*. Lifting and carrying the deity with the *mañjam* is a most taxing duty. When several *nādasvarams* play together the *mallāri* or even *nāṭṭai rāgam*, the total music inspires the carriers with an unusual heroic spirit, and the people, whatever the weight of the *mūrti* on the *mañjam*, lift and carry it with great ease. From the moment of lifting the deity on to the shoulders, *nāṭṭai, ārabhi, śrī,* and *varāḷi rāgams* are played. Then there is a schedule to be played on each street beginning from the east and on each of the corners. This schedule of systematic organised way of playing *rāgams*, informs the people around, merely by the *rāgam*, of the position where the deity has come in course of the procession along the streets. Many of the people have some duties along the streets and the particular *rāgam* reminds the people concerned of the next duty for which they have to get ready. Finally when the deity goes to the *paḷḷi-arai* (bed-chamber) *nīlāmbarī* is played. This is the *meghā rāgam kuriñjī paṇṇ* and the song is called *kadavaipāṭṭu*, song for closing up. This has been the *nādasvaram* tradition (temple) that has been passed on from generation to generation over the centuries.

Tiruvārūr temple observed the *āru kāla pūjaigaḷ* (six *pūjās* a day). The morning one is *uṣā kāla pūjā* (early morning) followed by *kāla saṁdhi*, then *ucchi kālam*, in the evening *sāya rakṣai*, the *eranḍām kālam* (night) and finally the *ardha jāmam* (midnight). Totally in a day the *nādasvaram* players played for about five hours for the deity as a ritual. The six *pūjās* also had prescribed *rāgams* to be played. For *uṣā kālam* it was *bhūpāḷam, bouḷi, māyāmaḷava gouḷa*, and *malayamārutam*. For *kāla saṁdhi* it was *bilahari, kedāram, navroj, kurinji, danyāsi, sāveri, śuddha sāveri* and *ārabhi*; for the afternoon the *rāgams* chosen were *madhyamāvatī, maṇiraṅgu, bangala, śuddha bangala*. For the *sāya ratchai* (evening) it was *kalyāṇī, śaṅkarābharaṇam, toḍī, bhairavī, kamboji* and *yadukula kamboji*. The *eranḍām kālam* had *āhiri, kanaḍa, ānanda bhairavī, mohanam*, etc. and the last one the *ardham* had *nilāmbarī, lalita, vasanta*, etc. Ramasvāmi Dīkṣitar, father of Muthusvāmi Dīkṣitar, had formatted the *rāgams* for the *nādasvaram* players and the *tāḷams* for the dancers and the percussion players (the *pañca mukha vādyam* and the *śudda matthaḷam*). The tradition of six *pūjās* with the strict *rāgam* pattern has been brought down to twice a day with limited time for playing the instruments for almost the past thirty years. There also used to be a percussion instrument called *kiḍupāṭṭī* in those days. Though it looked very much like the *thavil* the player used two sticks instead of his hand. It was a very special instrument and was played for all the temple festivals and *pūjās*. Even in those days very few people had mastered this art, which was very popular at weddings *nādasvaram* concerts also. Especially played during the *thani āvarthanam*, this instrument is almost forgotten and so are the artistes. They say that the late Naṭeśa Piḷḷai who played in the early 1970s was the last player to have played this instrument. The *raktthi meḷam* was something very exclusive to Thiruvārūr. The *raktthi* used to be played during all the days of the festivals. Once the deity was brought out of the *sanctum sanctorum* to the streets specific *rāgams* used to be played followed by *raktthi meḷam*. The *raktthi* used to be highlighted, particularly on the day of the *r̥ṣabha vāhanam* (the bull). There were four *nādasvaram* players, accompanied by two *thavil* artistes. Always the beat was in *chāpu tālam*. At Tirukaḍaiyūr the *raktthi* was a little different. There is a festival to mark the *Yama saṁhāram* when the *rāgam* prescribed was *kanda* followed by *raktthi* in *kanda*. The *raktthi* is a kind of *taṭakāram*, i.e. it has no *sāhityam* (words).

The tradition of singing in temples is less than 500 years old as there were not that many composers earlier. There were more instruments then. The *devadāsīs* also played a very predominant role in the Tiruvārūr temple till the 1940s. Muthusvāmi Dīkshitar *kr̥tis* were sung in the temple by the *devadāsīs* as part of the music ritual.

The most popular among them was "Tyāgarājasvāmi Namaste" in the *begada rāgam*. A number of Dīkṣitar's compositions belonged to the repertoire of the *devadāsīs*; the *nādasvaram* musicians perform several of them today. The *devadāsī* participation in the ritual of *dīpārādhanā* was her most characteristic task in the *nityārcanā* (daily worship). The tradition was that the *devadāsī* should offer *kumbhadīpa* and recite a *śloka* and perform the *puṣpāñjali*.

The Role of Tavil in Temples

Tavil is a percussion instrument that is a must for the *nādasvaram*. A *nādasvaram* cannot be imagined or played without the *tavil*. Both the instruments complement each other. A very unique characteristic feature about the *tavil* is that while all other percussion instruments accompany the main instruments, the *tavil* will have to start even before the main instrument, the *nādasvaram,* begins to play. The *tavil* begins to play the particular *tāla* that the *nādasvaram* artiste is about to play and only then the *nādasvaram* begins to play. To play a percussion instrument like the *tavil* one needs to have a sound and technical knowledge of the nuances of *layam*. There are a lot of mathematical calculations involved in playing this instrument and this percussion instrument has set the guidelines for all the other percussion instruments. One can easily say that it is the mother of all percussion instruments. The instrument that was hitherto played only as an accompaniment to *nādasvaram* is today played with other instruments and even used by the dancers in their concerts. Thus the accompanying instrument *tavil* enjoys the unique position of being played even before its main instrument the *nādasvaram*.

When the deity of a temple is brought from his or her sanctum outside the temple the practice in any temple is for the *tavil* to play the *alārippu* first. It is just a series of *jāti*s put together in a systematic *layam* (beat) pattern. This *alārippu* differs from the *alārippu* that is performed by a dancer on the stage. It was known as the *mellapraptthi* in olden days and this was the first item that had to be performed by the dancers during their recital. Likewise, this item had also to be performed by the *thavil* artistes in their recitals. This would always be in the five *attcharas* (beats) and set only in the *kandagathi*. The significance of this system is to make the devotees aware that God is superior to the five forms, and a number of other important features all connected to the number five. Any beginning of ritual to the Almighty should be in this number form and this has been prescribed in the Āgamas with due explanations. This five-number system is applied in both Śiva and Viṣṇu temples till this day.

Other Instruments Played in the Temples

Given below are names of most of the instruments played in the temples of Tamil Nadu: *nādasvaram, tirucinnam, ekkalam, mukhavīṇā, gouritāḷam, kombu, navuri, othunādasvaram, pullānghuḻal, śaṅku, thuthuri, bali-*

matthaḷam, kavanna-matthaḷam, śudda-matthaḷam, tavil, berigai, candrapirai, chenḍai, dakka, damāram, dungi, damavādyam, davandai, iḍakkai, jaggi, jayaberi, kanakathappaṭṭai, mr̥daṅgam, muttu, nagārā, periyaudal, cinna-udal, sanna-udal, thappu, thimilai, virakaṇḍi, sekanḍi, vānka, thakkai, tāḷam, brahmā-tāḷam, kai tāḷam, kuḷi tāḷam, maṇi, kaimaṇi, kothumaṇi, semakalam, kidikiṭṭi, vīṇai and *geṭṭu.*

In the villages *udukai, pampai and kaicilambu* were some of the musical instruments used by the folk artistes in their music rituals.

Pāri nāyanam an instrument akin to the *nādasvaram* that used to be played in a very low *śruti* (key) is an age-old instrument that is played in the Tiruvārūr temple. This particular instrument continues to be played to this day by the artiste who hails from the seventh generation of *pāri nāyanam* artistes. He strictly adheres to the recommended tunes and beats laid down by Ramasvāmi Dīkṣitar, father of the great composer Muthusvāmi Dīkṣitar who has completely formatted the music traditions for this temple.

Similarly the *pañcamukha vādyam* is a huge percussion instrument that is found only in the Tiruvārūr temple and Tiruturaipūṇḍi. The instrument is played in this temple by the artiste who belongs to the seventh generation of artistes and follows the ritual pattern as laid down by the temple authorities.

Unique Percussion Instruments

KIḌĪKIṬṬĪ

It is an age-old instrument that is almost unheard of in the temples these days. This was very much used till about forty years back. It played an important role in the *periameḷam* especially when the *tavil* artiste had to do the *layavinyāsam* (highlights of that particular *tāḷam* or beats).

This percussion instrument is occasionally heard at the Tiruvārūr temple today. One temple where this instrument is still heard is at Kīḻvelūr Kediliy Appar temple where it is a part of the daily music tradition. But it is done more as a part of the ritual as it is just taken by somebody (not trained to play) from the *nādasvaram* group and just beaten for a few seconds and put back. *Śudda mattalam* is another rare percussion instrument that is played only in the Tiruvārūr temple by the artiste who hails from a family that has been playing this instrument for more than six generations. This instrument resembles the *mṛdaṅgam*, but is a bigger and longer version of the *mṛdaṅgam*.

THAKKAI

This instrument called the *thakkai* is used in the Śrīraṅgam temple during the Vaikuṇṭha Ekādaśī festival.

GHEṬṬU VĀDYAM

In the Āvadaiyār temple, the *gheṭṭu vādyam*, which is a percussion instrument, is played daily. This instrument is used only for maintaining the pitch (*śruti*) and the beat (*layam*). It is unique because it is a stringed instrument, which cannot play tunes, but can be used only as percussion. This instrument is not played anywhere else in the entire country and today is almost out of use.

VĪṆĀ

In Śrīraṅgam, *vīṇā* is played twice a day — once in the morning, during *Tirupaḷḷieḻuci* and late in the night during *ardhajāma pūjā* (*ekāntam*). During the ten days of Vaikuṇṭha Ekādaśī festival, the *vīṇā* is played every night. The *vīṇā* players follow the deity around the temple. In the month of Cittirai (April–May) during the festival, the hymns of Kulaśekara Āḻvār are sung accompanied by the *vīṇā*.

SURAMAṆḌALAM

In Vaithiśvaran temple, several years ago an instrument called *suramaṇḍalam* — a small instrument resembling a harp — was used during the music rituals. This has been inscribed in the stones of the temples, where it also says about the honorarium (*māniyam*) received by the *suramaṇḍalī* artistes.

MUKHA VĪṆĀ

We can find a *mukha vīṇā* made out of stone in Āḻvārthirunagari (Tirunelveli district) and a *nādasvaram* made out of stone in Kumbheśvar temple (Kumbakoṇam district). But there is no information about the role they played in the music rituals.

SARVA-VĀDYAM

In the Ceyyūr temple that is situated about 70 km from Chennai, a unique music tradition used to be followed till a few decades ago. This was performed during the yearly festival. This ritual would start with songs from *Tevāram, Tiruvācakam, Tirupugal̤*, etc. followed by a *puṣpāñjalī*. After this *mr̥daṅgam* and *brahmattālam* would be played. Songs like *gītam, varṇam, kr̥ti,* and *padam* followed this. Then, several instruments like flute, *mukha vīṇā, tirucinnam,* etc. are played. It concludes with a *bhujaṅga nr̥tyam* (snake dance). This unique form of worship with 72 music rituals, which used to last for 4 hours, is known as the *sarvavādya val̤ipāḍu* (worship) and was done only in this temple. This ritual has not been observed since 1960s.

In the Tiruval̤undūr Parimaḷaraṅgan temple and Cidambaram Govindarāja temple, both of which are Vaiṣṇavite temples, a number of music traditions are followed to this day. In these temples, the Navarātrī festival is celebrated in a big way. On all the nine days, the Goddess (presiding deity) comes out of her sanctum, accompanied by the music of *mallāri* followed by the *ratthi* and *pallavī* within the rounds of the temple, before she reaches the God's sanctum. There she exchanges garlands with her Lord. The priest removes the garland from the God, carries it on his head dancing to the beats of the *nādasvaram* and percussion instrument which play especially composed songs for the *mālaimār̤r̤u* (exchange of garlands) ritual. The specified *rāgam*s for these songs are mostly *māñji, kuriñji* and *navroz*. Everyday, five different songs are sung and this ritual happens on all the nine days. When the Goddess returns to her sanctum, the *Tiruvandikāppu* is done. The *eccarika* is played after which she goes into her chamber. The *lālī* or the *ūñjal* songs (lullaby) are played and if the festival continues the next day, *mallāri* will be played.

In the olden days a commonly used word in the temple was *naṭṭu-muttu. Naṭṭuvam* or *naṭṭu* was a small *mr̥daṅgam* that was hung on the neck and beaten by the dance teacher known as *Naṭṭuvanār*. He would say the *jāti*s and play the instrument to the dancer's movement. This came to an end with the decline of the *devadāsī* cult.

The Āgamas have very clearly specified how the instruments should be played, in which direction the artistes should perform, etc. The *vīṇā* artiste should sit in the eastern side. In the southern side, wind instruments are played and percussion instruments on the northern side. In some places, the *naṭṭu-muttu* is played in the southern side, the singers in the northern side while the wind instruments will be between them. The dancers will be right in the middle. All these traditions were followed in the temples for a very long time.

In some temples the *kuravañci* (dance-drama) was performed during festivals. In many temples, they were sixteen ways of worship. After this, there was a tradition of singing the *pañca purāṇam* — singing songs from the seven *Tirumuṟais* like *Tevāram, Tiruvācakam,* and *Tirupallāṇḍu.* While these songs were sung instruments like the *yāḻ* (harp) used to be played. But the *yāḻ* was completely stopped after the tenth century. Later instruments like the *vīṇā* and the flute were played. The north-Indian instrument *sāraṅgī* was prevalent in those days, mainly in the Tirunelveli district.

In a temple near Tiruccirāpaḷḷi, Tiruverumbūr temple, the *uḍukkai* and *tāḷam* are used while singing the *Tevāram.* Unlike the *Tirupadikam* sung in the Śaiva temples, which were sung with tunes, the hymns from the *Nālāyira Divya Prabandham* (by Āḻvārs) were not sung with any specific tunes. The reason attributed to this is that nobody had set specific tunes for these and hence these were mostly chanted. This was known as *prabandham sevittal.* Instruments are not accompanied in this tradition.

A unique way of chanting these hymns from the *Nālāyiram* with actions by the priests known as *araiyar*s can be witnessed to this day during festivals at Śrīraṅgam, Śrīvilliputtūr and Āḻvārthirunagari. The *araiyar*s belong to a hereditary family of priests who not only sing the hymns, but also mime and explain the *Pāsuram*s. They also wear a traditional headgear and have a *tāḷam* that is used as they perform. The *araiyar*s are the only ones given the privilege of wearing a headgear in front of God.

PAÑCAMUKHA VĀDYAM

This instrument is a huge metal one with wheels attached to it and contains five percussion instruments in one big barrel-like metal container. (See photograph). There are only two such instruments: one in Tiruvārūr and one at Tiruturaipūṇḍi. There is an icon of Lord Naṭarāja playing this instrument in Tirupunkūr temple in Tanjāvūr district. There is also one bronze icon of Lord Naṭarāja playing this instrument in Uḍaiyārpāḷayam and one in Cidambaram temple opposite to the *sanctum sanctorum* under the stone chariot (*kal-ratham*). Here we find him playing this instrument with eight heads. This instrument is played regularly both at Tiruvārūr and Tiruturaipūṇḍi. Muthusvāmi Dīkṣitar's father, Ramasvāmi Dīkṣitar, systematized the playing of this instrument at Tiruvārūr.

ŚUDDHA MATTALAM

This is again a percussion instrument that accompanies the *pañca mukha vādyam* particularly in Tiruvārūr and Tiruturaipūṇḍi. (See photograph). At Tiruvārūr the player Thambi Appā Piḷḷai, the disciple of Muthusvāmi Dīkṣitar, used to play this instrument and today the seventh generation from the same family plays this at Tiruvārūr strictly following the tradition formatted by the senior Dikṣitar.

KAÑJIRA

Kañjira was mostly used for community singing (*bhajanai*) in temples and during Mārgaḻi month outside the temple (streets).

ḌAMĀRAM

Ḍamāram is usually taken along the four streets around the temple along with the *utsavamūrti* during temple festivals.

NAGĀḌĀ

Carried on elephants and taken in procession during temple festivals. It was also used during war by the kings in olden days.

DUNDUBHI AND BERĪ

These percussion instruments again were used like the *nagāḍā* during processions at the time of temple festivals and also during war times.

THAVAṆḌAI

Thavaṇḍai was played during festivals in Mariamman (Goddess) temples.

PAMPPAI AND UḌUKKAI

They were commonly played in Mariamman temples particularly during festival processions.

CANDRA PRABHAI AND SŪRYA PRABHAI

Made with a combination of iron and hide it was commonly played in Māriamman temples during festival processions. It is played at Kāḷahasti during festivals and also in some temples during the *Brahmotsavam* festival.

KANAKA THAPPAṬṬAI

It is played during Tyāgarāja's dance procession at Tiruvārūr and also a popular instrument in Śiva temples in Sri Lanka, as an accompaniment for *nādasvaram*.

PULLUVAN KUḌAM

It is usually played in Kerala temples. Sounds and acts like a resonator while a stick is beaten on a mud pot that has a mouth covered with hide and twine tied around it.

PERIYA UḌAL AND CINNA UḌAL

Made of wood and covered with hide. They are played daily at Śrīraṅgam temple. At Kāñcī it is played daily as the *naivediyam* is taken around. At Thiruvānaikāval it is played when the Gurukkaḷ performs the morning *pūjā*.

KIḌĪ-KIṬṬĪ

Played as an accompanying instrument to the *nādasvaram* and is not seen much in the Tamil Nadu temples these days.

DANGA

A two-piece instrument and placed on the horse while playing. The player would play the instrument while God was taken around in procession during temple festivals.

DANGI

Played as an accompaniment for *mukha vīṇā* (a smaller version of the *nādasvaram*) in temples. *Mukha vīṇā* is played regularly at Uḍupi Śrī Kṛṣṇa Temple in Karnataka.

DABBI PALAGAI

Played at Kāñcī Varadarāja Perumāḷ temple. *Jayabheri, vīramalahari* also belong to the same percussion group.

KUṆḌALAM

This instrument is a *tāḷa* instrument and is usually played for dummy horse dance particularly during temple festival processions.

PUJARI KAI CILAMBU

This instrument is made with bronze or brass with some metal balls placed inside to give it a tinkling effect. It is an instrument to keep up the correct beats (*tāḷa karuvi*).

This is generally used in Māriamman temples in Tamil Nadu specially while singing lullaby for the Goddess and is usually in the *sarva laghu*.

JĀLRA

This is once again for keeping up the tempo or beats while singing in the temples and used more for community singing (*bhajana*) and is also a must for *kathākalākṣepam* (musical discourses).

KUḺI TĀḶAM

It looks almost like the *jālra* and is compulsory for singing of *Tevārams* and Tirupugaḻ. This instrument is also known as *kuḻimaṇi.*

BRAHMĀ TĀḶAM

It is a bigger version of the *jālra*. It was regularly used in a temple musical ritual known as the *sarva-vādyam*. This particular tradition used to be a very popular form of an art tradition in a temple at a village called Ceyyuru about 70 km from Chennai on the way to

Pondicherry. The *sarva-vādyam* used to feature different art forms in music, dance, instruments, drama, etc. and was always a part of the main *utsavam* (festival). This instrument is also known by other names like (1) *Naragamja vādyam*, (2) *Tyāgarāja vādyam*, (3) *Rāja vādyam*, (4) *Dagora vādyam*, and (5) *Hindustani dagora vādyam*.

SEMMAKALAM

This instrument is played in a lot of temples especially during the Mārgaḷi month. It is also used as an accompaniment for singers. Pilgrims who take a pledge to walk while visiting any shrine also play this instrument as they sing and walk along. It is a common sight to see people playing this instrument and singing together while trekking up to Tirupati hills.

CHIPLA

This instrument is made of wood and is generally used for keeping a beat. Usually used by people who give religious discourses and also commonly used in community singing.

VILLADI VĀDYAM

In olden days people were specially trained to play this instrument in temples.

MUTTU

This is a smaller version of the *mṛdaṅgam*. Once upon a time it was a popular instrument. It was played at the Tiruvārūr temple during the temple festival when the presiding deity Lord Tyāgeśara was taken in His palanquin. This instrument was also played at the Tiruvānmiyūr (Chennai) temple. The beats were called "Aāḍum Tyāgeśara" and "Oḍum Tyāgeśara" depending on the beats.

VĪRA MAṆḌALAM

Huge (long) *mṛdaṅgam* played only in temples, now not very common.

KUDI MEḶAM

It is also known as the *koil meḷam* and is an essential part of the *nādasvaram* group or set.

SAṄKHU

It is the conch and used as a *upa pakka vādyam* (additional and optional) for *nādasvaram* and is still used in all the temples.

TIRUCINNAM

An instrument about two and half feet long made of dual metal pipe. *Tirucinnam* is played during daily worship rituals like the *nitya-kāla pūjā* etc.

KOṀBU

This instrument is about four to six feet long and is made of brass. It is played in some very old temples during the regular rituals. In olden days it used to be played in palaces and also during wars.

GHEṬṬU VĀDYAM

This rare percussion instrument was played only in Āvuḍaiyār temple near Pudukoṭṭai. An icon playing this instrument is engraved in a very old temple at a village called Hāle Ālūr near Mysore in Karnataka.

EKKĀḶAM

This instrument was played regularly during temple festival processions and is still played in a few temples down South.

PĀRI

This instrument was generally played when the *maṭhadhipati* (chief priest) of the temple went in or out of the temple.

GINNERI

This string instrument is exactly like a lyre and used to be played in temples of Andhra Pradesh particularly in Kurnūl, Anantapur and Cuddapah districts. And we find information about this instrument in old Sanskrit texts mainly. This instrument was mainly used in folk music. We find in the Basavanguḍi temple at Bangalore, an icon of an artiste playing this instrument.

PAÑCA VĀDYAM

An orchestra of five types of musical instruments, it is conducted during all the major *pūjās* in the temples of Kerala. The instruments are: *kombu, śuddha mattalam, thimila, eḍakka* and *ela tālam.*

The number of instruments increases in proportion to the place where it is conducted. (Inside the temple, outside or during festivals and *pūrams* in Kerala.)

AṢṬA DAŚA VĀDYAM

In olden days eighteen instruments used to be played in most of the temples during Āgamas. In some temples they were also a part of regular rituals and also during festivals. In Pudukkoṭai Brahadāmbāḷ temple 32 instruments were played. The basic idea was that the entire village would hear the sounds of all these instruments being played as a band. The sounds would be carried even outside the village and the neighbourhood villagers would also rush to the temple on hearing the music. It was like a signal to denote that the *pūjā* had started.

Here is a list of the 18 (*aṣṭa-daśa*) instruments:

1. *Bheri*
2. *Mṛdaṅgam*
3. *Mattaḷam*
4. *Tāḷam*
5. *Kākalam*
6. *Dundubhi*
7. *Dūriyam*
8. *Tumburu*
9. *Vīṇā*
10. *Veṇu*
11. *Nūpuram*
12. *Mathukam*
13. *Ḍinḍima*
14. *Ḍamarukam*
15. *Tavalla*
16. *Shabdha*
17. *Banava*
18. *Padākam*

13

Dance Forms as Rituals in Temples

AMONG art forms dance enjoyed a very special place in temples and was given topmost priority. It was patronized by all the kings and important people connected to the temples (*maṭhadhipatis*). We have Lord Naṭarāja performing His Celestial dance at Cidambaram. The earliest dancers were the *devadāsīs*, and dance was performed only at temples as an offering only for the gods. The Āgamas mention of a dance that used to be performed by the *devadāsīs* of the Śiva shrines before The Lord and Goddess Pārvatī, known as *śuddha nṛttam*. This used to be a presentation of the *karṇams*. This number did not have any song but was only set to beats of different counts for the *jatis*.

There was another number known as *miśra nṛttam* that was performed based on a story from the Purāṇas or an incident from the Epics or Purāṇas. When the dancers performed at the temple for an audience during a festival like Navarātrī or Ārudra Darśana, etc. it had a few items of dance numbers and was known as *kevala nṛttam.* There were occasions when the *utsavamūrti* would be taken around within the temple and the *devadāsīs* would perform the *pañcamūrti kavuthuvam;* especially when all the five *mūrtis* like Vināyaka, Muruga, etc. were brought out together this was performed. They also would perform a few items like *padams*, etc. Other *devadāsīs* — the singers — would sing the *Tevārams*, etc.

Some of the other dances performed in temples during festivals were:

Pallakku Naḍanam (Palanquin dance)

Siṁha Naḍanam (Lion dance)

Navasaṅdhi Naḍanam (9 Directions dance)

In temples of Tanjāvūr district where Tyāgeśa (they are known as Viṭaṅka Kṣetras) is worshipped the dance that was performed was known as *vaidika naḍanam*. The deity Tyāgeśa is decorated in all His finery and brought out of the *sanctum sanctorum* and placed in a palanquin. Dances would be performed as He is taken around the temple. The palanquin movements would be in the dance form with dance beats to the playing of a number of instruments. There are a number of dances named according to the beats as follows:

Ajaba Naṭanam

Unmatta Naṭanam

Turaṅga Naṭanam

Bruṅga Naṭanam

Kamala Naṭanam

Haṁsa Naṭanam

In the Cheyyūr temple where the *sarva-vādyam* tradition was observed, 72 different art forms were performed. Several instruments were played during this yearly festival at the Vasanta *maṇḍapam*. The festival would start with the singing of the *Tevāram, Tiruvācakam, Tirupaḷḷāṇḍu, Tirupugaḷ* and other songs. This would be followed by the dance item known as *puṣpāñjalī* (more of an invocatory piece). The next item would be the performance of a dance item known as *bhujaṅga nṛttam* performed along with several accompaniments like *tirucinnam, flute, daṅga, mukha vīṇā*, conch, *bhujaṅgasuram, navuri*, etc. This entire ritual will last for more than four hours. *Vādyams* (instruments) for all the dance forms mentioned above included a number of percussion instruments. But the main percussion used is the *śuddha mattalam* and the *kanaka tappaṭṭai*. Besides in the Tanjāvūr districts, this dance is also performed at the Tiruvoṟṟuyur and the Tiruvānmiyūr temples (both are in Chennai) and another famous temple, the Tirukaccūr temple. While the dance is performed during the special festivals the presiding deity is taken around the temple in a palanquin in dancing movements,

Tyāgeśa is called *Āḍum* (dancing) Tyāgeśara, *Oḍum* (running) Tyāgeśara and *Asaiyum* (moving) Tyāgeśara.

Dances were performed also in some Vaiṣṇava temples. In Teraḻundūr temple in Myilāḍuthurai and in Cidambaram Govindarāja temple (housed in the Naṭarāja temple itself), Navarātri festival used to be a very grand affair. The Goddess would in all her finery come to the *maṇḍapam* and be taken around the temple on all the nine days. She would be taken to Perumāḷ's *sannidhi* to the accompaniment of the *mallāri*, followed by *ratthi, pallavī,* etc. (played on the *nādasvaram*). There the God and Goddess would exchange garlands. The *arcaka* would do the garlanding ritual to the beats of the instruments that is exactly like a dance number.

Navasaṅdhi Nṛttyam

According to the Āgamās, the *navasaṅdhi nṛttyam* has (*pratyega*) specific *rāgams, tāḷas* and *vādyams* (instruments) for each *saṁdhi* (direction). Some of the names are:

Sama pādam

Bhujaṅgam

Maṇḍalam

Bhujaṅgatirasam

Dhaṇḍa pādam

Kuñjitam

Bhujaṅga lalitam

Sandiya

Ūrdhva pādam

The Āgamās also lay specifications for singing of the *navasaṅdhi* — the *paṇṇ* related to each direction was specified and they had to sing according to these specifications.

Araiyar Sevai

Temples are places where our art and culture are housed and preserved for posterity and sanctity. One such great and ancient art, the "Araiyar

Sevai" is preserved to this day among the Vaiṣṇavite temples. In this art form the hymns (*Pāsurams*) composed by the Āḻvārs are sung with mime or action (*abhinayam*) for the *utsavamūrti*, i.e. the deity who is taken out in procession during the temple festivals. This form of singing with miming or action is known as "Araiyar Sevai". The *araiyars* are known with different names like — "Vinnapanchevan, Naṁpaḍuvan, Isaikārar, Thambiranmār", etc. The (*sevai*) service performed by the devotee to his God is what the "Araiyar Sevai" means in Tamil. This art form is further classified into different forms — *koṇḍaṭṭam* (singing the praise of the God), *abhinayam* (action), singing in tune to the *Pāsurams*, and conveying the meaning of the hymns (*Pāsurams*). The founder of this art form is Tirumaṅgai Āḻvār. He is supposed to have sung his hymns with tunes and mimed them to the presiding deity at the Śrīraṅgam temple during the "Kārthigai festival." He also is supposed to have requested the deity to accept his ring and acknowledge it as an equal to the Vedas (Vedasāṁyam) so it could be performed during the sacred month of Mārgaḻi (15 December - 13/14 January) on the "Śuklapakṣa Ekādaśī" day when the "Adyayana Utsavam" (festival) was performed. It seems God also agreed to this request and ever since this art form has been practised as a tradition (ritual) during the Mārgaḻi month and Ādi month in some particular Vaiṣṇava temples — i.e. Śrīraṅgam, Āḻvār Tirunagari, Śrīvilliputūr, and Tirukkuṟuṅguḍi. This art form began during the latter half of the eighth century CE and was a regular ritual in the above Vaiṣṇava temples during the Mārgaḻi month during the 10-day festival beginning from the first day after the new moon and the full moon. But somehow it stopped in between and then again was revived during the tenth century by Nāthamuni. Śrī Nāthamuni's contribution to Vaiṣṇavism is immense. It was he who edited and compiled all the four thousand hymns in the *Nālāyira Divya Prabandham*. It was also he who brought about the method of reciting the *Nālāyiram* as well as chanting as and setting the format for the *araiyar sevai*. Born in Vīranārāyaṇapuram (also called Kāṭṭumannar Koil) near Cidambaram he was requested by the king of Vīranārāyaṇapuram to compile the *Nālāyira Divya Prabandham* and also to make it available and accessible to all the

Vaiṣṇavites. He also entreated Nāthamuni to make the hymns available in the form of "*iyal* and *isai*" — (dance and music). Nāthamuni belonged to the earlier part of the tenth century and was well-versed in music and also in Yoga. It is believed that Nāthamuni had taught his two nephews the *Nālāyiram* completely and with their help also composed the tunes (*rāgam*) and beats (*tāḷa*) for all the hymns. This also came to be known as *deva gānam* and *divya isai*. With the help of his nephews he also formatted the *Araiyar Sevai* in the Śrīraṅgam temple. He brought about the performing of this art form in the temple during the Mārgaḻi month beginning on the day after the new moon day to the *daśamī* (10th day). This used to take place during the afternoons and hence to this day is known as *pagal patthu* (ten afternoons). On these ten days the first 1000 of the *Nālāyiram* are sung and acted with the formatted tunes set by Nāthamuni. Similarly *Tiruvāimoḻi thirunāḷ* observed from the day of "*Ekādaśī*" for ten nights when the *Tiruvāimoḻi* composed by Nammāḻvār would be sung and enacted (dance form) during nights. This festival to this day is observed and is called *Ira patthu* (meaning 10 nights). The twenty-day festival is known as *pagal-patthu-ira-patthu* and is also known as *Adyāyanath Tiruviḻā*. Nāthamuni not only formatted the music and steps for this dance and music but also laid specification for the costume that is followed to this day. The performing artiste wears a cone-shaped cap, marked with the Vaiṣṇavite symbol on it. Nāthamuni was a great exponent of music and could identify any *tāla* at the very beginning of the beat. He was supposed to have used "Yoga-Mārga" in this art. Thus this art of dance and music took a divine form culminating together Veda, Purāṇa, Āgama and the Nāṭya-Śāstra.

Performance of Araiyar Sevai

Araiyar Sevai is performed only before the *utsavamūrti* (the deity that is taken out in the procession during festivals) of the temple. This art form is performed in the temple only during the sacred month of "Mārgaḻi" (15 December to 13/14 January), during the *pagal-patthu and ira-patthu utsavam*, i.e. (10-day and 10-night festival). This festival is held in three important Vaiṣṇava temples at the same time —

Śrīraṅgam, Āḻvārtirunagari and Tirukkuṟungṅḍi. Only in Śrīvilliputhūr — the birthplace of Āṇḍāḷ (one of the 12 Āḻvārs) it also takes place during the month of Ādi (15 July to 14 August), Mārgaḻi and Thai (15 January to 14 February) (when Āṇḍāḷ gets married to the God at Śrīraṅgam). *Araiyar sevai* during the olden days was performed at a number of Vaiṣṇava temples. But now it is confined to four important Vaiṣṇava temples only — Śrīraṅgam, Śrīvilliputtūr, Tirukkuṟuṅguḍi and Āḻvārtirunagari. In Karnataka at Melkoṭṭai (a very important and significant temple for the Vaiṣṇavites near Mysore) this art form is only in the form of music. Here the *araiyar* only sings but does not mime or dance though he dons the traditional *araiyar* costume. There is no special make-up or costume for this art form. The special cap wound with silk scarf adorned on the deity and two floral garlands adorned on the deity given to the performer (*araiyar*) are all that is worn by the performer. The *araiyar* carries the *tāḷa* in both his hands, which is called the Āḻvār. No other instrument is used. Only when *Paḷḷupāṭṭu* is sung he uses (dances to) the *mṛdaṅgam*. He starts by beating the *tāḷam* and singing the *kondāṭṭam* (songs in praise of the deity) and then goes on to sing the *Pāsurams* (hymn to be sung on that particular day). When he completes the *Pāsurams*, he mimes (*abhinaya*) the song, placing the *tāḷam* in his hip. Through the miming the entire meaning of the song is depicted. The action (*abhinaya*) is done putting good use to the eyes, facial expression and also steps by using deftly the feet and also other body movements. This art is also called "the art of the eyes" (*dṛṣtikāvyam*). After this he explains the hymn word by word with proper word modulation. After this he once again goes back to the *koṇḍāṭṭām* with the *tāḷam* (praise of the deity) and then concludes. All the hymns chosen for the dance are those that have been formatted by Nāthamuni, in the tenth century, and no change has been made in the order or the selections of the songs. The tunes (*rāgams*) also depict the moods of the songs. There are two methods in the presentation of the *Nālāyira Divya Prabandham*. In the first method the Vaiṣṇavites chant all the four thousand hymns in a big group called the *ghoṣṭī* (group). There is no tune in this method. It is purely a recitation of the hymns. In the second method the songs are sung set to the tune by the *araiyars*. In this music, the tunes are very old and ancient and were originally set by Nāthamuni. Today the first system is more common in most of the Vaiṣṇava temples. The second system prevails only in Śrīraṅgam, Śrīvilliputtūr, Āḻvārtirunagarī and Melkoṭṭai.

Dramatic Aspects in Araiyar Sevai

This is performed before the *utsavamūrti* (the deity that is taken out during festivals). The *araiyar* stands in the middle facing the deity. On either side of the performer the audience sit and some also sit behind him. This sitting arrangement by itself brings in a feeling of togetherness between the performer and the audience. There is no difference of any kind as men women, and children of all sorts sit together in rapt attention watching the performer. There is only a divine feeling and the appreciation of the art, bringing the artiste and the audience irrespective of class, creed and sex closer. The *araiyar* enacts the different roles — i.e. mother, daughter, etc. — all in one — it is the production of art at its best in divinity and aesthetics — all in one.

Historical Facts about Araiyar Sevai

Some stone inscriptions of Kulottuṅga Coḷa (CE 1070–1120) at Śrīraṅgam temple register the honours bestowed upon the *araiyar* at that temple. In the Varadarājasvāmi temple in Kāñcīpuram, in the stone inscription (1242), we find that there were 22 *araiyars* in the temple during that period and they were all patronised by the king. They were not merely performing artistes according to these inscriptions. They were also highly respected by the kings, nobles and were looked upon as people who were serving God. According to the inscriptions the *araiyars* were also found to be artistes who appreciated other artistes and treated them with a lot of respect. There are a lot of traditions attached to both the Vaiṣṇavite temples and Śaivite temples and we owe it to the Āḻvārs and the Nāyaṉmārs who have contributed to this rich tradition of art and culture blended with *bhakti* (divinity). Though over the years the traditions have been diluted, and even stopped at a number of places, they still remain and attract devotees who throng these temples to get the feel of the rich music traditions and also the divinity and spirituality attached to these traditions.

Folk Dances

Folk dance forms are usually conducted outside the temple premises. The dancers are invited to perform during the annual festivals and usually move with the processional deity during the *Ūrvalam* (taking the deity around the streets surrounding the temple). Some such dance forms are *Poi-kāl kuthirai* (dummy horse dance), *Mayilāṭṭam* (peacock dance), *Oyilāṭṭam, Karagamāṭṭam* (with the decorated pots on their heads) and *Tappaṭṭam* (with small handheld drums), *Kolāṭṭam* and *Kummi* performed as a part of temple festivals in urban areas. *Terukūthu,* a dance drama with themes from the mythology and folklore is conducted all night during these festivals. *Kāvaḍiyāṭṭam* is a dance offering to Lord Muruga where the devotee carries the *kāvaḍi* (a decorated, arched wooden plank) with milk, peacock feathers, etc. *Kāvaḍi cindu* is a specific tune played for the *kāvadiyāṭṭam.*

14

Festivals in Temples

THERE are three aspects to every festival in a land. There is the ritualistic aspect — the various steps of its celebration, whether it is in a home or a temple, the performance of *pūjā*, the preliminary arrangements, etc.

The second is the legend aspect — the ancient stories that had grown around it, which had caused the origin of festival, the benefits attained by some who had celebrated it early in the history of the society and so on.

The third is the philosophical or the esoteric aspect, which gives significance to the celebration and which has kept it alive through many centuries. In many the philosophical aspect may not be fully explicit, but a social significance may be apparent.

People in Tamil Nadu have a way of celebrating great people — by observing their birth or death anniversaries. The Vaiṣṇavas celebrate the day of birth of the Āḻvārs and Ācāryas, while the Śaivas celebrate the day of the *mukti* or passing away of their Nāyaṉmārs and Ācāryas.

The festivals seem to constitute the eternal spirit of India, and more so in Tamil Nadu. We do not know when exactly the celebration of the festivals as a society or the state came into existence. But we can say that it started right from the time men organized themselves into a civilized group or society. Saint Tirujñāna Sambandar mentions a series of monthly festivals for the twelve months, which were popular in his day (seventh century). Most of then continue till this day both in the manner of celebration and in their significance. Festivals are the outward social expression of the communal joy of the people and have helped to retain the best of the past culture and by celebrations in the present, hand it down to the future generations. Festivals, mostly conservative, do not lend themselves easily to changes but continue to be rigid and open a window to peep into the past.

The mode of observance of festivals has not changed. Lamp, incense, camphor, fragrant flowers, sandal, turmeric and *kumkum* with the betel leaves, banana fruits and coconuts form an inseparable part of any festival. Even if the electrical lamps have replaced the oil lamps, one oil lamp in a corner will always be placed symbolically. Camphor was introduced during the fourth to sixth century CE in order to replace the oil lamps then used for *ārādhanā*. The *kolams* and festoons are the part of the decorations for any festival. Baths, fasts (vigil in some cases), dip in auspicious rivers and seas, circumambulation, tying of an auspicious, yellow string around the neck or the wrist, new clothes, etc. have helped continue the ancient culture and kept the glamour and glory of the festivals over centuries. The various songs and dances have also made their contribution in the preservation of that culture.

The Śaiva and the Vaiṣṇava festivals dominate the ones that are celebrated in Tamil Nadu. Vīnāyaka, Skanda, Śakti and Śiva festivals can be brought under Śaivism, while those related to Rāma and Kṛṣṇa and others like Vaikuṇṭha Ekādaśī and Kaiśika Ekādaśī will fall under Vaiṣṇavism. Sarasvatī *pūjā,* New Year day and Poṅgal belong to both. But all this in reality does not detract from the concept of the ONE God in Hinduism.

There is continuity in the festival celebrations and the festival culture of Tamil Nadu, which is hardly to be found elsewhere. Several factors have contributed to this continuity. The chief factor is the large number of temples that stud the state. Even small villages have large temples for Śiva and Viṣṇu. All the temple festivals involve the entire society around, through daily *ārādhanā*, processions and music rituals particularly, playing the *nādasvaram*, singing of devotional songs, distribution of *prasāda*, etc. Besides, the songs of the Nāyaṉmārs and the Āḻvārs in the temples was another integrating force of permanence.

Although temple festivals appear to be only religious, they are not mere temple celebrations but do involve some social values. There are more than a dozen important festivals observed in temples that take us around the calendar. These have been celebrated for centuries before Indian independence was won and long before the spirit of nationhood in the modern sense took shape. Starting from the first day of Chittirai — Tamil new year day (April) — we have festivals right until Panguni — *Śrī Rāma Navamī* (March).

Some of the most important temple festivals are regulated in a manner that helped the pilgrims to make their tours conveniently and at leisure. Devotees had been by religion and custom enjoined to visit the important festivals at the major temples at least once in their lifetimes.

Temple festivals have given rise to a large number of new poetic patterns and motifs. The best known is the Pāvai song in Śaivism and Vaiṣṇavism. The song is associated with the pre-dawn bath in the month of Mārgaḻi and going around the temple and village streets. Saint Āṇḍāḷ sang *Tiruppāvai* and Saint Māṇikkavācagar sang his *Tirvempāvai*. Both the songs are the best odes by the two saints to their respective religions and the Tamil people in general. Tirupallāṇḍu is another song purporting to pray for long life to the Lord himself so that he may shower his grace on mankind for all time. Periāḻvār first sang this song on Viṣṇu and it is very popular in the Vaiṣṇavite temples even today. Two centuries later Sendanar — a Harijan *bhakta* — sang a *pallāṇḍu* on Naṭarāja during the *Ārudhradarśana* car festivals and today it is equally popular in all Śiva temples. Toṇḍaraḍippodi Āḻvār, who sang his first wake-up song on Lord Raṅganātha at Śrīraṅgam, composed Tirupaḷḷieḻuci — a song intended to wake up the Lord in the temple. Māṇikkavācagar followed him on Lord Śiva at Tiruperundurai. All these songs form part of the temple rituals. Similar songs sung on temple festival occasions are many. They are modelled on the rituals and the folk patterns of songs suited for such occasions. In many temples, there are songs for different types of festivals.

Oduvārs sing verses from the *Tevāram* and this is an item of interest because it gives literary and musical training to many devotees in the society. The fact that the Coḷa emperors had made liberal endowments to temple *oduvārs* for singing *Tevāram* songs had helped literary taste as well as music to be developed among the masses in those days.

Religion was the soul of all activity in Hindu society and dance also had assumed great importance. In temple rituals, *gīta* (music), *vādya* (instrumental music) and *nṛttya* (dance) were the three *upacāra*s at the end of the 16 *upacāra*s. Coḷa monarchs had made numerous endowments in all the major temples for these three. They had continuously been existing as essential features of temple activity through more than ten centuries.

The *Teppotsava* (float festival) is a popular festival in temples, which have large temple tanks. Tiruvārūr, Madurai, Tiruviḍaimarudūr, Kumbakoṇam and Mylapore are some of the temples where this festival is celebrated. One of the major traditions in this festival is the *nādasvaram* orchestra going by a tradition of playing tunes formatted exclusively for the festival. The *nādasvaram* is played followed by the hymns sung by the *Oduvār*s and there are other cultural events like music concerts and dances. The *Brahmotsava* is an annual feature in all Śiva and Viṣṇu temples of Tamil Nadu. The festival takes place usually for 10 days and some temples have festivals on different occasions and even more than once. On all the days of the 10-day festival, the chief deity is taken around the main streets called the *māḍa vīdi* (the streets along which the temple car is drawn) on different *vāhana*s, always accompanied by *nādasvaram* orchestra, singing of the Vedas, *Tevāram* or *Nālāyiram*s as the case may be. All these festivals take the Lord to the doors of the devotees and aim at making even those who had been denied temple admission have a *darśana* of the Lord at close quarters.

The famous Kapālīśvara temple at Mylapore performs a festival for the Aruvathimūvar (the 63 Śaiva saints or Nāyaṉmārs). Such a great festival for all the saints at once is not conducted at any other shrine. On this particular day all these saints (bronze images) are taken out in procession along the main streets around the temple. *Nādasvaram* music and *Tevāram* singing are parts of the rituals observed during this festival.

The birthdays of the 12 Āḻvārs are observed as festivals in the Vaiṣṇavite temples by singing of hymns from the *Nālāyiram*.

Temples of Tamil Nadu observe several festivals all round the year. Navarātri festival is celebrated for nine days in most temples in south India. Cultural activities play an important role in the celebration.

Dhanur Māsam (15 December–13/14 January), is observed as a sacred month in Śiva and Viṣṇu temples in all the south Indian states.

Well known is the *Pāvai* song in Vaiṣṇavism and Śaivism. The song is now associated with the pre-dawn bath in the morning of the Mārgaḻi month and going round the temple and temple streets — *Tiruppāvai* in Vaiṣṇavism and *Tiruvempāvai* in Śaivism. Both, the *Vaikuṇṭha Ekādaśī* in honour of Viṣṇu and the *Ārudra Darśanam* in honour of Śiva occur in the sacred month of Mārgaḻi. They also signify the integration in the two *vaidika* religions, Śaivism and Vaiṣṇavism. Members of both the sects get up early in the morning before dawn, have a good bath, and attend pre-dawn temple service. Songs heralding this month have been sung in all these temples known as *Pāvai Pāṭṭu* (Tiruppāvai and Tiruvempāvai) composed by the two great saints Āṇḍāḷ and Māṇikkavācagar. Legends say that Āṇḍāḷ melted away in the form of Lord Raṅganātha at Śrīraṅgam and Māṇikkavācagar in the form of Naṭarāja at Cidambaram. The traditions originated in the land several millennia ago and were perpetuated by these two saints in the eighth and the ninth centuries. The *pāvai* songs that are sung to this day at the temples are some of the richest legacies of the Tamils. (The *Nālāyira Divya Prabhantham* (four-thousand poems) in the Tamil language is the Veda for the Vaiṣṇavas. During a period of ten days before *Vaikuṇṭha Ekādaśī* and another ten days after the *Ekādaśī* the recitation of the *Nālāyiram* is made at Śrīraṅgam and it is called the *Adhyayana Utsava*. On some special days during this period, the *araiyar* (a privileged class of temple priest) performs a kind of dance for the *Tiruvāimoḻi* of Nammāḻvār. This festival thus coincides with a celebration calculated to glorify the many Āḻvārs and their poems that are masterpieces of Tamil literature. Saint Māṇikkavācagar had sung his most moving *Tiruvācakam* hymns (656) verses. They are all set to music but the *paṇṇ*s (tunes) had not been specified. They are generally sung in *mohana rāgam*. A lot of value was attached to singing in the divine presence in the temples. The three components were incorporated into temple services as *gītam*, *vādyam*, and *nṛttyam* (vocal singing, instrumental music and dancing.) The service of singing was part of the *caryā mārga*, among the four pathways to God in Śaiva Siddhānta termed as *caryā*, *kṛya*, *yoga*, and *jñāna*. The four *samaya* *ācāryas* Appar, Tirugnāna Sambandar, Sundarar and Māṇikkavācagar are considered to represent the four pathways respectively. Māṇikkavācagar had taken many of his poetic motifs from folk-lore and folk songs. Starting from Perundurai and Uttarakosamangai, having Cidambaram as his destination (as ordered by Lord Naṭarāja) he visited many places and witnessed children, particularly girls (*pāvai*) playing games and he methodically utilised their folk songs which being so simple and natural seemed to echo his longing for union with Lord Śiva.

These are some such songs:

Tiru-Empāvai	girls going for a bath
Tiru-Ammānai	girls playing with cowries (shells)
Tiru-Porchunam	girls pounding bath powder for the Lord
Tiru-Kottumbi	chasing the dragonfly
Tiru-Tellenum	girls patting each other's shoulders in pairs
Tiru-Challa	playing with rings
Tiru-Pū-alli	plucking the lily from the tank
Tiru-Tolnokkam	a game
Tiru-Ponnūsal	playing on the swing
Tiru-Paḷḷieḷuci	waking up the Lord

Yearly Festivals in Temples

TAIPŪSAM

The deity is offered *pradakṣiṇā* on a chariot. As the deity is taken towards the chariot, the musicians should play *pāras rāgam*. From there to the eastern *gopura* (temple tower) the *meḷas* should play as usual. From the Panthal of the Dancing Piḷḷayār (Gaṇeśa) *pāras rāgam* should be played followed by *Mallāri*. Then proceeding towards the four-pillared *maṇḍapa*, a *pada* in *bhairavī rāgam* and *aṭa tālam* should be performed. Other *rāgams* to be played are the *śuddhasaveri varṇam*, a *pada* in *dhanyāsi rāgam*, and the *tāḷas* specified are *miśra tālam* and *tripuṭa tāḷam*.

Pankuni Utsavam

This festival lasts for 27 days and used to abound with *padams, varṇams* and other compositions that were related to the repertoire of the *devadāsīs*. It is also one of the two ritual occasions (the other one during *Ārudra Darśanam* in December) during the entire year when the presiding deity is shown dancing the *ajapa naṭanam*. The procession carrying the God on the *ṛṣabha vāhana* (bull mount) during this festival would halt in front of the king's palace for two hours for two hours to enable the *devadāsīs* to perform *varṇam, jātisvaram, padam* and *tiḷāna*. They also performed a *varṇam*, specially composed by Dīkṣitar, for this occasion — Tyāgarājapālaya in the *rāgam aṭaṇa*. At the tail end an *Aṣṭapadī* was also performed. Another important feature during this festival is the procession on the temple chariot (*rathotsava*). The temple chariot of Tiruvārūr is famous for its size and its fine workmanship. Nowadays it has become impossible to pull the chariot because of its size and it requires immense man-power to pull it.

Vasantotsava (Spring Festival)

This festival included the performance of the dance-drama — "Tyāgeśara Kuravañji" also called "Tiruvārūr Kuravañji." This tradition ceased in the beginning of the last century to be replaced by a full-fledged dance concert (*sadir-katcheri*) that came to an end in the 1940s with the *devadāsī* tradition.

Āḍi Pūram Festival (Teppotsavam)

A float was pulled around the large temple tank (*kamalālaya*) thrice. The first round would feature music by the *nādasvaram* artistes "Periya Meḷam." One of the main compositions played by them was "Śrī Nīlotpala Nāyakī" (presiding deity) in *rāgam rītigowḷa*. In the second round the "Cinna Meḷam" would enter the float. The *devadāsīs* and their accompanists who constituted the small band would sing and dance and one of the highlights was "Kamalāmbike" in *rāgam toḍī*. The last round of the float gave the singers, the Oduvārs, to perform the *Tevārams*. The festival continues minus the dance by the *devadāsīs*.

Puraṭṭāsi Masam Niraipani Festival

This festival is celebrated during September-October when Tyāgarājasvāmi is supposed to give a special audience to Indra who lives in Tiruvārūr due to a curse. During this festival both the *cinnamurai* and the *periyamurai devadāsī*s used to sing and dance while the procession (*purappāḍu*) is going on. Special songs for this occasion were the *ūñjal pāṭṭu* while the gods were gently rocked to sleep.

Mārgaḷi Māsam Ārudra Darśanam

This is a festival held in honour of the asterism of Ārudra (Śiva). It is related to Śiva in the form of Śiva Naṭarāja (Śiva as the king of all dancers). This form of Śiva indicates his Rudra aspect of the cosmic destruction of all impure, gross forces by means of His Cosmic dance that burns all impurities to retain only the purest substance, namely gold. The most important aspect of this festival was the *kautuvam*s performed for several deities by the *devadāsī*s. The *nādasvaram* band still follows the similar processional routine. The most famous Ārudra festival celebrations however take place at Cidambaram. The aspect for which Tiruvārūr is famous is the processional dance, the "Ajapa Naṭanam" that is executed by the deity Himself. Actually, it is the bearers of the platform on which the deity is placed, who dance the particular *naṭanam*. The seven dances performed are *Unmatta Naṭanam, Parvarataraṅga Naṭanam, Kukkuṭa Naṭanam, Bhṛṅga Naṭanam, Ajaba Naṭanam, Kamala Naṭanam, Haṁsapada Naṭanam*. These dances might be connected with the seven *cakra*s through which *kuṇḍalinī śakti* ascends. All these dances need a particular choreography and the accompaniment of the *śuddha mattalam* drum.

The procession of God Naṭarāja on the morning of Ārudra Darśanam still follows the same processional route. Till the 1940s regular patterns in the music and dance rituals for all festivals were followed by the *devadāsī*s. The *rāgam*s and the *tāḷa*s were prescribed and strictly followed by the artistes of the temple.

The format is as follows:

The performers dance by the show of their hands in different ways, befitting the sixteen forms of offerings (*ṣoḍaśopacāra*). After the camphor light offering (*karpūram āratī*) is over, they will offer prayers with flowers, called *puṣpāñjali*. Then, the Lord will be taken round the *prākāra* when the big *meḷam* (*Periameḷam*), i.e. *nādasvaram*, will be played till it reaches the east main street, outside the temple. From the middle of the east main street, the *Naṭṭuvanār*s and those playing on *suddha matthalam* and *mṛdaṅgam*, will, according to the tenets of Bharata Nāṭyam, perform *meḷāprāpti* that has already been explained. They will recite *Collukethu Stotra*s on Vīnāyaka, Subrahmaṇya, Īśvara, Tyāgārāja and Sundaramūrti. Afterwards up to the end of the south main street, they will call out *jati*s prepared in different *tāḷam*s and also *Jati Chollukatus* called *tatakāra*s prepared in *rāgam*s like *siṁhananda*. Then, in the whole of the west main street and the north main street, *meḷā vādyakāra*s (percussion artists) will play on the *nādasvaram*, songs and *pada*s of Muthu Tānḍavar, etc. At the junction of north street with east street called *Īśānya Dik*, Śivācāryas will recite ślokas in praise of the Lord. After this the *Oduvār*s will sing *Tevāram* songs in praise of the Kṣetra and the Lord. Then the *Rudrakannikā*s will together sing *Tevāram* songs of the Kṣetras at the end of which camphor light (*karpūram āratī*) will be offered and *vibhūti* (holy ash) will be distributed. During the last stage of the procession, i.e. from the north end of the east main street to the middle, the *Rudrakannikā*s will sing *Tevāram*s. When the procession reaches the middle of the east main street, just opposite the main *gopuram* of the temple, the Amman (Goddess) will be separated from her Lord Naṭarāja and taken in an angry mood inside the temple. But their quarrel will be set right through the timely intervention of Sundaramūrti Svāmigaḷ, who will act as mediator. After the reunion Tīrthavāri will be performed. The *Rudrakannikā*s bearing "Thaṭṭu Dīpas," mṛdaṅgists and Naṭṭuvanārs bearing *tāḷam*s, will go round Lord Naṭarāja and Śivakāmasundarī twice when the *sarva vādya* will be sounded. After this, the *sarva vādya* will be stopped and all the *Rudrakannikā*s will either sing *puṣpāñjali* or *maṅgalam* to the accompaniment of *mṛdaṅga tāḷam*. Then the *Rudrakannikā*s will complete the third round to the accompaniment of *tāḷam* and *maddhaḷa*. The procession will end with the offering of camphor light after which, the deities are then taken to be installed in their original place when the *Rudrakannikās* will sing *Ullas* and *Yaccarika* (*Eccarikais*) in praise of the Kṣetra. After their installation, there will once again be camphor light offering and the *Rudrakannikās* will return to their respective houses.

Until the third decade of the last century, Naṭṭuvanārs and *Rudrakannikās* have been performing this holy service in their respective Kṣetras (temples) where they had rights.

Festivals Associated with Specific Stars in a Month

Taipūsam

Māsi makam

Paṅguni Uttiram

Cittirai Pourṇami (star Cittirai)

Vaikāṣi Viṣākam

Āni Anuṣam

Āḍi Pūram

Āvani Tiruvoṇam Avittam

Puraṭṭāsi — Navarātri

Aippasi — Dīpāvaḷi

Kartigai Pourṇamī (star Kartikai)

Mārgaḻi — Ārudra darśanam — Pāvai festival

Special New-Moon Days

The gods and goddesses of the temples are taken to the nearby river or the sea for a ritualistic bath. The devotees also have a bath here and proceed to visit the temple.

Thai Amāvāsai

Āḍi Amāvāsai

Mahāḷaya Amavasai (the first day of Navarātri festival).

Citra Pourṇami is a special Full Moon day when Goddess Mīnākṣī is given in marriage to Lord Sundareśvar a (Śiva) by Aḻagiri Svāmi (Viṣṇu). The festival is conducted at the Mīnākṣī temple in Madurai along the river Vaigai.

15

Inscriptions having Music Information in the Temples

IN a number of temples we find details about the kind of honour, the honorarium, respect and privilege the artistes performing in temples enjoyed from the days of the Pallavas and the Coḷas. At the Bṛhadīśvara temple in Tanjāvūr we find the inscription — *āriyam pāḍuvor mūvarukku tamiḻ pāda oruvanukku* . . . ending with *koṭṭi madallam* and find the following word *kīḻ kaṇṇaku* at the bottom with the order of the king. This was supposed to have been inscribed during the king's (Rājarāja Coḷa) 29th birthday. There were two types of singing in the temples — *Āriyan tamiḻ* and *Āriyakūtu.* These two methods differed from each other and were accompanied by different percussion instruments. Their fee structure as fixed by the king is mentioned on these inscriptions.

At Pudukkoṭṭai in Kuḍumiyānmalai we find inscriptions datable to the seventh century. The then ruling king has inscribed about his *guru* in music Śrī Rudracārya and shows his reverence for his *guru* by mentioning the disciple's respect for the *guru*. He has inscribed on a rock 14 ft long and 13 ft wide just behind the Singanāthar temple. On this rock he also mentions a special title conferred on himself *saṅkīrṇa jāti* for his versatility. *Saṅkīrṇam* also refers to classification of *tāḷams*. This inscription shows the advanced development of music technically then. The inscription mentions the four classifications of the *tāḷams* namely *catuśram, tiśram, miśram* and *kaṇḍa* and suggestively classifies a number five leaving everyone wondering whether the creator was the king himself.

At Arichanallūr we find inscriptions dated back to second century with words identical to *tāḷa māṭrās* in three parts as — *tha-thai-thā thai.*

In Tirumayyam near Pudukkoṭṭai we find the three classifications of the Gandharva music and also the names of instruments and words like *Abhinaya kūthu.*

In temples like Tiruvaṇṇāmalai the inscription says there were more than thousand *devadāsīs* attached to the temple in the year CE 1336 during the time of King Vallāla.

There was an instrument called the *svaramaṇḍalam* a thousand years ago. This resembled a *yāḻ* but was smaller. This was played as an accompaniment while the singer used to sing at the temple. This information is inscribed in the Vaitīśvaran temple. The inscription also gives details about the remuneration given to the artiste. Similar information is found in Tirucendūr temple, Tiruvāvaḍuturai, etc.

The temple at Bṛhadīśvara temple at Tanjāvūr gives us a lot of information on percussion instruments played during the regime of Rājarāja Coḷa like *mattalam, uḍukai, vīṇā, tumburu, bheri, yāḻ , kuḻal, kombu, tāḷam, murasu, mālari,* etc. and also about visiting artistes from other temples like Tiruvengāḍu and Tillai. Interesting information on the *śrībali, naivediyam* during early morning at the *bali pīṭam* accompanied by a number of instruments is also inscribed in the Bṛhadīśvara temple at Tanjāvūr. It says — *mattalam-eṭṭām* (8) *tāḷam onrām* (1) *karaḍigai-onrām Kaṇḍai ārām,* and *thimilai onrām.* The *Tamiḻ* word denotes numbers and it says *śrībaliku koṭṭuvān* (will be played during the *bali*).

This *śrībali* ritual is followed in almost all the Kerala temples to this day and the *pañca vādyam* accompanies the *naivedyam* (*prasādam*). In some temples like the Padmanābhasvāmi temple in Trivandrum and the Guruvayūr temple we find that the elephant is also taken around the temple.

At Candragiri Tirumalai temple, we find inscriptions giving us information that Tirupāvais were sung during the *Puraṭṭāsī* month *Tiruviḻa* (the Navarātri festival falls during this month) and the special *prasāda* made of rice that was offered to Āṇḍāḷ. The inscription mentions the quantity of rice that was allocated by the king for this purpose.

At the Bilvamaṅgaḷa Āgamalīśvarar temple there is this inscription — *ippāṭin pāsurathin* . . . mentioning particular hymns sung during the reign of the King Kulaśekara Tevan.

At Tiruvaiyāru — Pañcanadīśvarar temple the remuneration given by the king to temple dancers and singers has been inscribed. The inscriptions also mention the remuneration given to the accompanying artistes. We also find that artistes were classified as male and female in the inscription at Ulagamadeveśvarar temple at Tiruvaiyāru as *Gandharvar* for males and *Gandharliyār* for females.

16

Sculptures of Dancers and Musicians in Temples

In south Indian temples the most noteworthy aspect is the structure and the carvings of the sculptures. Beginning from the *gopurams*, we find a whole lot of sculptures done on granite depicting gods, goddesses, dancers, women and artistes playing instruments all done very minutely and importance given to every little detail. A day is not enough to study the icons and sculptures or to appreciate their beauty. One is dumb struck when one enters the main *sanctum sanctorum* as one has a first glimpse of the presiding deity. The beauty leaves you breathless and *bhakti* (devotion) is evoked.

Once we come out the beauty of the engravings and the sculptural splendour leaves one spellbound. The architecture of each and every temple in south India goes to prove one point — "There is Divinity in beauty." It would be an extremely tiresome task to make an account of the music-related sculptural representations in Tamil Nadu temples. Almost all the temples have atleast a few to offer. The ones that stand out for their profusion of sculptures are Sucīndram (musical pillars), Dārasuram, Mahāliṅgapuram, Tiruvaṭṭaru, Tiruerukathampuliyūr and a number of other temples in Karnataka, Andhra, etc.

It is a common feature to find several dance poses (*karaṇas*) engraved on the temple walls. A few temples which have displayed several *karaṇas* of Bharatanāṭyam are as given below.

- Tanjāvūr Bṛhadīśvara temple, Cidambaram Naṭarāja Temple — The name of the *karaṇa* is mentioned below each of the poses represented here.
- Bagūr near Pondicherry, The Thiruvaḍigai temple (one of the

eight *vīraṭṭānam* temples of Śiva) is noted for its 108 *karaṇas*.

- Kumbakoṇam Śāraṅgapāṇi koil
- Thirubhuvanam temple
- Both Śiva and Viṣṇu temples in Kāñcīpuram
- Dārāsuram temple.

We also find musical steps and pillars in stone at Suchindram temple, Dārasuram, Madurai Aḻagar temple, Kalakāḍu temple, Tirunelveli Nellaiappar temple and Tāḍikombu temple near Dindigul in Tamil Nadu. A number of temples in Kerala and Karnataka display such sculptures.

A number of instruments like flute, *vīṇā, nādasvaram, yāḻ, mattalam, uḍukka, tirucinnam, bheri,* etc. are represented in the sculptures, usually on the *gopurams*, walls, *maṇḍapams*, pillars or the temple chariot. This only goes to show that music and musical instruments were indispensable for worshipping or communicating with God.

17

Unique Music Traditions in Some Temples

SOME very unique music rituals in some of the temples are still being followed today.

In Tiruveṅkādu temple (near Cidambaram) there is a rule that first the *Mohana rāgam* should be played in the morning followed by the *mallāri* in *Gambhīra Nāṭṭai rāgam*. It was considered that the *Mohana rāgam* was exclusively meant for the presiding deity Aghoramūrti (Śiva), hence this *rāga* was not played anywhere else outside the temple in this town and not even for any occasions like weddings, religious or cultural or social festivals. This tradition is observed to this day.

In the temple at Vedaraṇyam (near Nāgapattinam) they had certain formatted music traditions. Early morning *pūjā* is observed with *Bouḷi rāgam*, in the next *pūjā* — 8-9 a.m. *Kedāram* or *Danyāsi* is played and in the noon-12.30 p.m. *Śrī rāgam* or *Maṇiraṅgu* should be played. Evening 5-6 p.m. *Kalyāṇī rāgam* is played, and in the night only *Begada* was played. Later, the ninteenth-century Dīkṣitar's "Tyāgāraja Yoga Vaibhavam" in the *rāgam Ānanda Bhairavī* was introduced instead of *Begada*.

In the *devī*'s (Goddess) *sannidhi* (*sanctum sanctorum*) *Kedāragouḷa* or *Sahāna rāgams* were played and in the nights *Cakravāham* was played. During festivals first *nādanāmakriyā* used to be played and only then the *Gambhīra Nāṭṭai Mallāri* was played. In the mornings *Mallāri* to the *miśra chāpu Tāḷam* used to be played and in the evenings the *Taligai Mallāri* was played. But this *mallāri* was not played in the three speeds. *Miśra Chāpu Tāḷam* was handled when deity was given holy water bath with the conch (*śaṅkhābhiṣekam*).

During the wedding festival (Kalyāṇa Utsavam) songs in *Nāṭṭaikuriñjī rāgam* was sung by the *devadāsī*s who also sang the '*Oḍapāḍalgaḷ* (boat songs) and the *Oñjalpāḍalgaḷ* (swing). Once the *devadāsī* system came to an end, these songs began to be played by the *nādasvaram* artistes.

In the nights after the *dīpārādhanā* was over hymns like *Tūngu sudaranaiya jothi* and *Yāḷai paḷittha moḷiyāl*, etc. (*Tirumuṟai*) were sung and later came to be played on the *nādasvaram*. In the Tiruvaḷapudhūr Māṇikkavannar temple during the *Tiruvādirai* festival, the presiding deity would leave the *sanctum sanctorum* with the *mallāri*, but half way through — the *nādasvarm* would be stopped. Only the *Nattu* and *Muttu* (percussion) would be played. Then when the deity reaches the western street the *nādasvaram* artiste would play Muthuthāṇḍavar's songs till it reaches the temple.

In Avuḍayārkoil temple, the *nādasvaram* should be played only opposite to the *sanctum sanctorum* near the *balipīṭam*. When the deity was taken outside the *sanctum sanctorum* the Periameḷam would be played before the sanctum and continue till the first *maṇḍapam* (hall). Another unique feature about this temple was the playing of a very unique and now dying instrument called *geṭṭhu vādyam* (more about this temple in the chapter "Temples of Tamil Nadu"). This *vādyam* used to be played in Tirukutrālam and Tenkāsi temples where a unique way of performing the *dīpārādhanā* (lamp offering) was done. The *nādasvaram* artiste would first play the *Ānandabhairavī rāgam* in the *ādī-tāḷa* and then continue the same *rāga* in *Miśra Cāpu Tāḷa*. While the *nādasvaram* artiste played the instruments to this prescribed *rāga* the *arcaka* (priest) would bring the *dīpa* (lamp) dancing to the beat of the music. While this tradition was done by the *devadāsī*s once upon a time, this tradition is still done today but by the priest. This ritual lasts for about fifteen minutes and the other instruments that are played during this ritual are — *śaṅkha* (conch), *mṛdaṅgam, tavil* (percussion instruments), *otthu* (accompanying *nādasvaram* and the *tāḷam* (small instrument to keep track of the beats). This ritual or tradition is known as the *tāṇḍava dīpārādhanā*.

In the temple at Vāsudevanallūr in Tirunelveli district during every Friday and during festivals, a unique tradition was observed. The temple priest had to go around the *balipīṭam* offering food to the God followed by the periameḷam. When he came near the north-east corner the periameḷam would stop playing. Then he would say *thakkri-thāḷam*, and on hearing the command the Naṭṭuvanār would say the *guru-laghu-guru* a *jāti* comprising of twenty *akṣara*s (beats) and the periameḷam would play this beat.

In the Kanyakumārī temple during the *Tiruveṇpā* festival the *devadāsī*s used to sing the *Ūnjalpāṭu* (songs sung while the deity was put on a swing and gently moved up and down.) Now this tradition of singing songs does not exist. Instead the *nādasvaram* artistes play on the *nādasvaram*.

In the Cidambaram temple, the playing of the *rāgam*s and music forms by the *nādasvaram* players have been formatted and it is to a great extent followed even today, particularly during festivals. The main reason for this is because these players have been playing there for generations.

On the first day of any festival only *ārabhi* or *dhanyāsi rāga* has to be played. In the night *śaṅkarabharaṇam rāga* is played. On the second day, *rīthigowla rāga* played, third day *māyāmāḷavagowḷa*, fourth day *chakravākam* are played. On the fifth day till the deity reaches the *vāhana* (carrier in which the deity is placed) called as "Teruvadaithan" only *nādasvaram* can be played, followed by *nattu* and *muttu* will be played. On the sixth day *ṣanmugapriya* or *toḍī* should be followed. Seventh day *kambhoji* or *varāḷi*, on the eighth day the *odakūru* song in *nādhanāmakriyā rāgam* will have to be played. On the ninth day — the day the temple car is brought out to take the deity out, the *Ther* (car) *mallāri* should be played. When the deity reaches the *āyiramkāl maṇḍapam* (thousand pillared hall) *Eccarika* songs set in *āhiri* and *nīlāmbarī* are played. These songs have to be followed by any one *padam* (dance song) on the presiding deity. On the eleventh day *husseni rāga* has to be played. These are the music traditions that were formatted for the Cidambaram temple and are followed to this day.

In all the temples, whether it is Vaiṣṇavite or Śaivite, the general rule is that no songs should be played by the *nādasvaram,* when the deity is taken out in a procession. But the Tiruvārūr temple is an exception and does not follow this tradition. The music traditions standardized in this temple are very unique in character, and are entirely different than those at the other temples.

During temple festivals they follow a set pattern of playing specific *rāgas*. In the mornings, *śrī rāgam* or *kalyāṇī* should be played, in the afternoon *begaḍa* or *toḍi* and in the nights *kedāragowḷa* and *yoganam* should be played. Thus there is a standard and a long list of *rāgams* that have been prescribed and is followed even now. The day, Lord Paraśurāma is taken out in the temple car, till the landmark called *vimocanapandal, paraz rāgam* should be played after which till the *kīḻagopuram* (tower below) *mallāri* should be played. Again at the sanctum of Nartana Gaṇapati *paraz rāgam* will have to continue. When the deity reaches the four pillar *maṇḍapam* the *padam* set in the *rāgam bhairavī* should be played; when it reaches the south-east end *danyāsi rāga padam* should be played. At the end of the procession when the deity reaches the end of the street a *kṛti* (song) set in *punnagavarāḷi rāga* should be played. On the day of the car festival in the morning *bhūpāla rāga* should be played while the *tavil* will have to observe the *miśra gati* (a particular beat) followed by the *tisra gati* and then the *sarva laghu*. After this the *nādasvarm* artiste will play a *kattaḷai padam* set in the *tirupuṭa tāla*. Once the deity enters the inside of the temple *padams* set in the tune of *pantuvarāli, asāveri* should be played. When the deity is placed on the car the *Ter Mallāri* should be played. But for this the *nādasvaram* should not be accompanied by the *Tavil,* instead an instrument called *Kidikiṭṭi* is played. When the car starts moving a *padam* set in *Tirupuṭa tāḷam* should be played. When it reaches the fourth corner the *Periameḷam* has to be stopped. Songs (folk-type) like the *lālī* (lullaby), *ūñjal* (swing) and *nalaṅgu* (should be sung by the *devadāsī*s. With the end of the *devadāsī* system in the late 1940s the singing of the prescribed songs has been stopped, but continues to be performed by the *nādasvaram* artistes on their instruments. After the singing of the prescribed songs by the singers the *Ter Mallāri* will have to be played before the day's programme concludes.

The *Āḍi Pūram* festival in the Tiruvārūr temple also needs special mention. On this particular day the *Teppotsavam* (float festival) is observed. The deity leaves the temple to get into the float in the temple tank to the playing of *mallāri* in the first round. At this juncture the *rāga* prescribed is *śaṅkarābharaṇam varṇam* followed by *kṛtis* in Garuḍanāga — *kāpi rāga*, and *rīthigowḷa rāga*. After this, the *tavil* set to the *miśra gati* (beat) will be followed by the *nādasvaram* in the *kalyāṇī rāgam*. After this a *kṛti* in *sāma rāga* and a *padam* in *āhiri rāgam* have to be played. In the second round the *Cinna Meḷam* should be played and in the third and final round hymns from the *Tirumuṟai* should be played. Nowadays, music concerts are performed by eminent artistes instead of these traditions.

Tiruthuraipūṇḍi (Near Tiruvārūr)

In Tiruthuraipūṇḍi where we find the *pañcamukha vādyam* the rituals are followed strictly according to the Āgamas. There are five *pūjā*s for the main deity Piravimarundīśvarasvāmi. Everyday the following instruments are played four times a day: the *mattalam, nādasvaram* and *tāḷam*. Every night at 8 the percussion instrument *lavandai* is played and at 9 p.m. the *thirucinnam* is played. The yearly festivals are the 15-day festival during the Citira Month (April-May) and during this festival on the fifteenth day the Deity goes on the *Ṛṣabha vāhanam*. Thousands and thousands of devotees assemble to get a glimpse of the deity's feet. And the *pañcamukha vādyam* is played in the presence of the presiding deity honouring Him. Each day (15 days) the deity goes on different *vāhanam*s and in the evenings there is a lot of music. *Tevāram*s concerts, music concerts, Veda chanting, etc. are done with great pomp and grandeur.

The Navarātri festival for Goddess Periya Nāyaki Thāyār is also observed in a big way with dance and music. The Ādhirai festival for Candra Cūdāmaṇi Thāṇḍavar (deity of the temple) and Ṣaṣṭi festival for Lord Murugan are other important festivals of this temple. In this temple the *nādasvaram* and *mattalam* artistes have been playing for more than five generations.

Oppiliappan Temple

It is one of the very important 108 holy Vaiṣṇavite temples sung by the Āḻvārs. Suprabhātam in Sanskrit (symbolically waking up the Lord in the morning) was composed for this temple several centuries ago. Every month Śrāvaṇam day is very important in this temple and thousands of devotees gather to worship the Lord. Nārāyaṇa manifested here on the Śravaṇam day in the month of Paṅguni (March-April). Viśvarūpa *sevā* in this temple is very popular. Lord Oppiliappan married Bhūmi Devī on the day of Śrāvaṇa in the Tamil month of Aippasi (October-November). To celebrate this event, every year a twelve-day music and dance festival is held commencing with the Tirukalyāṇam (holy wedding of the Lord with his consort). There is no separate shrine here for the Goddess. She sits with the Lord in the main sanctum. Lord Oppiliappan is never taken outside the temple without his consort. All the food offered to the Lord at the temple are made without salt. Salt in any form or food item is not allowed to be taken beyond the sanctum of Garuḍa. *Pūjā*s are performed six times according to the Āgama Śāstras. Starting with the Viśvarūpadarśana when the *Suprabhātam* is recited, it continues to the singing of *Tiruppāvai* and Vedapārāyaṇam. Every night the *Divya Prabandham* and the *Vedapārāyaṇam* are chanted. Besides the Tirukalyāṇam, the other annual festivals are the *Panguni Brahmotsavam* and the float festival in the tamil month of Thai (January-February). Śrī Rāmanavamī is celebrated for 10 days with a lot of music and dance events. On the concluding day Kanakābhiṣekam and Rāma Paṭṭābhiṣekam are conducted.

Other Festivals

Vaikasi (May-June)	—	*Vasantotsavam* for 6 days concluding on the Śrāvaṇam day.
Āvaṇi (August-September)	—	*Pavitrotsavam* for 5 days
Purattāsi (Sept.-Oct.)	—	*Brahmotsavam* for 9 days. Small chariot drawn on the last day is called *go-ratham*.

Mārgaḻi (December-January)— *Adhyayana Utsavam* for 10 days and 10 nights +2 days. (Pagalpatthu Rāppatthu)

Festivals of the Tirunangur Divyadesams (12 of 108 Tirupatis)

TIRUMAṄGAI ĀḺVĀR MAṄGAḶAŚĀSANA UTSAVAM AND GARUḌA SEVAI MAHOTSAVAM

This festival is dedicated to 11 gods every year for 3 days. The idols are taken on Garuḍa. *Maṅgaḷaśāsanam* stands for praying for the welfare of all beings. While people usually approach God requesting personal favours, great *ācāryas* worship for the well-being of God Himself and all the other beings. These great savants — the Āḻvārs — were people who went to Him and sang *pallāṇḍu* (live for many more years). Hence their prayers came to be known as *maṅgaḷaśāsanam*. The greatest among them was that of Periāḻvār. But Tirumaṅgai Āḻvār had visited all the Divya Deśams (108 Tirupatis) and was one up on the other Āḻvārs. He was also given the title *Nalu-kavi Perumāḷ*. He was always travelling and singing the praise of the Lord. Even today he is taken around these 12 shrines known as the Tirunāṅgur Divya Deśams on Thai Amāvāsai (new moon).

On this day, Tirumaṅgai Āḻvār leaves early in the morning. He is given a holy turmeric bath in the Kāverī before he sets out on his journey. All the 11 deities are brought to Tirunāṅgur Nārāyaṇa Perumāḷ temple (the twelfth temple). Tirumaṅgai Āḻvār is taken before each god. The first *Pāsurams* of each deity is sung after which he is honoured with the *parivattam* and the *prasādam*. The honours are supposed to be received from Manavāḷa Māmunigaḷ — the *ācārya* of the *āḻvārs*). This event is celebrated in the month of Thai (Jan-Feb.).

Tirunāṅgūr is situated between Sīrkaḻi and Tirukaḍayūr. Temples that participate are as follows:

- Sīrkaḻi
- Tiruveḷḷakuḷam
- Tirunāṅgūr
- Tirumenikūḍam

- Kīḻcālaī
- Tiruvāḷi
- Kavalambāḍi
- Tirunagari
- Tirukuraiyalūr (Tirumaṅgai Āḻvār's birthplace)
- Pārthanpaḷḷi
- Talaichaṅgāḍu
- Maṅgaimaḍom

All the temples are accessible from Sirkaḻi and lies within a 40 km radius.

Nine Important Temples of Ceṭṭināḍ (also referred to as Tirupati) and Kundrakuḍi

- Velanguḍi
- Iranikovil
- Ilayāthanguḍi
- Surakuḍi
- Māthūr
- Nemam
- Illupakuḍi
- Vairavanpaṭṭi
- Piḷḷayārpaṭṭi

All these temples are old and conduct various annual and monthly festivals. The most important among them is Piḷḷayār-paṭṭi. The 6 ft idol of Lord Gaṇeśa had his tusk on the right side. He has two hands instead of four with the *modakam* in the right hand. The story goes that when Gaṇeśa killed Gajamukhāsura, he prayed to Lord Śiva at this place. Vināyaka Caturthī celebration here goes on for 10 days. He is taken outside on different *vāhana*s every day accompanied by music and dance. Among these temples, Iranikovil, Illupaikuḍi kovil and Vairavanpaṭṭi koil, built around seventh century by the Pāṇḍya kings are famous for the sculptural works.

Kundrakuḍi is in Sivaganga district, about 10 km from Kāraikuḍi railway station. The hillock on which the temple is built is about 40 m high. The temple has two parts Malaikovil and Kīḻkovil (hill temple and hill-bottom temple). The main deity is Lord Murugan and the major festivals are Taipūsam and Paṅguni Uttiram each last for 10 days.

18

Centres that Promoted Temple Art Forms

It is said that the soul of a nation is enshrined in its temple, in its literature and in its arts. All the three have been belived to be born from God, and are highly venerated in our land. Fine arts in India have always been looked upon as things divine and have all along been used as a vehicle for spiritual pursuits. Music apart from its aesthetic appeal was viewed by the ancient sages as conducive to heavenly bliss, the *parokṣa* and *aparokṣa* knowledge. That *saṅgīta* is a means to the triple concentration of mind, body and speech, a *sādhanā* to spiritual realization, has been unanimously extolled by poets, philosophers and saints. The *saptasvara*s have been held in such veneration that they are considered not only equal to *mantra bījākṣara*s but are also the very abodes of Goddess and aid in the attaintment of *mokṣa*. The basic sound *auṁ* has been adored in India as *nādabrahma* or the manifestation of the Lord. Of the two aspects of God namely, the abstract or the *nādamaya rūpa,* and the concrete or *Devatāmaya rūpa,* the Vāgeyakkāras composers worship the former form in their songs.

Tanjāvūr

If south India is considered a huge temple of learning, Tanjāvūr may well be identified as the *sanctum sanctorum* radiating spiritual and cultural inspiration. The temple, which arose as a symbolic representation of the religious faith and devotion of the people necessarily included the cultural adjuncts. The fine arts found their highest form of expression in the temple and grew as handmaids to religion and religious worship. Tanjāvūr has been famous as the motherland of many a sterling devotee, saint composer, philosopher, scholar, proficient in many branches of learning, *Bhāgavatas*, illustrious musicians and dancers. Tanjāvūr has all along been the stronghold of Hinduism since the period of Coḷa imperialism. The long line of pious and accomplished rulers who were noted for their liberal patronage, a living tradition of the devotional music of *Tevāram* and *Prabandhans*. The dance and dramas in temples, the rise of saintly souls, saint composers and musicians, the spiritual influences of the temple and its annual festivals have contributed to the accumulated cultural wisdom of Tanjāvūr which grew to be a centre of devotional music and dance in south India. The devotional music of Tanjāvūr may be dealt with under the following headings:

I. Temples as promoting centres of musical learning and

II. The religious institutions such as *Bhajana Harikathā* and their contribution to the devotional music of south India.

Temples as Centres Promoting Music Traditions

With the development of the *bhakti* movement in the seventh and eighth centuries in south India, the great Coḷas who were devotees of Lord Śiva studded the land with temples and endowed richly with land and wealth for the perpetual conduct of religious worship. The historic Bṛhadīśvara temple at Tanjāvūr is symbolic of the cultural wealth of the whole of south India. The temple came to dominate Tanjāvūr as Tanjāvūr dominated the rest of south India. It grew to be not only a place of worship but also a cultural centre with regular establishment of *odhuvars*, *araiyars*, dancers, instrumentalists, musicians, sculptors and painters. Singing of *Tevāram* hymns, *Tirupallāṇḍu*, *Tiruvāimoḷi*, *Divyaprabandham*, performance of *Kuravañji nāṭakam*, musical plays and dance formed an integral part of daily worship in the temples, and this fact has been attested by the evidence of inscriptions and documentary evidences dating from Coḷa period. The Nāyaks were great *bhaktas* of Lord Raṅganātha of Śrīraṅgam and Rājagopāla Svāmi of Mannārguḍi, while the Marāṭhās were well known for their devotion to Lord Tyāgarāja of Tiruvārūr. The devotional music forms such as *Tevāram, Divyaprabandham, Lālī, ūñjal, Saraṇu, Hecarika* and *Mallāri* tunes, the *Raktthi meḷam, Kavutthuvam* and the *Sthala kīrtanas* constitute the live music of temples and are still sung at specific time of worship. The *navasandhi* and *Pañcamūrti Kavutthuvams* are sacred dance items performed regularly during the *Brahmotsavam* festivals. The *Mallāri* music of the *nādasvaram* usually sung in the tune of the *nāṭṭai* has its unique structure and significance. Usually the *Mallāri* will be played to mark the different stages of worship in temples as such. At the beginning of the procession called *Puṛappāḍu* these tunes are played regularly by the *nādasvaram* players. The music of *Mallāri* indicated the commencement of the particular worship in the temple. It is said that it was Rāmasvāmi Dīkṣitar who systematized the *Mallāri*, which is now being performed at Tiruvārūr. The *pāri nāyanam*, which is the pride of Tiruvārūr temple, is played during particular occasions. The contribution of the temples in the preservation and development of music and dance may be dealt with under the following general headings:

I. The *Sthala kīrtana*s or musical compostions in praise of the presiding deities of the various shrines (*kṣetras*) were composed by great *vāggeyakāra*s (composers) who were devout *bhakta*s of the Lord. These are of two kinds:

   a. *Group kīrtana*s: Usually these are a set of 5, 7, 9, 12 and 16 *kīrtana*s in praise of a particular deity of a shrine. They represent a garland of songs in which each song forms a unit in the chain.

   b. *Kīrtana*s in praise of the presiding deities, *iṣṭa devatā*s, gods and goddesses of the various shrines.

II. Musical plays like dance dramas, *Kuravañji nāṭakam* and others that were enacted during particular temple festivals.

III. Ritualistic music and music peculiar to various temples (*navasandhi kavutthuvam, sarva vādyam*)

IV. The musical instruments belonging to the stringed wind and percussion group that are used in music of particular temples, e.g. the *pañcamukha vādyam, pāri nāyanam* and *śuddha mattalam*.

The Sthala Kīrtanas

The great *vāggeyakāra*s who were God-intoxicated men of

extraordinary ability and transcendental experience considered music as a handmaid of religion, and a path to realization. They undertook extensive research and pilgrimage to various shrines and have sung soulful pieces invoking *bhakti* towards the presiding deities. These are called the *kṣetra kīrtana*s or *sthala kīrtana*s. These compositions form an enriching part of our repertoire on *bhakti*. The *kīrtana*s describe the greatness of the *sthala* in its historical and spiritual aspects. Information pertaining to the name of the presiding deity, the *sthala vṛkṣa*, the *puṣkariṇī*, the festivals, the special *pūjā*s if any, and the music and dance of that particular temple or area. The Śaivaite and Vaiṣṇavite saints of south India have adopted the practise of offering worship to the same deity through a garland of fixed number of songs. Almost every temple in south India has been sung upon by the *Tevāraka*s and they are known as *Pāḍal Petra Sthalaṅgal*. The *kṣetra kīrtana*s of some of our great *vāgeyakāra*s may be dealt with. Of the Trinity, Śrī Muthusvāmi Dikṣithar has to his credit a large number of group *kīrtana*s. The opening line of authorities of the *sāhitya* of the *pallavī* section of the songs with the *rāgam* and *tāḷa* are given with notations.

Music and Dance in Temple Festivals

The festivals connected with temples such as the *saptasthānam* festival at Tiruvaiyāru and the annual *Brahmotsava*s had special musical and dance items of worship. The temple festivals attracted a continuous stream of devotees from far and wide to participate in the spiritual and aesthetic experience. It was the thrilling sight of the procession of Lord Raṅganātha at Śrīraṅgam during the annual festival that inspired Śrī Tyāgarāja to compose songs in praise of Lord Raṅganātha mentioned earlier. Music, dance and drama found their highest expression in the presence of the deity taken out in procession. The music of the *nādasvaram* invariably marks the commencement of the festivals. In fact the *Periyameḷam* constituting the players on *nādasvaram* and *thavil* was the highlight. Originally the *Muddirasaṅghu* accompanied the *Periyameḷam*. Experts play the suitable *solkaṭṭus* on it. The deity in procession followed by *odhuvār*s, reciting the *Tevāram* hymns and the row of dancers performing the classical Bharatanāṭyam must have been a thrilling experience that inspired many a saint composer and a devotee. Folk dances and music such as *bommalāṭṭam* (puppetry), dummy horse shows and pantomime gave fresh significance to the occasions. Dramatic shows were represented in the temple on sacred themes such as *Manmatha Nāṭakam, Aḻagar Kuravañji, Tyāgeśa Kuravañji* and *Kumbheśvarar Kuravañji.* These were noted for the fine music, representative of the golden age of music. The music of *nādasvaram* heard over long distances heralded the sacredness of the temple and at the same time served to carry the thoughts towards the divine. The copperplate record of the eighth century CE, which has been recently discovered in the Nāgeśvara Svāmi temple at Kumbakoṇam, records a grant by the Nāgapāśa community towards the establishment of *Periyameḷam, Cinnameḷam, Vīṇākkarāram, nattumuttu* and others in the Kumbakoṇam temple. The copperplate is highly valuable as the figures of more than 30 musical instruments are engraved on it. These comprise seven varieties of stringed and percussion instruments, and nine kinds of wind instruments which include the *ekkāḷam* and *nādasvaram*. Other works like *Karaṇāgamam* and *Mahābhārata Cūḍāmaṇi* mention various musical instruments used in the temple music and in all these nādasvaram finds a honourable place.

Bṛhadīśvara Temple — Tanjāvūr

Tanjāvūr has become very famous since the time of the Imperial Coḷas and known as the seat of culture. Tanjāvūr became famous during the reign of Rājarāja Coḷa I and his grandson. Rājarāja I ruled during the period CE 985 to 1013. He built the magnificent temple called the Rājarājeśvaram, now known as the Bṛhadīśvara temple.

Festival Days

Every month the day of the ruling star *Sadayam* is treated of importance as that was the ruling star at the time of the Rājarāja's birth. The other festival is the Kṛttikā day in the month of Kārthikai. The annual festival is for 9 days celebrated in the month of Viśākha during which the drama of Rājarājeśvara is also enacted. Other festivals include *Pradoṣams* in Kārthikai and Aippasi. Last Fridays of Paṅguni and Āḍi months are celebrated. The deity is taken around accompanied by *Mallāri* played by the *nādasvaram*. Though a number of compositions were written during those times in praise of the deity, as a rule, only songs composed by Karuvur Tevar during the year CE 1112 are sung in the morning and in the night. The singers are known as *sevakarthās*. The *rāgams* for all these songs have been set to tune by Karuvur Tevar himself. During the days of Rājarāja Coḷa, the temple administrative officer got statues of Rājarāja Coḷa and his wife Lokamādevī made and presented them to the temple. After their death, they were installed in the temple and worshipped by all his people. These two statues were shifted to the Gautam Sarabhai Museum at Ahmedabad.

Daily Rituals

In the morning, *rāgams śuddha danyāsi* and *śrīrāgam* are played on the *nādasvaram*. Afternoon, *madhyamavatī* is played. In the evening at 5.30 *ṣaṇmugapriya* and *kalyāṇī* are played. Every night at 8.30, the presiding deity Bṛhadīśvara is brought to the *Paḷḷiaṟai* (sleeping chamber) of his consort Bṛhannāyakī in a *pallākku* (palanquin). This is done accompanied by *nādasvaram*. *Sevārthī* sings a couple of songs composed by Karuvur Tevar.

Tiruvaiyārū

The land of Tiruvaiyārū is cherished by all lovers of music. Surrounded by five rivers, groves and fields, resounding with the sound of the Vedic incantations and the divine call of the temple, the people who were intensely musical and spiritual, led a simple and *dhārmika* life here. Sanctified with the footsteps of the Śaivate and Vaiṣṇavite saints who worshipped the deities with garlands of devotional songs, this place has the hallowed lustre of being associated with the trinity of music.

Tiruvaiyārū is the 61st first among the 276 Śaiva shrines sung by the 63 Nāyaṉmārs. There are six important Śiva shrines that are equivalent to Kāśī. They are Tiruvāñjiyam, Tiruveṅkāḍu, Tirumayilāḍuturai, Tiruviḍaimaruḍūr, Triucaykāḍu and Tiruvaiyārū, which come foremost among these. Most important festival observed in the Tiruvaiyar temple is the Eḻūr Viḻā (festival of seven villages) that happens in the month of April. During this festival, the main deity along with his consort is taken in a glass palanquin to Tirupaḻanam,

Tirusotrututurai, Tiruvedikuḍi, Tirukaṇḍiyūr, Tirupūnthuruthi and Tiruneythānam. The festival is also known as the wedding procession of Nandithevar. Among many great devotees who have witnessed the event and walked with the deity, one was Tyāgarāja Svāmigaḷ who has composed nine *kṛti*s on this deity.

The *saptasthāna* music festival held at Tiruvaiyārū is not only of religious but also of musical significance. The seven sacred shrines in the Tanjāvūr district namely Tiruvaiyāru, Tirupaḻanam, Tirucoṟṟuturai, Tiruvedikkuḍi, Tirukkaṇḍiyūr, Tiruppūntururuti and Tillaisthānam are considered as representatives of the seven manifestations of God. The same have been conceived in the body of the human being as the seven *cakra*s or the principal seats of *nāda* (sound). The concept of *saptasthāna* according to the tāntric interpretation represents the seven sound manifestations of the fundamental *praṇava oṁkāra* as *akāra, ukāra, makāra, ardha mātrā, nāda, bindu* and *unmani.* The respective deities join the presiding deity of the shrine of Tiruvaiyārū in its procession to the other six *kṣetra*s and finally all of them are brought to Tiruvaiyārū, which is also called *amānasika kṣetra*. Śiva is said to have offered *pūjā* to the *liṅga* in the guise of an *ācārya* in this place known as *Jīvanmuktipura* in *Brahmavaivarta Purāṇa*. A number of compositions from the *vāggeyakāra*s invoking the presiding deity of Tiruvaiyārū are available. In the *saptasthāna* festival, music and *bhajana* parties accompany the procession of the Lord. It's said that Saint Tyāgarāja used to lead the *uñcāvṛitti bhajana* groups during that occasion. Famous musicians like Paṭṭanam Subramanya Iyer, Mahāvaidhyanātha Iyer and other Bhāgavatas participated in this function. The beautifully decorated palanquins carrying the deities must have inspired Sahāji to compose the *Śaṅkara Pallaki Sevā Prabandham* wherein the realistic description of the palanquin has been depicted by the royal composer (*Śaṅkarabharaṇa rāgam* song *Siṅgārapallakī*).

What began as a Veda Pāṭhaśālā by the Sarabhoji Mahārāja long ago, is the Tiruvaiyārū Music College that promotes various fine arts today.

On the occasion of the *Brahmotsava,* in the Tanjāvūr Big temple, the *Sarabendra Bhūpāla Kuravañji Nāṭakam* was enacted regularly. Evidence from records point out the enactment of Rajarājeśvara Nāṭaka in the same temple. The singing of *Tiruvisaippa* of Saint Karuvur Devar has been considered a special feature in this temple at Tanjāvūr. There is a special dance platform facing the Naṭarāja shrine for the purpose of holding such items. During the occasion of Aṣṭakkoḍi workshop the dancing girls attached to the temple perform certain dances in a group before the shrine of the goddess.

Ritualistic music and dance of temples occupy a dignified place in the history of a country's music. The role of music, dance and drama in the annual festivals of the temple is precious and testifies to the religious significance.

Religious Discourses

Before the advent of *Harikathā* as an art form of disseminating spiritual knowledge there were in prevalence in the past, the *purāṇa paṭhanam* and *Harikathā ālāpana* or the religious expositions by the priest or the religious head in the temple *prākāra*s, *bhajana maṇḍapa*s, *maṭha*s and other sacred places of worship. References to *granthika*s and *purāṇapaṭhanam*, recitation of *Tevāram* and religious exposition, *ākhyāyāna* are available in epigraphs dated as early as the tenth century CE. These were philosophical and religious discourses intended to uplift the masses to a higher spiritual level. Bhoja in his *Śṛṅgāra Prakāśa* defines *ākhyāyana* as an exposition of a mythological story with music and dance. The reference to Kathaka's art is also useful as it is to this form of religious instruction that the *Kathā Kalākṣepa* is to be traced. Kālakṣepa is literally spending time. A happy blend of philosophy, poetry, music and *abhinaya* became Harikathā in later days. It was from *kīrtana* form that south Indian music made more impact on Harikathā. The Maharashtra *bhajana*s were a regular feature in the various *maṭha*s established by the pioneering missionary work of Maharashtra saints. The people of Tañjāvūr attended these in large numbers. The devotional songs were *pada*s, *abhaṅga*s, *pañcapadī*, *ovi*, *dhindi*, *sākhī*, etc. The south Indian *bhajana* tradition was nourished in Tanjāvūr in Marudanallūr, Kumbakoṇam, Varahūr and Govindapuram. Śrī Tyāgarāja conducted *ūñcavṛtti bhajana*s and *cāturmāsya bhajanas* with longing devotion. For this purpose he composed the *divya nāma saṅkīrtanas* and *utsava sampradāya kīrtanas* and *heccarikas*. With the advent of Marāṭhā rule in Tanjāvūr and due influence of famous saints Sadaśiva Brahmendra and Bodendral, the Marāṭhā *kīrtana* in Tanjāvūr was made possible. The modern day *bhajana* repertoire extends to *Bhadrācala* Rāmadāsa, Tāḷapakkam composers, Nāmadeva, Tukārāma, Śrī Purandaradāsa, Peddadasari, Mīrābāī, Jayadeva, Nārāyaṇa Tīrtha and a number of *nāmāvaḷīs*.

Tirukogarṇam

Situated 2 km from Pudukkoṭṭai town, this temple is more than a thousand years old. Pudukkoṭṭai district contributed a number of artistes in the field of music and drama. This place used to be a centre of a lot of cultural activities. The temple at Tirugokarṇam attracted large number of devotees right through the year. It had a unique music tradition where *Tavil* without the *nādasvaram* was played for the presiding deity Goddess Bṛhannāyakī. *Vīṇā* was the main instrument and was played every morning and evening. Sadly, the temple is deserted today and there are no musical instruments played for want of funds. The temple car that was once used during festivals was found in a dilapidated state, not very different from the temple itself. Āḍi Pūram and Cittirai are the only festivals observed. Again these are conducted with no fanfare. During the 10-day celebration of Āḍi Pūram, the Goddess is taken to the temple tank everyday for a *pūjā*. The Goddess is taken to each of the 7 *maṇḍapams* on 7 different days. The music rituals have stopped ovet the last 10 years.

Śrīraṅgam

Śrīraṅgam is a small town on the outskirts of Tiruccirāpaḷḷi town. This town attracts millions of pilgrims all the year round, in particular the Vaiṣṇavite devotees. The congregation of pilgrims becomes unprecedented during the main festival of *Vaikuṇṭha Ekādasī* that falls in the Tamil month of Mārgaḷi corresponding to December-January. The festival continues for a period of 30 days. Śrīraṅgam is spoken of as a paradise on earth (Bhūloka Vaikuṇṭham). Some festival or the other takes place throughout the year. The idol of Śrī Raṅganātha (the presiding deity) is very impressive and one who worships Him is believed to get all his desires fulfilled and attains *mokṣa*. This temple-complex was considerably expanded during the period of the Coḷas and Pāṇḍyas and was patronized by the Hoysaḷas, and the Vijayanagar kings and all these kings have patronized and developed this temple during different periods and contributed to the richness of its architecture in some way or the other. This is the most important among the 108 Divya Deśams (sung and glorified by the 12 Āḻvārs in their *Nālāyira Divya Prabandham*) of the Vaiṣṇavites. There are 21 *gopurams* (entrance towers or gateways) in the temple spread over an area of 156 acres. The temple is so big that a stranger who enters it without a guide cannot find his way out. One of the kings of the south who undertook the construction of the *maṇḍapam* with 1000 pillars was attacked and defeated by his enemy when the work was in progress. So the *maṇḍapam* was left incomplete. There are only 936 pillars now. The images are carved out on these pillars and attract attention and reveal the remarkable talents of the sculptors of those days.

Music Rituals at Śrīraṅgam

DURING REGULAR DAYS

In the early mornings, Viśvarūpa Darśanam takes place. After waking up the Lord in the morning, the *abhiṣekams* are done and the *vīṇā* is played. The *Pāsurams* are played on the *vīṇā* for one hour and a few Tyāgarāja *kṛtis* are included. A horse, a cow and an elephant are brought in as a part of the ritual to witness the *abhiṣekam*. As the concluding part of the ritual, the elephant trumpets thrice calling out to Śrī Raṅganātha as Raṅga . . . Raṅga . . . Raṅga. . . .

There is a regular playing of the *nādasvaram* in the morning between 7.30 a.m. and 8.45 a.m., in the afternoon and in the evening. During the month of Mārgaḻi, i.e. 15 Dec. – 14 Jan. the *Pagal Patthu* is sung along with a 10-day festival *Araiyar Sevai*. For all the 10 days *Irapatthu* is sung before the public commencing on the *Vaikuṇṭha Ekādaśī* day.

On all the 10 nights there is a special music tradition called the *Ekānta Sevai* when six artistes play the *vīṇā* and walk along with the *utsavamūrti* around the temple. The devotees are allowed to walk along with the deity and the *vīṇā* players, till they reach the *sanctum sanctorum*. After this the *vīṇā* players play for some more time and disperse. Very small children are not allowed and one is allowed only against a paid ticket for this crowd-restricted programme.

Kuttrālam and Tenkāsi

Kuttrālam is a famous Śiva shrine in the western part of Tirunelveli. It is also a popular health resort famous for its waterfalls. The temple is dedicated to Śrī Tirukkutrālanāthar. The Śaiva saints Tirunāvukarasar, Māṇikkavācagar and Paṭṭinathār have poured forth their feelings of spiritual ecstasy in soul stirring lyrics. Inside the temple there are three shrines. Three major festivals of ten days each are celebrated in a year. Cittirai festival is celebrated during 14 April – 14 May and Aippasi festival is celebrated during October-November.

The most important festival that is celebrated during Mārgaḻi (December) is the Ārudra day. *Tāṇḍava Dīpārādhanā* representing the cosmic dance of the Supreme Being is offered on this day. The temple contains many inscriptions relating to Coḷa and Pāṇḍya kings and their varied services between the tenth and fifteenth centuries. The name Kuttrālam is derived from the word *kuttrāl,* the name of a forest tree under whose refreshing shades God is said to have seated Himself in the company of His consort. Tenkāsi is within one km of the Kuttrālam temple. Dedicated to Lord Naṭarāja, Kuttralam is one of the five *sabhā*s where Lord Naṭarāja is dancing the Cosmic Dance (celestial dance) candour. Nearby is the Kūthanār temple said to be the predecessor of the present main temple. Here again the *Ārudra Darśanam* is observed in the month of Mārgaḻi. The Tāṇḍava Dīpārādhanā is a beautiful ritualistic dance performed by the *arcaka* (priest) with a lit up lamp in his hands to the accompaniment of the music of the *nādasvaram* and percussion. The *dīpam* (lamp) is called the *aḍukku dīpam* that contains 108 wicks all burning simultaneously.

Tiruvārūr

Tiruvārūr is one of the seven sacred places of Lord Tyāgarāja. It is a great pilgrim centre, throughout the year, particularly in the month of

Cittirai (April-May) when the most important festival, the annual festival of Lord Tyāgarāja is performed. It has been the most important centre in south India of music and dance culture and of temple arts in particular. The temple which is gigantic in structure is visible from a distance of several miles.

The colossal structure of the temple can be well imagined from its length of 846 ft with breadth of 666 ft. On the western side of the temple there is a famous tank known as Kamalālayam where Goddess Kamalā (Lakṣmī) took her birth. It is considered as the biggest temple tank in the whole of India. To be born in Tiruvārūr is *mukti* — so they say of this old city, which is rich in arts and culture. The Trinity — Tyāgarāja, Dīkṣitar and Śyāma Śāstrī — were all born here. One of the oldest temples, the Tyāgarājasvami temple, generously endowed by the Coḷa kings, is situated in the heart of the city. The beautiful temple tank, the thousand monolithic pillars, the granite stone chariot and the gigantic wooden temple car speak volumes of the glorious rich culture that was and the rich legacy of Tamil Nadu.

The great composer Muthusvāmi Dikṣitar has left sets of *kṛti*s on several deities of the Tiruvārūr temple — twelve *kṛti*s on Śrī Tyāgarāja (presiding deity), nine *kṛti*s on Goddess Kamalāmbāḷ, nine *kṛti*s on Goddess Nīlotpalāmbāḷ, nine *kṛti*s in praise of the nine planets (*navagraha*), 16 *kṛti*s in praise of the Gaṇapatis (all from the same temple) and 5 *kṛti*s on the 5 *liṅgams* found within the same temple. The most unique and important fact about Tiruvārūr is that the introduction of playing the *nādasvaram* in the temple as a ritual started here. Legend has it that Tiruvārūr temple is the oldest among all the temples and was built by heavenly beings and not by any king. The divine *nādasvaram* also is supposed to have originated from here. Tiruturaipūṇḍi, not very far from Tiruvārūr is the only other temple where the *pañca mukha vādyam* is played.

The Naṭarāja Temple of Cidambaram

The famous Naṭarāja temple is situated at Cidambaram which is on the main railway line from Chennai to Tanjāvūr at a distance of 132 miles from Chennai. This temple is also known as Ponnambalam and

Tillai. In this temple Śiva is seen in the dancing posture of *ānanda tāṇḍavam*. Naṭarāja is supposed to have performed the *ānanda tāṇḍavam*, i.e. the dance of bliss, in the presence of His consort Śivakāmasundarī (the presiding goddess of the temple) and all the gods and *ṛṣis* and the two devotees, Patañjali and Vyāgrahpāda, who were allowed to witness it. Cittsabhai is the innermost portion of the temple, the *sanctum sanctorum*. This is the place where Lord Śiva performed His cosmic dance. The whole figure stands on a lotus referred to in connection with the *kuṇḍalini śakti*. Thus the dance represents all the fivefold acts of God. The form of the Lord can be described as the synthesis of religion, science and art. The Lord is represented here with His left leg raised up in a dance pose (in all temples of the south, where Naṭarāja's idol is worshipped, the left leg is found to be lifted in dancing posture, but there is an exception to this at Madurai where the right leg is lifted).

Cidambaram is a modest township located in Tamil country on the Coromandel Coast, north of the delta of the Cauvery river. With no mountains, not even a hill to block its horizon there stand alone the monumental towers of its temple, a major axis of Śaivism and the main sanctuary devoted to Śiva Naṭarāja, master of the cosmic dance. This edifice where gods of the Śiva pantheon live together in harmony with a few figures of Vaiṣṇavism today covers 13 ha in the city centre at it heart. Naṭarāja himself cohabits with Govindarāja (Viṣṇu). Rituals overlap without any problem but not without a certain detachment from each other: Vaiṣṇavite priests are almost systematically absent from Śaiva solemnities. The temple's history marked by schisms no doubt helps to explain these minor breaches of affection: the icon of Viṣṇu for example was thrown into the sea in 1127 on the orders of King Kulottuṅga Coḷa II and only rehabilitated in 1539 during the reign of Kṛṣṇadeva Rāya, sovereign of Vijayanagara. But beneath the golden dome of the principal sanctuary, the cult of Naṭarāja has always been practised. Rituals take place regularly and without interruption like an activity necessary to the equilibrium of the phenomenal world.

Naṭarāja appears here in three equally venerated forms: an anthropomorphic statue, a stone *liṅgam* — the phallic symbol of Śiva

— and an invisible *liṅgam* unable to be represented constituting the first of the five elements called *ākāśa* in classical philosophies and conventionally translated as "ether." This element, unlimited, empty and formless, is thought to be consubstantial with the temple of Cidambara, the cosmological brother of the temples of Kāḷahasti, Tiruvaṇṇāmalai, Tiruvānaikāval and Kāñcīpuram where the *liṅgams* symbolize air, fire, water and earth respectively. Just like the five elements of earth these five temples are supposed to have been born from primal matter *prakṛti* and constitute "the egg of *Brahman*" the universe in its totality.

Music Traditions in Cidambaram Temple

An interesting and perhaps unique feature of the Naṭarāja temple at Cidambaram is the system of management. The temple is controlled by a class of brāhmaṇas called Dīkṣitars, (Tillai Mūvāyiravar) whose ancestors came to Cidambaram from Antarvedi. They are the hereditary trustees of the temple, who since time immemorial, have been regulating temple activities along democratic lines. Private donations are what enable the temple to conserve its independence and its priests to preserve, as much as possible, their ritualistic traditions. The term "Dīkṣitar" itself means "he who makes oblations" and is usually applied to an exclusive group of brāhmaṇas learned in Vedic lore with a number of sacrifices (*yajña*) to their credit. Tamil literature confirms the antiquity of the *Dīkṣitars*. In the *Tevāram* hymns, one of the Śaivite saint-poets says, I am the servant and devotee of "Tillai Mūvayiravar." Sekkiḻār too, refers to the "Tillai-Vāḻ Anthaṇar." Apart from its great literary and religious background, few temples in south India have such a rich musical tradition as Cidambaram. Over the centuries, Naṭarāja has inspired devotional music of exceptionally high quality and some of the grandest forms of art have evolved around Lord Naṭarāja. The *Tevārams* and many literary works in Tamil, and the wealth of poetic literature that has been inspired by Cidambaram and Naṭarāja, are a remarkable proof of the hold of Naṭarāja and his cult on a succession of devotees over the ages. The impact on the tradition of Carnatic music and Bharatanāṭyam has been equally strong and notable. Of the Trinity of Carnatic Music, Muthusvāmi

Dīkṣitar (CE 1775–1834) is an honoured name. It is on record that Cidambaram was among the many sacred places Dīkṣitar visited in the course of his long pilgrimage in south India. In the holy precincts of the Citsabhā in Cidambaram, Dīkṣitar went into musical ecstasies, to the delight of his devotees who had collected at the temple at the time of his worship. Other composers who composed songs on Naṭarāja and Goddess Śivakāmī were Aruṇagirināthar (fifteenth century), Muthutāṇḍavar (sixth century), Tyagārāja (eighteen century), Muthusvami Dīkṣitar (eighteenth century), Śyāma Śāstrī (eighteenth century), Gopālakṛṣṇa Bhāratī (eighteenth century) and many other poets, musicians and composers, eternally sanctified, venerated by all Carnatic musicians have left hundreds of pieces recounting the life of the temple and its gods.

However, musicians of this temple are little known; they descend for the most part from a particular community destined to knowledge and not to service. Therefore unlike *Periyameḷam or Cinnameḷam* they did not participate in regular ritual activities, coming rather to the temple to express their devotion, sing or play out of regular hours. Many of them attached to the princely court were dependent on a patron. Only with the dawn of the twentieth century, and the disappearance of royal patronage, did musicians migrate little by little to towns, looking for new opportunities. Thus, the importance of the temple or palace court was lessened in favour of the concert hall, a new place, with a shorter and more concisely defined performance time. Music, however, underwent no significant changes apart from a progressive decline of improvized form in favour of written compositions. At the same time dance was leaving the temple for the stage, not without struggle. The musicians of the *Cinnameḷam*, seconded by those of the *devadāsī*, female dancers and musicians in the service of the cult, and the *naṭṭuvanār*, dance teachers, formed an autonomous ensemble. Like *Periyameḷam* musicians, their blood brothers, they were entirely devoted to the temple and participated fully in the rituals. A succession of decrees declared dancing in temple precincts forbidden. Dancers left the sanctuaries and active life in general; *sadir* dancing or *sadir āṭṭam* became Bharatanāṭyam dancing under pressure from the brāhmaṇa communities; the *mukhavīṇā* oboe was too loud for the stage hence replaced by the flute, and strictly ritual repertoire was abandoned.

It is no doubt in this moving back and forth from palace to temple from sanctuary to public places that *Periyameḷam* repertoire, immensely rich, unique, shared, inherited or borrowed is best explained. Each musical form, even each piece, can in fact come from different traditions. Strictly instrumental repertoire is in part specific to *Periyameḷam*. Only oboists and drummers in a temple context play *Mallāri* and *raktti meḷam*. *Rāgam* or *ālāpana* improvized preludes that permit an exposition of the mode are also played by professional Carnatic musicians; but the *rāgam*, elaborated for several hours during temple processions, remains the speciality of master oboists. Pieces, devotional songs for the most part, belong either to Carnatic repertoire, mainly forms like *kṛti* or *kirttanai*, *sampradāya kīrtana* and Tiruppugaḻ or to stage or ritual dance repertoire, to *ūñjal* for example in which the *nādasvaram* perpetuates the forgotten voices of the *devadāsī*. Beyond the Carnatic world, *Periyameḷam* borrows not only from temple hymn traditions like the *Prabandhams* of Vaiṣṇavites and *Tevāram* of Śaivites but also from popular traditions, like pilgrim or domestic songs. This so-called "art music" orchestra has no qualms about borrowing from popular music for specifically liturgical music, mixing genres, from the altar to the temple courtyard, from the home to the street-corner. The *Mallāri* — it has no name other than the *tāḷam* in which it is played — is played in front of the palanquin and the divine image before the procession gets underway. The *Mallāri* cannot be played in any mode other than *Gambhīra Nāṭṭai*, with its overtones of force and heroism, for it is meant to strengthen the palanquin-bearers with the energy necessary to carry out their task. No procession, whether a daily ritual or a temple pageant, can begin without playing *Mallāri* which explains its presence in the *Periyameḷam*. During the 11-day *Brahmotsava* of Cidambaram, Āchāḷpuram S. Chinnathambi Piḷḷai and his troupe perform nearly twenty distinct *Mallāri*s. No *Mallāri* can be repeated during this time. If from one piece to the other, a rhythmic cycle is identical, then the melodic line must change, in which case, both

Mallāri, though different, will be called similarly by the name of the cycle. Such rules, variable from one temple to another, mean that *Periyameḷam* musicians have to have mastered uncommon *tāḷam*, for example *khaṇḍa jātī tripuṭa tāḷam*, *saṅkīrna jātī jampa tāḷam*, or *saṅkīrna jātī tripuṭa tāḷam*. A *Mallāri* always begins with an *alārippu*, a rhythmic prelude sub-dividing the beat into five. Then comes the exposition of the mode, or *rāgam*, followed by the piece, first as a simple melodic theme, then developed according to a principle of rhythmic diminution and augmentation called *trikāla* (literally: three speeds). The *Mallāri* recorded here respects this kind of structure. Its melodic line is thought to have been composed by Cidambaram Rādhākr̥ṣṇa Piḷḷai, or borrowed by him from his teacher, Cidambaram Vaidyanāthan Piḷḷai. *Raktti meḷam*, unlike *Mallāri*, is always played in the same *tāḷam*: *miśra chāpu*; the mode however can change. This is an improvised form of which only one short melodic line is composed beforehand. The *Raktti meḷam* is more predominant in Tiruvārūr. *Raktti meḷam* is always played after *rāgams* are played elaborately during the deity's procession (*pur̥appāḍu*.) The Raktti *sampradāya* (tradition) also differs from temple to temple. The *vīdhi bhajana* sung during the early hours of the day led by the veteran *bhajana* artiste Rajah Bhāgavatar, was an inspiring part of the daily routine of Cidambaram many years ago. Rendering of compositions of *Tevāram* pieces and also popular compositions of Gopālakr̥ṣṇa Bhāratī, Muthu Tāṇḍavar and Pāpanāśam Śivan was a regular feature.

Religious festivals are celebrated with great pomp. The *Brahmotsava* of the Tamil months Mārgaḷi (15 December – 14 January) and Āṇi (June-July) lasts for eleven days when the images of Śiva, Pārvatī, and Murugan up front are paraded in imposing processions, solemnly winding down the four streets surrounding the temple. Whether these rites are simple or complex, the temple festivals have a definite, stratified structure. The ritual calendar is well known to devotees from all over India, who throng the temple to implore the blessings of the gods. During the festival nights of *Āṇi Tirumañjanam* and *Ārudra Darśanam* the temple *āsthāna nādasvaram* players play the *Mallāri* in *Nāṭṭai* when Naṭarāja and Śivakāma Sundarī are taken out in procession and finally after they offer *darśana* to thousands of devotees on their way back to the thousand-pillared *maṇḍapam Ārabhi* is the chosen *rāgam* that is played. The 11-day long *Āṇi Tirumañjanam* festival has been following the same pattern of music rituals for more than two hundred years.

Day 1	Haṁsadhvani or Śaṅkarābharaṇam *Rāgam*
Day 2	Rītigowḷa *Rāgam*
Day 3	Māyāmāḷavagowḷa or Pantuvarāḷi
Day 4	Cakravākam *Rāgam*
Day 5	Pañca *Rāgam* — The *Pañcaratna kṛtis* of Śrī Tyāgarāja
Day 6	Toḍī *Rāgam* or Ṣaṇmukapriya
Day 7	Varāḷi *Rāgam* or Kāmbhoji
Day 8	Nādanāmakriya *rāgam*
Day 9	Muthuthāṇḍavar *padam* in Devaghāndāri *rāgam*
Day 10	Muthuthāṇḍavar *padam* in Ārabhi *rāgam*

On the eleventh day (concluding day) the image of Naṭarāja is taken in the *pallaku* (palanquin) and the *rāgam* chosen for this occasion is *Useni* or *Bhairavī*. Six *pūjā*s are performed everyday — from the waking up of the Lord (Tirupalliyeḻuci) to the *Ardhajama pūjā* (when the lullaby is sung). The burning incense, the lighted camphor, the beat of the drums and the music of the cymbals, the chime of the majestic temple bell, the Oduvār's rendering of the *Tevāram* hymns and Naṭarāja's perfumed *vibhūti* — these create an atmosphere which is spiritually uplifting and emotionally satisfying. Each of the six daily *pūjā*s is inspiring — from the *pāl naivedyam* (offering of milk to the Lord when He wakes up in the morning) to the *ardhajāmapūjā* (when the lullaby is sung). At the end of each *pūjā*, the processionists complete their perambulation of the Kanaka *sabhā* and they round off the ceremonial music with the notation, *tat-tat-tagum*, rendered thrice. Therein lay the music, the mysticism and the majesty of Naṭarāja and His Cosmic Dance. Cidambaram takes one "to the very back of beyond, in point of time," to the blessed vision of Naṭarāja.

Kāñcīpuram

Conjeevaram is the English name of the ancient city, Kāñcīpuram. It is situated about 75 km from Chennai and is a district headquarters. Like all ancient cities which are located on the banks of rivers, Kāñcīpuram is also situated on the banks of the river Vegavatī. The city stands foremost among the seven ancient sacred cities of India. The history of Kāñcīpuram can be traced back to several centuries before the Christian era. The place finds its name in Patañjali's *Mahābhāṣya* written in the second century BCE. *Maṇimekalai*, the famous Tamil classic, and *Perumbānaṟṟu Paḍai* a great Tamil poetical work, vividly describe the city as it was at the beginning of the Christian era. From the fourth to the ninth century, Kāñcī was the capital of the Pallavas who ruled over the territory extending from the Kṛṣṇā river in the north to the Kāverī in the south. The Pallavas built a number of beautiful temples. Mahendravarman I, one of the most illustrious among the Pallava kings, was a great scholar and musician and also a playwright. Kāñcī is regarded as one of the three most important centres of Vaiṣṇavism, the others being Śrīraṅgam and Tirumalai (Tirupati). It is also regarded as one of the four Vaiṣṇavite centres in south India, with the addition of Tirunārāyaṇapuram in Mysore. Poigai Āḻvār, one of the first three Āḻvārs, was born here and Śrī Vedānta Deśika, the great Vaiṣṇava Ācārya was also born here. It is also said that six out of sixty-three Śaivite Nāyaṉmārs belonged to Toṇḍaimaṇḍalam of which Kāñcī was the capital. Kāñcī is popularly known as the Benares of the south. The Śaivite strong-hold is Big (Periya) Kāñcī and the Vaiṣṇavite stronghold is Little (Cinna) Kāñcī.

Kāñcīpuram is of great importance both to the Śaivaites and Vaiṣṇavites. 20 of the 108 Tirupatis are situated here. Śakti Pīṭham (the Kāmākṣī Amman Temple) and the Kumarakoṭṭam (Subrahmaṇya temple) are also here. The centre of attraction in Viṣṇu Kāñcī is the temple of Varadarāja Svāmi situated on the top of Hastagiri or Elephant Hill. One has to ascend 24 steps up the hill to reach the *sanctum sanctorum*. Lord Varadarāja is in standing posture facing towards the west with his gracious looks. The figure is huge in size with four hands holding the insignias of *śaṅkha, cakra* etc. — richly decorated with jewels. The Vijayanagara kings contributed to the architectural expansion of this temple. There are five *prākārams* around the temple, with high outer compound walls. The whole temple covers an area of about 23 acres. The four temples I visited to study the music traditions were the Varadarāja Svāmi temple, the Ekāmbareśvara temple, the Kāmākṣī Amman Temple and the Kumārakoṭṭam temple. *Nādasvaram* and drums play an important part in the Varadarāja Svāmi temple and the age-old tradition is followed during the daily *pūjās* as well as festivals. Eminent musicians are invited for festivals particularly for the *Āḍi Pūram* festival that is celebrated during July-August. The *nādasvaram* players strictly adhere to the Vaiṣṇava *sampradāyam*.

At the Kāmākṣī Amman temple, the nādasvaram has a set pattern everyday. The instrument is played thrice a day with the Oduvārs singing the *Tevāram* twice a day. During festivals the *nādasvaram* is played for a long time and outside artists are invited.

At the Ekāmbareśvara temple, the *nādsavaram* is played twice a day and the *Oduvār* sings the *Tevāram* twice a day.

The Kumārakoṭṭam temple is situated between Śrī Ekāmbareśvara Temple and the Kāmākṣī Amman temple. It is very auspicious to offer prayers every Tuesday and Kṛtikai in this temple. The two most important festivals celebrated in this temple are Skanda Ṣaṣṭhī immediately after Dīpāvaḷi in October-November and Vaikasi festival in April-May every year.

In this temple, the sacred *Kanda Purāṇam* written in praise of Lord Muruga by the saintly scholar Kaciappa Sivācāriar was first released.

The scholar-saint Aruṇagirināthar who authored the Tirupugaḷ has composed the Tirupugaḷ song Arivilāpitthar eulogizing Lord Muruga presiding over this temple. In this temple the *Tevāram* is sung four times a day while the *nādasvaram* is played thrice a day.

19

A few Important Centres to Visit

WITH all those who read this book I would like to share some information about some important centres or towns from where you can visit a number of temples mentioned in my book. Travelling to these places with some good planning can make your travel very simple, interesting and relaxing. Travelling by road or travelling by train and landing up in the centres mentioned and thereafter hiring cars is not only economical but also time saving and you can be sure that you can cover more of places this way. The travel should be planned out in such a way that you set your travel early in the morning and finish visits by 11 a.m. Between 11 a.m. and 4.30 p.m. almost all temples will be closed. This would be ideal time to plan the second half of the day's travel and visit more temples and get back to your room by 8 p.m.

In and around Chennai

You will find a number of temples in and around Chennai that are very old and personified by the savants.

1. Kapālīśvarar temple (around Kapālīśvara temple itself you will find six old temples) *Keśava Perumāḷ, Mādhava Perumāḷ, Virupakeśavara Perumāḷ, Valīsvara Perumāḷ, Muṇḍakannī Amman Perumāḷ, Kārnīśvara Perumāḷ.*
2. Gaṅgādīśvaran temple at Purasavalkam.
3. Kandasvāmi temple,
4. Kachalīśvarar Temple,
5. Kālikāmbaḷ temple,
6. Kr̥ṣṇa temple.

(Items 3–6:) In the broadway area

7. Tiruvoṟṟiyūr temple (10 km from central station).
8. Tiruvānmiyūr temple near Adyar.
9. Śrīperumbudūr temple,
10. Tirumaḻisai temple,
11. Tirumullaivāyil temple,
12. Tiruninṟavur temple,
13. Tirupāchūr temple,
14. Tiruvaḷḷur temple,
15. Tiruvālaṅgāḍu temple,
16. Virincipuram temple.

(9–16: All within 60 km from Chennai on the Bangalore Highway.)

17. Nityakalyāṇaperumāḷ temple,
18. Tirukaḻukuṉṟam temple,
19. Ceyyūr temple,
20. Tirunīrmalai temple.

(17–20: On the way to Mahābalipuram)

Kāñcīpuram

Nearly 100 temples in and around Kāñcīpuram can be visited in a couple of days.

Cidambaram

From Chennai to Cidambaram there are a lot of temples as you go on the East Coast Road like Mayilam, Tiruvendipuram, etc.

From Cidambaram to Kuṁbakoṇam again a number of temples can be covered like — Vaitīśvaran temple (Lord Vaitīśvaran is the eternal doctor as His name signifies and he is the healer of 4,448 diseases and people with chronic ailments come to Him and have a holy dip in the huge temple tank here) between Cidambaram and Sīrghāḻi, Kāṭṭumannār Kovil (the birth place of Nāthamunigal), Śrīmuṣnam, Tiruveṅgaḍu and Mayilāḍuthuṛai. From Mayilāḍuthuṛai to Kumbakoṇam there are nearly 30 temples and you can also visit the famous old town Pūmpuhār and the Tarangambāḍi Fort on the seashore (built by the Dutch and of historical importance where the war of Tranquibar was fought).

At Mayilāduthuṛai there are several temples and during the month of Aipasi (15 October – 14 November) a dip in the Kāverī is supposed to be very auspicious. The entire month is oberved as sacred for both known as the *Kaḍai muḻukku* on all thirty days and the *Muda muḻukku* in the month of Karthigai (15 Nov. – 14 Dec.). This is observed by both Vaiṣṇavites and Śaivites.

Tiruccirāpaḷḷi (Trichi)

At Tiruccirāpaḷḷi you have the Ucchi Piḷḷayār temple, the Śrīraṅgam temple, the Tiruvānaikaval temple, and within a very short distance, you have the very famous Samayapuram Māriamman temple, the Virāli Malai Murugan temple, The Vayalūr Murugan temple, Uraiyūr, Guṇaśīlam, Anbil, Lālguḍi Śiva temple, etc.

From Tiruccirāpaḷḷi it is less than two hours to Pudukkoṭṭai and from there you can visit Āvudayār kovil, Tirumayyam, Tirukogarṇam, etc. These places are also of archaeological importance. Āvuḍaiyar kovil is noted for its architecture and intricate sculptural work. It is one of the oldest temples and has also a very special place for Mānikkavācagar. One can also proceed to Chettināḍ from here. The cave paintings and fort in and around Pudukkoṭṭai are also worth visiting.

Kumbakoṇam

Kumbakoṇam is the city where devotees throng to have a dip in the Kāverī and visit some of the oldest temples. At Kumbakoṇam there are more than a dozen important temples like the Śārṅgapāṇi temple (noted for its sculptural splendour), the Kumbeśvara temple and the Cakrapāṇi temple. The famous Mahāmaham bath (Puṣkar) takes place at Kumbakoṇam and is one of the biggest temple festivals in India when millions of people from all over the country come to have a holy dip in the tank once in 12 years. Kumbakoṇam is the centre for the Navagraha (nine) temples and the Tirunangūr temples (12 Tirupatis). From Kumbakoṇam to Tañjāvur you can visit a number of temples including Svāmimalai, Oppiliappan temple, Tiruviḍaimarudūr, Sarasvatī temple, Patīśvaram, Tiruvaiyāru, Mannārguḍi, Vaḍuvūr (Rāman temple), etc. and reach Tañjāvūr. Temples noted for beautiful sculptures like Dārasuram, Gaṅgaikoṇḍacoḷapuram (a replica of the Tanjore big temple) are also very near Kumbakoṇam, Tiruviḍaimarudūr.

Nāchiyār kovil is famous for its stone Garuḍa. It is the only temple where the presiding deity is taken on the stone Garuḍa who is also the *utsavamūrti*. The Garuḍa here is a huge one, made of granite. On the festive occasions, when he carries Perumāḷ on his shoulders, it takes only four people to bring him down the first four steps. In the next steps he becomes heavier and 8 people are needed, and thereafter 16 people are needed to carry him with the *mūrti* it then becomes 32 and finally 64 when he with Perumal on his shoulders are brought down. Again going back to the *sanctum sanctorum* (elevated with a lot of steps leading to the main door) the same procedure starts from 64, which is finally reduced to 4.

Tanjāvūr

At Tañjāvūr there is the famous Bṛhadīśvara temple, The Baṅgāru Kāmākṣī temple, the famous Punnainallūr Māriamman temple, etc. and as you proceed to Tiruvārūr you can visit temples like Nannilam (Vadanyeśvarar where you have a *sanctum sanctorum* for Lord Yama).

Tiruvārūr

At Tiruvārūr you can visit the Tyāgarājasvāmi temple, the birthplace of the Trinity (Saṅgīta Mummurthigal) and a few temples like Pulivalam, Reṇukā Devī temple, all in the town, and proceed to Nāgapaṭṭinam and visit the famous temple of Saturn at Tirunallāru.

Nāgapaṭṭinam

Again you will find some very famous temples enroute from Tiruvārūr to Nāgai like the famous Sikkil-Singāra Velan temple, Kīvalur Śiva Temple, Tiruthuraipūṇḍi, and at Nāgapaṭṭinam the Perumāḷ temple (one of the 108 Tirupatis — Soundararāja Perumāḷ) the Śiva Temple and the town's presiding Goddess temple.

Madurai

At Madurai you have the famous Mīnākṣī temple, the Tiruparankunram (Murugan's Ārupaḍaivīḍu), Aḻagar kovil (108 Tirupatis) and Paḻmudhircolai (Arupadaivīdu).

From Madurai there are temples to be visited like Paḻani, Śrīvilliputthūr and covering a few more temples in Ramnad distict like Tirupullāṇi, Devipaṭṭinam, Navapāṣanam, etc. you can reach Rāmeśvaram.

Thirunelveli (Nellai)

A stay at Tirunelveli for 3-4 days, and you would have seen some of the oldest and most beautiful temples in and around Nellai. The Tamaraparani river flows gently all the way as you pass some of the breathtaking scenes. The Nava-Tirupatis are all within 20 km around Nellai. At Nellai you have the most famous Nellaiappar temple whose consort is Kānthimathī. Kovilpaṭṭi, Kṛṣṇapuram, Śaṅkaran Kovil, Tirupuḍaimarudūr, the most beautiful Kaḻugumalai Murugan, Nagarkoil are some important temple towns. Temples around Nellai are very ancient and beautiful.

From Nellai you can proceed to Tenkāsi, Kuttrālam, on one side, or to Tirucendūr and go on to Sucīndram, Kanniyākumāri etc.

Conclusion

TEMPLES in those days gave equal importance to worship, music and dance. The artistes who performed in the temples gave the same importance to their art as worshipping God. They were focused on promoting their art and not interested in money or publicity. There was a genuine effort to preserve the art that was handed down to them by their forefathers. No compromises were made in the quality of art according to the likes and dislikes of the audience. It was at those times, that appreciation of these art forms was at its zenith. Art was considered sacred and artistes held a lot of respect in the society. But sadly, from the beginning of the twentieth century, traditions have slowly been compromised and due to the change in people's lifestyle and advancement in science and technology, a number of art forms have slowly died. The abolition of the *devadāsī* system brought a full stop to the dance traditions in the temples. Very few temples today continue to observe the music traditions that were followed by their forefathers. Lack of funds and interest, changes in the socio-cultural backgrounds and Western influences are some of the reasons why we are left with no more than a few inscriptions to convey the cultural heritage of these temples. Let us take a moment to look back at time and admire the devotion and conviction of the Āḻvārs and the Nāyaṉmārs who travelled great distances (even to north India) at a time when transportation can barely be called thus. What they have achieved is humbling especially today when mankind has taken everything for granted. The artistes who have been playing over generations have slowly moved into other more lucrative professions. Several of these temples now have government appointed musicians for their day-to-day rituals.

In Kerala and coastal Karnataka to large extent music traditions in temples are still being followed with a few compromises. This can be attributed to the reasons like:

- Respect for traditional values still present among the people.
- Minimum government interference and most of the temple artistes continuing to be hereditary.
- Awareness to preserve art forms even among the common people.
- Worshipping God in temples is still a part of their daily routine and is instilled even in the children.
- Temple serving as a centre for cultural activities continues to attract in the crowds even today as it was centuries ago.

Several musicians and temple officials who were spoken to during the study, felt that lack of a system for archiving these rituals will leave the future generations bereft of cultural heritage. There were suggestions that a light and sound show or documentaries in the old temples could give a common man an insight into the glorious past of these temples. Inclusion of these in the school curriculum may be able to control this decline to a certain extent. One of the oldest instruments, *nādasvaram* has no takers now. Even until a few years back, *nādasvaram* concerts were held during music festivals. But today it is reduced to an instrument played during weddings or at temples. The artists do not get recognition or monetary benefit to continue playing at their own initiative. Media can play an important role here in recognizing the artistes and the temples they perform in. This will take them closer to the general public. Awareness on the part of every individual citizen that temples were not only places of worship but also a centre for culture and social activities will go a long way in preserving our socio-cultural heritage. Apart from being rich sources of information for the history of India, they are also celebrated as a tourist's delight because of their architectural beauty. Preserving our temples and their traditions will not only enhance the nation's economic standing but also give us a chance to relive the past.

1. Golden Gopuram of Thirumala Thirupathi Devastham.

2. Thiruvarur Temple.

3. Nādasvaram artists and group getting ready to perform at the Temple.

4. Thiruvarur Temple tank.

5. Inside the Thiruvarur Temple.

6. Bari Nayanam artist at Thiruvarur temple being interviewed by the author.

7. Bari Nayanam artist — Sri Selvaganapathy, Thiruvarur.

8. Pañcamukhavādyam at Thiruvarur Temple.

9. Inscriptions at the Bṛhadīśvara Temple detailing the performing artists at the temple.

10. Tanjore Bṛhadīśvara Temple, Gopuram.

11. Another view of Tanjore Bṛhadīśvara Temple.

12. The Nandi at the Bṛhadīśvara Temple.

13. Musical instruments of the folk artists.

14. Nādasvaram artist at Tanjore Bṛhadīśvara Temple.

15. Ela Thalam.

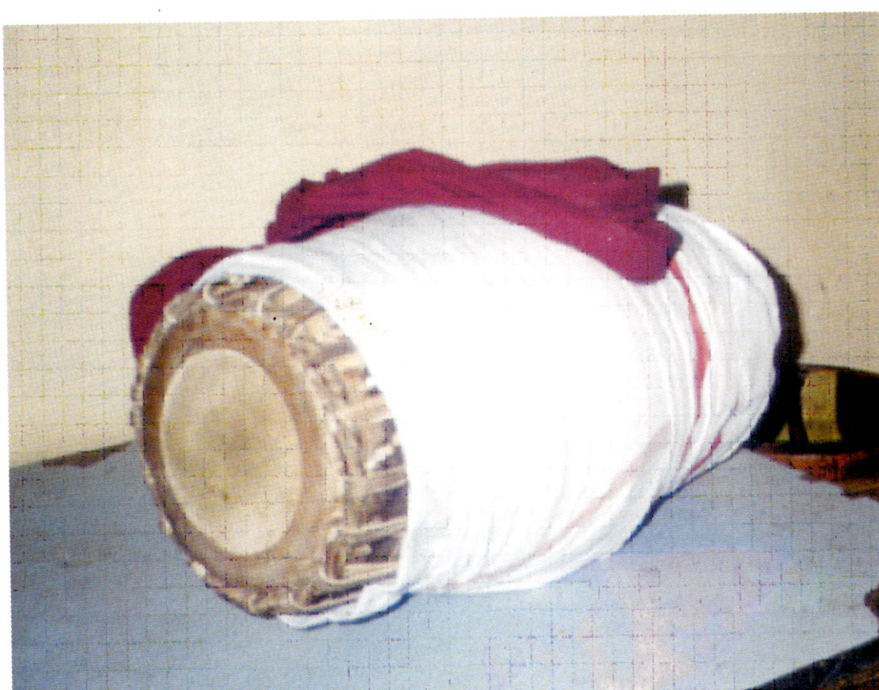

16. Mathalam.

17. Śaṅkha (the conch).

18. Kolattam.

19. Kavadiyattam.

20. Folk music conducted as a part of the temple festival.

21. Kapālīśvarar Temple, Mylapore, Chennai.

22. Getting ready for Theppotsavam, Mylapore, Chennai.

23. An old picture of the Mylapore Temple tank, Chennai.

24. Naṭarāja Temple at Chidambaram.

25. An old photograph of the Periyamelam at Chidambaram Temple.

26. A temple door at the Kutralam Śiva Templewith engravings of musicians performing.

27. Kutralam Temple.

28. Azhwar Thirunagar.

29. Azhwar Thirunagar.

30. Inside view of the Azhwar Thirunagar Temple .

31. The idols of the twelve Azhwars in Venugopalswamy Temple, Muvva (Andhra Pradesh).

32. Sri Ramanujacharya, Sri Perumbudur.

33. Birth place of Sri Ramanuja Sriperumbudur.

34. Thirumazhisai Temple (near Chennai), the birth place of Thirumaḷisai Āḻvar.

35. Peyazhwar's Birth Place at Chennai.

36. Idols of Sri Nadhamunigal, Sri Alawandar at Kattumannar Kovil.

37. Arayar Sri Srinivasa Varadachariyar displaying the head gear used in Arayar Sevai.

38. A photograph of Sri Srinivasa Varadachariar in his Araiyar Sevai costume.

39. Hyms of the Trinity (Nayanmars) inscribed
on the walls of Virupākṣeśvarar Temple at Chennai.

40. An Oduvar pointing out to the picture of Nayanmārs with Manickavachanar.

41. Avadiyar Koil — The sanctum sanctorum of Manickavachakar.

42. Manickavachakar Sannidhi — Avadiyar Koil.

43. Lord Viṣṇu seated on the Garuḍa during a festival at Kañcīpuram.

44. .Kañcī Kāmākṣī Amman Temple, Kañcīpuram.

45. Kumarakottam Temple at Kañcīpuram.

46. Vedaparayanam at a temple in Kañcīpuram.

47. Kumarakottam Temple, Kañcīpuram.

48. Story of Karaikkal Ammayar as seen on the Thiruvalangadu Temple tower.

49. Nādasvaram artist performing inside the Thiruvalangadu Temple.

50. Enterance view of Pudukottai Temple.

51. Enterance to sanctum at Pudukottai Temple

52. Inscriptions on the Walls of Pudukottai Temple.

53 Aerial view of Madurāī Mīnākṣī Temple.

54. Gopuram of Madurāī Mīnākṣī Temple.

55. Inside view of Madurāī Mīnakṣī Temple.

56. Enterance to Thiruparangrundram.

57. Thiruparang Kundram Temple.

58. Enterance to Pazhamudhir Solai Tample.

59. Pazhamudhir Solai Temple.

60. Entrance of Gangaikonda Coḷapuram Temple.

61. Gangaikonda Coḷapuram Temple.

62. The Nandi at Gangaikonda Coḷapuram.

63. Side view of Gangaikonda Coḷapuram Temple.

64. Thavil artist at Gangaikonda Coḷapuram Temple.

65. Entrance to Azhagar Temple.

66. Inside view of Kalazagar Temple.

67. Marundīśvarar Temple, Thiruvanmiyur, Chennai.

68. Oduvar reciting from the mandapam at the Thiruvanmiyur Temple.

69. Entrance to the Cheyyur Temple.

70. The Oduvar and Nādasvaram player at Thiruvottriyur Temple, Chennai.

71. Vasantha Maṇḍapam at Cheyyur where Sarvavādyam was held.

72. A teaching session of the Divya Prabhandams at the Thirupati Thirumālā Temple.

73. A festival at Thirupati Thirumālā Temple.

Bibliography

Arunachalam, M., *Musical Traditions of Tamil Nadu.*

———, *Festivals of Tamil Nadu.*

Azhwar Charitram, Thiru Dharmapuri Adheenam.

Chaitanya, K., *History of Dvādaśa Jyotirliṅgams.*

Chaitanya, Krsna, *India — The Land and the People — Kerala.*

Chari, S.M.S., *Philosophy & Theistic Mystisicm of the Azhwars.*

Das, R.K., *Temples of Tamilnad.*

Dey, C.R., *The Music and Musical Instruments of Southern India and the Deccan.*

Dornakal, V.S., *The Music of India.*

Jayabalan, S., & N.V. Parthasarathy, *108 Thirurpathigalil Thiruvuruvangal.*

Kersenboom, Saskia C., *Nitya Sumangali.*

Krsnan, Nagarkoil, *Arul Petra Nayanmaarkal.*

Kulendran, Gnanambikai, *Karaikkal Ammaiyar — Mother of South Indian Music.*

Kulendran, Ngana, *Deiva Thamizhisai.*

Kuppuswamy, Gowri & N. Hariharan, *Readings on Indian Music.*

Library, Sampradaya, N.C.P.A — *Journals —1984 to 1987.*

Macdonell, Arthur A., *A Vedic Reader for Students.*

Murugavel, N.R., *Arubathumoovar.*

Murugavel, *Panniru Thirumurai.*

Nagarathar Nalam Kaakum 9 Unnadha Thirupatigal, Chinmaya Publication.

Natarajan, B., *The City of the Cosmic Dance.*

Rajagopal, *Marundeeshwarar Temple.*

Ramesan, N., *The Thirumala Temple.*

Sadashivam, K., *Devadāsī System in Medieval Tamil Nadu.*

Sambamurthy, P., *South Indian Music,* Book 1 to Book 6.

Sapthagiri Magazines.

Shree, P., *Periyāzhwār.*

Sita, S., *Tanjore — As a Seat of Music.*

Sree, P., *Divya Prabandha Sāram.*

———, *Thiruvempavai.*

Sthalapuranam books of several temples mentioned in the book, published by temple authorities.

Sundaram, B.M. (Tamil University Tanjore), *Ālaya Vazhipādukal.*

———, *Ālayapāttil Isai.*

Tallotte, William, *Temple of Cidambaram booklet.*

Thiru Arul Mozhi, R.K. Mutt.

Thirugnanasambanda Swamigal, Śaiva Siddhanta Mutt.

Thiruvācakam, Śaiva Siddhanta Mutt.

Thiruvācakam, Thiruvavaduthurai Atheenam.

Varadachary, V., *Pañcaratragama.*

Venkatesan, S., *Arayar Sevai.*

Venkitasubramonia Iyer, S., *Religion Art and Culture.*

Index

abhaṅga hymns, 128

abhyāsa ghanam (*alaṁkāram*), 36

Abinaya kūthu, 171

Ācārya bhakti, 54

Ādi-Grantha, 128

Āḍi Pūram festival (*Teppotsavam*), 166, 179

Adyāyanath Tiruvilā̤l, 156

Āgama tradition, 114-15

Āgamas, 145

Ā̤lvār Hymns, Recitation of,
 Adhyayana Utsavam, 103, 105
 Dhanur Māsa Sevā, 101
 Erāpatthu, 104-05
 Kalyāṇa Utsavam, 99
 Kārtikai Dīpotsavam, 101
 Nitya Utsavam, 100
 Other Deities Utsavam, 101
 Pūlaṅgi Sevā, 99
 Punarvasu Utsavam, 100
 Puraṭṭāsi Brahmotsavam, 102-03
 Pvaitrotsavam, 101
 Rohiṇī Utsavam, 99
 Śrāvaṇa Utsavam, 100
 Śrī Jayanti Utsava, 100
 Thomāla Sevā, 98-99
 Tirumañjana Sevā, 99
 Tiruvātirai Sevāi, 100
 Vasantotsavam, 100-01

Ā̤lvārs, 21, 38, 45, 43, 51-76, 111-12, 128, 130, 161, 163-64, 181
 dates of, 52
 divine roots, 52-53
 Divya Prabandham of, 56-62

amānasika kṣetra, 190

Āmukta Mālyada, 62, 64, 75

ānanda tāṇḍavam, 195-96

Āṇḍāḷ, 54-55, 59, 61-64, 75
 Nāciār Tirumo̤li, 55
 Tiruppāvai, 55

Āndhra Vidya, 2

Āṇi Tirumañjanam festival, 201

anukramantas, 7

Appar, 111

Araiyar Sevai, 60-61, 127, 145, 154-58, 164, 185, 193
 dramatic aspects, 158
 historical aspects, 158
 performance of, 156-58

Āraṇyakas, 5

Āriyakūtu, 170

Āriyan Tami̤l, 170

Ārunagirinathar songs
 Ārupaḍaivāḍu, 47
 Kāñcī group, 47
 Lord Śiva, Five Sabhais of, 48
 Lord Śiva, Vīrattānangal of, 48
 Pañca Bhūtha Sthalaṅgaḷ, 47

Aruvathimūvar festival, 163

Aruvathīmūvar utsavam, 24

Aṣṭa Daśa Vādyam, 151

aṣṭākṣara rahasyas, 57

āsthāna vidvāns, 119

Avesta, 6-7

Banava, 151
Berī, 146
Bhāgavatameḷa, 134-35
Bhajana Harikathā, 185
bhajana style, 15, 48, 126
bhakti mārga, 20-21
bhakti movement, 9, 14-17, 22, 62-64, 111, 114-15, 128-29, 132-33, 185, 187
Bhaviṣyottara Purāṇam, 77
Bheri, 151
bhoga maṇḍapam Śrīraṅgam, 78
Bhūdath Āḻvār, 82-83
Bhujaṅgatrāsita Nṛttyam, 120
bommalāṭṭam (poppetry), 187
Brahmā Tāḷam, 148-49
Brahmotsava, 163, 186-87
Tirumala, 87-91
Candra Prabhai, 147
carmaśloka rahasyas, 57
Carnatic Music, trinity of, 43, 112
Ceṭṭināḍ Temples, 182-83
Chipla, 149
cinnameḷam, 124, 166
Cinna Uḍal, 147
Community Singing, 126-27
Comparative Study Āḻvārs and Nāyaṉmārs, works of, 111-13
Contemporary Devotional Music, 127-33
Dabbi Palagai, 148
Ḍamāram, 146
ḍamuru, 2
Ḍamarukam, 151
Dance Forms, 117, 120, 152-59
dance poses, 173-74
Danga, 147
Dangi, 148
dāsya rasa, 16
Deiva Tamiḻ Isai, 37
See also Tevāram
deva ganam, 57, 156
devadāsīs, 124-25, 140, 152, 167, 171, 177
devarnama, 133
dhenu-mudrā, 116
Ḍinḍima, 151
Divyanāma Kīrtana, 130-31
dohā, 15
Draviḍa Veda, 97
See also Nālāyira Divya Prabandham
Dundubhi, 146, 151
Dūriyam, 151
dvaya rahasyas, 57
Eccharika, 122-23, 144, 177
Ekkāḷam, 150
Eḻuisai Eḻunarambinosai, 32
Emperumānaḍiyār, 124
See also devadāsīs
Festivals, 3, 160-69
float festivals, 125
See also Teppotsavam
Folk dance, 158-159
Folk Music, 135
gheṭṭu vādyam, 143, 150, 176
Ginneri, 150
gītā, 12
See also vocal music
Gīta-Govinda, 129-30
Godhā Sthuti, 70
Guru-Paramparā Prabhāvam, 61
hanumad vīṇā, 2
Harikathā, 131, 191
Hinduism, revival of, 19-23
Hymn, development of, 17
indexes, 7
Instrumental music, 32, 36, 41, 136-51
Mukha Vīṇā, 109
Pāri Nayam, 109
Sannidhi Ḍol, 109
Suddha Maddhalam, 109
Isai Pā, 58
Iyar Pā, 59
Jālra, 148

jñaṇa maṇḍapam
Melkoṭe Tirunārāyaṇapuram, 78
Kaikāṭumurai, 116-17
Kaiśikī Ekādaśī, 63
Kākalam, 151
Kālakṣepam, 133-34
Kāmikāgamam, 12
Kanaka Thappaṭṭai, 147
kañjira, 146
Kanninur Siruthambu, 57
Karagamāṭṭam, 159
Kāraikkāl Ammaiyār, 43-45, 112
Karaṇas, 173-74
karma, 5
Kathā Kalākṣepa, 191
Kaṭṭalai (Commandments), 43
Kāvadi Sindu, 40
Kāvaḍiyāṭṭam, 159
Kavuthuvam, 116, 185
Kiḍīkiṭṭī, 142-43, 147
Kīrtana, 15-17, 186
Koil-Oḻugu, 61
Kolāṭṭam, 159
Kombu, 150
Kouthuvams, 120
Kṛtī, 111
Kudi Meḷam, 149
Kulaśekhara Āḻvār, 59, 73, 76-78
Perumāḷ Tirumoḻi, 55
Kuḻi Tāḷam, 148
Kummi, 159
Kuṇḍalam, 148
kuravanji (dance-drama), 120, 145, 185
laya, 2
Lord Veṅkaṭeśwara Temple, 74-110
lyrical hymn, 15
Madhurakavi Āḻvār, 54, 60, 75
Kaṇṇiṇur Sirattāmbu, 54, 57
Mahā Nārāyaṇa Upaniṣad, 77
Maṇavāḷa Māmunigaḷ, 70-71, 100, 181
maṅgalaśāsanam, 21, 64-65
Māṇikkavācagar, 162, 164
mantra, 16
Mārgaḻi Māsam Ārudra Darśanam, 167-68
Mathukam, 151
Mayilāṭṭam (peacock dance), 159
mattaḷam, 151
Meḷakāra Kāṇi, 119
metre (*chanda*), 9
mṛdaṅgam, 151
Mukha Vīṇā, 109, 143
Mukundamāla, 65
Music Discourses, 133-35
Music information on inscription, 170-72
Music Traditions, 175-83
Cidambram Temple, 197-201
Devadāsīs, contribution of, 114-18
Śrīraṅgam, 193-94
Tamil Nadu Temples, 119-23
Music, role of
Vedas, 5-10
Musical forms, 117
Muttu, 149
nādasvaram, 45, 115, 120-21, 137-40, 166-67, 176-77, 187-88, 194-95, 203
Cinna Mallāri, 121
Mallāri, 121, 138-139
Ratthi, 121-22
nāda-tāḷa, 48
Nagāḍā, 146
Nālāyira Divya Prabandham, 45, 52, 61-62
Nāmāvaḷī Kīrtana, 130
Nambiāṇḍār Nambi, 24, 33
Nammāḻvār, 54, 59, 78
Periya Tiruvandādi, 54
Tiruvāymoḻi, 54, 59
Tiruviruttam, 54
Nānmukhan Tiruvandādi, 82, 84
Nāthamuni, 57, 60, 155

Nāṭya Kāṇi, 119
Nāṭyaśāstra, 62
Navarātri festival, 179
navasaṅdhi nṛtyam, 116, 153-54
navavidha bhakti, 127
Nāyaṉmārs, 21, 24-49, 128, 161
  See also Sivan Adiyars
nindā stuti, 63
nirūpaṇam, 133
nṛtya, 12
Nūpuram, 151
Oḍakūru, 123
Oduvār, 34, 36, 41-42, 120, 127, 162-63, 168, 185, 187, 203
Oppiliappan Temple, 180
otthu, 60
Oyilāṭṭam, 159
padākam, 151
padhigam pattern, 43, 45, 111-12
Padmāvatī Temple, Tirucānūr, 91-96
  Annual Festivals, 95-96
Pallakku Naḍanam (Palanquin dance), 152
Pamppai, 147
pāṇars (music masters), 114
Pañca Vādyam, 150
pañcamahāpuruṣas, 126
pañcamūkha vādyam, 142, 146, 179
Pancaratra Agama, 94, 96-98
Pankuni Utsavam, 166
Pannisai, 36, 42-43, 45, 49, 111-12
Pannangam, 40
Panniru Tirumuṟai, origin of, 34-35
paṇṇ-murai, 35
paṇṇ-nothiram, 138
Pāri Nāyam, 142, 150, 185
pāvai songs, 164
percussion instruments, 135, 140, 142-51, 153, 171
periāḻvār, 54, 59, 80, 82-83
  periāḻvār Tirumoḻi, 54
  Tirupallāṇḍu, 54, 59, 62
Periyameḷam, 123, 187
Periya Purāṇam, 34
Periya Uḍal, 147
Perumāḷ Tirumoḻī, 74, 76
Peruvangiyam, 120, 137
  See also nādaswaram
Pey Āḻvār, 53
Pidaran, 41
poetical metres, 128-29
Poi-kāl kuthirai, 160
Poygai Āḻvār, 53, 80, 81, 83, 202
Prapannāmṛtam, 74
prapatti-bhakti, 14
prastotā, 8
pratihāra, 8
Pujari kai Cilambu, 148
Pulluvan Kuḍam, 147
Puraṭṭāsi Masam Niraipani festival, 167
puruśārtha, 51
puṣpa maṇḍapam Tirumalai, 78
Pūtattār Āḻvār, 53
rāgam vakaikaḷ 103 (*paṇṇs*), 61
Raktthi meḷam, 140, 185
Religious Discourses, Thiruvaiyaru, 191
Ṛgveda, 6-8, 16
rituals (sixteen), 116
Rudrakannīkas, 168
Saint Māṇikkavācagar, 111
Sakoda Yaḷ, 37
Samavedic Music, 8-10
Sambandar, 111-12
Saṁhitās, 5
sandham (beats), 49
Saṅkhu, 150
Saṅkīrṇam, 170
Sannidhi Ḍol, 109
santa rāsa, 16
saptasthānam festival, 187
Sarva-Vādyam, 126, 144-45

Semmakalam, 149
Shabdha, 151
Silappadhikāram, 62
Simha Naḍanam (Lion dance), 152
Śivagīti, 130
Śivan Aḍiyārs, 24
Śivavilāsam, 114
Saṁkīrtalakṣaṇa, 132
Spiritualism, 21
Śrī Annamācārya, 131-32
Śrī Govindarāja Svāmi Temple, Tirupati, 105-108
  Music Recitals, 109-10
  Utsavams, 106-08
Śrī Rāmānuja, 71-73
śrībali ritual, 171
Śṛṅgāra Kīrtana, 131
Sthala Kīrtanas, 185-87
Suddha Maddhalam, 109, 146, 167, 168
suddha nṛtyam, 117, 120
suddhangam, 36, 40
Sundarar, 111-12
Suramaṇḍalam, 143
Sūrya Prabhai, 147
svaramaṇḍalam, 171
svayamvyakta divya kṣetras, 85
Taipūsam, 165
Tāḷam, 151
tala-murai, 35-36
taḷa vakaikaḷ 103 (*otthu*), 61
Tamil Vedas, 124
tāṇḍava (Cosmic dance), 2
tāṇḍava dīpārādhanā, 176, 194
Tantrism, 16
Tappaṭṭam, 159
tattva, 51
Tavalla, 151
tavil, role of, 140-41
Temple art forms, 184-03
  Kāñcīpuram, 201-03, 205
  Kuttrālam, 194
  Naṭarāja Temple, Cidambaram, 195, 205
  Śrīraṅgam, 192-94
  Tanjāvūr, 184-89
  Tenkāsi, 194
  Tirukogarṇam, 192
  Tiruvaiyārū Temple, 189-92
  Tiruvārūr, 194-95
Temple Festivals, 125, 160-69
  Bṛhadāśvara Temple, 188-89
  Music and Dance, 187-88
Temple Sculptures, 173-74
Temples, 204-08
  Lord Veṅkaṭeśwara, 74-110
  role of, 18-23
  Tiruthuraipūṇḍi temple, 179
  Tiruvaiyārū temple, 189-192
Tenkalai, 70
Teeppotsavam, 94, 123, 163, 179
  See also float festivals
Terukūthu, 159
Tevāra Nāyagam, 41
Tevārathu-Cuṟṟukallūṟi, 41
Tevāram, 32-33, 116, 162-63, 168, 179
  Classification of, 35-38
  grammer in, 35
  in Temples, 41-42
Thakkai, 143
thampura, 2
Thavaṇḍai, 147
Thavil, 122
three speed pattern (*mukkālam*), 35-36
Tirucānūr Pañcamī, 94-96
Tirucendūr Temple dances, 117
Tirucinnam, 150
tirukoṭṭu maṇḍapam, 42
Tirukovai, 34
Tirumala Tirupati Temple, 85-87
Tirumaḻisai Āḻvār, 54, 59, 80, 82, 84
  Hanumān Tiruvandādi, 54

Truccanda Viruttam, 54

Tirumaṅgai Āḻvār, 55-56, 59

Periya Tirumaḍal, 56

Periya Tirumoḷi, 56

Siriya Tirumaḍal, 56

Tirukkuruntakam, 56

Tiruneduntāṇḍakam, 56

Tiruvelukurrirukkai, 56

Tirumuga Pāsurams, 34

Tirumurais, 31, 43, 61

classification of, 33-34

Tirunangur Divya-desams, festivals of, 181-82

Tirupallāṇḍu, 162, 185

Tirupati, history of, 78-96

Tiruppadhikams, 43

Tiruppalāṇḍu, 34

Tiruppāṇ Āḻvār, 55, 59, 75

Amalanādipirān, 55

Tiruppāvai, 40, 162

Tirupugaḻ, 46-49, 111-12

Tiruthuraipūṇḍi Temple, 179

Tiruvācakam, 34, 39-41, 164

Tiruvāimoḷi, 42, 185

Tiruvaiyārū Temple, 189-192

Religious Discourses, 191

Tiruvandādi, 34, 82

Tiruvandhikappu, 122

Tiruvempavai, 40, 162

Tiruveṇpā, 177

Tiruvisaipākal, 34

Toṇḍaraḍippoḍi Āḻvār, 55, 59, 162

Tirumālai, 55

Tiruppaḷḷieḻuci, 55

Transcendental Power, 3

Tumburu, 151

tyāga maṇḍapam

Kāñcīpuram, 78

Ubhaya Vedānta, 63

Udgaitha, 8

Uḍukkai, 147

ulvaccar (drummers), 114

Upaniṣads, 5, 17

See also Vedānta

Upaveda, 11

utsavas, 3

See also festivals

Vaḍakali, 70

vādya, 12

See also instrumental music

vaiṇikagāyaka, 2

Vaiṣṇava shrines (hundred and eight), 64-71

Vaiṣṇavism, 51, 71

Vāraṇamāyiram, 62

Vasantotsava, 165

vātsalya rasa, 16

Veda śikhārtha garbam, 74

Vedānta Deśika, 70-71, 92, 202

Vedānta, 5

vedānām sāmvedosmi, 8

Vedas, 5-10

Veṅkaṭachala māhātmyam, 79

Veṇu, 151

vicitra vīṇā, 2

Villadi Vādyam, 149

Vīṇā, 2, 143, 151

Vīṇāi Kāṇi, 119

Vira Maṇḍalam, 149

Viruda Karaṇa, 131

Viśiṣṭādvaita Vedānta, 51

Viṣṇu-Sahasranāmastotra, 130-31

Vocal Music, 124-35

wind instruments, 136

Worship, form of, 11-13

Yaḻmuri paṇṇ Isai, 38-39